Metaphors and Meanings

ESSAYS ON ENGLISH TEACHING BY GARTH BOOMER

Metaphors and Meanings

ESSAYS ON ENGLISH TEACHING BY GARTH BOOMER

Edited by Bill Green

PE
1065
.136
1988

AATE
1988

First published in 1988 by
AATE, Australian Association for the Teaching of English.

Text © Garth Boomer, 1988.
Editorial material © Bill Green, 1988.

LaserSet in 9/12 point Bookman by
N.S. Hudson Publishing Services Pty Ltd, Hawthorn, Victoria 3122

Printed in Australia by Australian Print Group

Australian C.I.P. data

Boomer, Garth.
Metaphors and meanings.
ISBN 0 909955 82 4.

1. English language – Study and teaching. I. Australian Association for the Teaching of English. II. Green, Bill. III. Title.

428'.07

ACKNOWLEDGEMENTS

The English Teacher, Research and Change' was published in R.D. Eagleson (ed.) *English In The Eighties*, A.A.T.E., 1982. 'Struggling In English' was published in *English in Australia*, No. 59, March 1982. 'Literacy, Power and the Community' was published in *Language Arts* (N.C.T.E.), Vol. 61, No. 6, Oct. 1984. 'Literature and English Teaching' is a revised version of a paper published in *Opinion* (S.A.E.T.A.), Vol. 13, No. 4, Nov. 1984. 'English Teaching: Art and Science' was published in *Language Arts* (N.C.T.E.), Vol. 52, No. 7, Nov. 1985, and also in Stephen Tchudi (ed.) *Language, Schooling and Society*, Boynton/Cook, Montelair, N.J., 1985. 'Zen and the Art of Languaging' was published in *Pivot* (Ed. Dept. of S.A.), Sept. 1977. 'Language, Learning and the Hyperactive' is an edited version of a paper published in the proceedings of the *Education Seminar on Hyperactivity*, Hyperactivity Association of South Australia, 1979. 'Curriculum as Narrative' was published in W.J. Crocker (ed.) *Developing Communicative Competence*, University of New England, 1980. 'Reading the Whole Curriculum' is a revised and rewritten version of a paper published in *VISE News* (Victorian Institute of Secondary Education), May/June, 1983. 'Coming of Age in Drama' was published in *Drama In Education*, National Association for Drama in Education, Vol. 5, Dec. 1980. 'The Politics of Drama Teaching' was published in Margaret Meek and Jane Miller (eds.), *Changing English: Essays for Harold Rosen*, Heinemann Educational Books, London, 1984. 'Negotiating the Curriculum' was published in Garth Boomer (ed.) *Negotiating The Curriculum*, Ashton Scholastic, Sydney, 1982 and also in James Britton (ed.), *English Teaching: An International Exchange*, Heinemann Educational Books, London, 1984. 'Negotiation Revisited' was published in *Interpretations* (E.T.A.W.A.), Vol. 16, No. 2, Nov. 1982. 'Teaching Against the Grain' was published in *Viewprints* (Victorian Institute of Secondary Education), No. 7, June 1986.

CONTENTS

	Foreword	vi
	Editorial Note	vii
	Dancing Lessons: An Introduction	1
	SECTION ONE: ON ENGLISH TEACHING	13
1	The English Teacher, Research and Change	15
2	Struggling in English	31
3	Coming of Age in Drama:	
	or, the Importance of being Ordinary	42
4	The Politics of Drama Teaching	55
5	Literacy, Power and the Community	68
6	English Teaching: Art and Science	80
7	Literature and English Teaching:	
	Opening up the Territory	99
	SECTION TWO: ON CURRICULUM AND LEARNING	109
8	Zen and the Art of Languaging	111
9	Language, Learning and the Hyperactive	118
10	The Curriculum as Narrative	127
11	Negotiating the Curriculum	139
12	Reading the Whole Curriculum	151
13	Negotiation Revisited	168
14	Teaching against the Grain	179
	SECTION THREE: ON TEACHER EDUCATION	193
15	Teachers Learning	195

FOREWORD

The Australian Association for the Teaching of English is proud to publish *Metaphors and Meanings*, a collection of essays on English teaching by Garth Boomer.

Well, obviously. No-one has contributed more to the teaching of English in Australia than Garth: life-long member of A.A.T.E., provocative and inspiring conference speaker, vigorous workshop leader, compelling writer, pace-setting president.

The essays in this collection, though, are not an exercise in nostalgia. As Bill Green points out in his Editorial Note, they speak to us as freshly today as they did on the public occasions when they were presented. Leaf through the pages. If 'metaphor' is a leitmotif of the collection, so is 'paradox'. Garth's writing is full of compatible contradictions: it is seriously playful, combative but inviting, conversational and rhetorical, grappling with the new while sustaining continuing preoccupations, poetic and yet full of lists, inventories, models, diagrams, questions, imperatives – a bi-cameral brain with all systems firing.

But when all these introductory words are done, we are left with a simple fact. The essays are talks to English teachers. Some readers will have the satisfaction of rediscovering a favourite keynote address. New readers will be challenged. For all readers Garth warns that the book has designs on our thinking and acting. And so it should. But, equally, it has designs on our intentions as well. It invites us to rediscover our enthusiasm and commitment to English teaching. It shows us ways to do this. In the current political and educational climate nothing could be more important.

And perhaps this is the final Boomer paradox. This *occasional* writing, as Garth describes the book, is also a solid statement of the profession's concerns: not a book for occasional browsing by English teachers, but a permanent resource and guide. A book to have within arm's reach.

It is with a sense of occasion that A.A.T.E. presents *Metaphors and Meanings*.

Margaret Gill
President, Australian Association for the Teaching of English
May 1988

EDITORIAL NOTE

This book involves a selection of Garth Boomer's papers on curriculum and English teaching. A number have been previously published. In some instances, this has been in state association and departmental journals, as well as conference proceedings, and hence they have been restricted in their availability and accessibility. In other instances, while the venues have been more public, the papers warrant reprinting here because such presentation provides them with what is arguably their best context. Several papers, including 'Dancing Lessons: An Introduction', are presented here for the first time. All have been edited so as to provide for coherence and continuity.

The principal impulse behind the collection was my conviction that Boomer's work in curriculum and English teaching represented a particularly significant achievement; moreover, that the project he had long been engaged in had an integrity, a distinctiveness and a coherence that was too easily obscured by the 'occasional' nature of his publications and presentations. A further concern was that his work represented a decisive decade in English teaching in Australia, and hence a collection of his papers would be a more than useful contribution to English teaching generally, in that it would provide a particular kind of historical record.

This is not to say, however, that the work is of historical interest only. Quite the contrary. My strong feeling is that it speaks vitally to our present concerns, which includes dealing with a general tightening-up in curriculum and schooling in the face of a widespread and deepening socio-economic crisis. The profession is under pressure, urged both to conform and to confirm. Boomer's concern with what he calls, here and elsewhere, 'teacher power' is something we need to seize upon and develop ourselves, in our own ways and in a manner consistent with our present circumstances, in the context of the late 1980s. The profession needs inspiration and encouragement, and a sense of its own possibilities: moral, intellectual and political leadership. It also needs the provocation of 'tactlessness', so as to unsettle its will to complacency. In my view these papers are eminently provocative, stimulating, inspirational and generative. They *energize* as much as they *agitate*. They urge and invite us to become better educators than we currently are, even as they acknowledge and are eloquent testimony to our present achievements: our *excellence*.

A few comments, then, on the collection itself. The title seeks to articulate a distinctive feature of Boomer's writing: its use of tropes and figures, especially metaphors, as a matter both of style and of pedagogy. This goes hand-in-hand with an insistence on *meaning* as the very heart of curriculum. The relationship between metaphor-making and meaning-making is a consistent emphasis in the collection – metaphor as a way of knowing and meaning, and hence crucially important in the practices of teaching and learning. This is something enacted and and embodied in the papers collected here, rather than explicitly discussed: a curriculum theory in 'the practical state', in several senses of that phrase.

The collection is organized more or less chronologically. This is both to give a sense of the consistency and integrity of Boomer's project in the period in question and to convey something of its evolution and development. Two things are worth pointing out. One is the constant engagement with problems and features of classroom practice. The other is a growing politicisation, which is linked to heightened awareness of the significance of *context* in curriculum generally. Hence, the increasing sensitivity to matters of *constraint* in teaching and learning, and the need to engage in collective, collaborative work, in classrooms and schools as well as in other sites.

The collection is presented in three sections. Section One ('On English Teaching') focusses on English teaching more directly, considering matters more or less specific to the English domain: literature, literacy, drama, and the role of the English teacher. It ranges from celebration to critique, and presents overall a particularly dynamic picture of English teaching in evolution.

Section Two ('On Curriculum and Learning') has a broader reference, although it certainly continues to speak to the concerns of the English classroom. The emphasis here is more on curriculum generally, or teaching and learning across the school curriculum and at various levels of schooling. It is noticeable that there is an increasing stress on curriculum politics in this section. Two points can be made here, with specific reference to English teaching itself. There is, firstly, clear indication in this section that English teaching cannot proceed in an insular fashion, disregarding more general issues of curriculum and the wider school context. This is a matter of some significance: the strong identification over this period of English teaching with what has been called language-and-learning theory. So the second point to draw attention to is the possibility that this identification has not always benefited English teaching and English teachers, in the subject-specific sense. The collection is, I believe, both suggestive and symptomatic in this regard – something which does not in the least lessen its significance or its value. After all, it invites us to carry on the task of theorising what it means to be an English teacher and what English classrooms are all about.

Section Three ('On Teacher Education') is an important and distinctive statement in professional development. In the original conceptualisation of this book, the paper published here, written in 1984, was counter-balanced by a paper written in 1974, also bearing the title 'Teachers Learning'. The aim was to show, very clearly, continuity and development in Boomer's work in professional development over the period 1974-1984. Space did not allow this. However, it is worth pointing out that for Boomer there can be only artificial separation of curriculum development from professional development, and that for him the teacher is at the very centre of curriculum change – both its achievement and its problematic.

Many of the papers here were originally generated for specific occasions. They need to be read with this in mind. However, the sense of a distinctive project is, I believe, unavoidable in the collection as a whole. As such, it is more than simply the sum of its occasions; rather, it reaches beyond them to provide an eloquent and articulate statement on English teaching itself.

Bill Green

DANCING LESSONS: AN INTRODUCTION

This is a book about a pleasurable struggle to know more about English teaching in particular, and teaching, in general. At least, it was pleasurable for me and I hope that some of the pleasure and some sense of the struggle will be conveyed to the reader. It is not just a personal struggle that I represent. It is important to understand it as a shared journey. There is an inseparable connection between my work and the work, through State and Territory networks, of the Australian Association for the Teaching of English which has nurtured, supported, challenged, taught and sometimes corrected me since its inception in 1965. AATE, I am pleased to say, has struggled and is prospering. The Association is, of course, people, and to those people I am greatly indebted.

For the encouragement to put this work together, and the critique to make it better than it would have been, I am most grateful to Bill Green and Margaret Gill.

The 'Writing'

You are invited to read a collection of short 'plays' about English teaching and education written between 1977 and 1984.

Apart from the last chapter, all this work is, in essence, script for performance, although it has been edited to make it more suited to the book form. It is *occasional* writing; the occasion usually being a conference, or a seminar, or a convention; the audience, usually teachers; the speaker, on a platform quite often with a microphone; the venue, some distance from schools.

When I write occasional pieces such as these, I hear my voice delivering the words and I imagine the dramatic tensions which will be built between me and my audience. The challenge is not to be as concise and as precise as possible, but to cast out related networks of meaning which, cumulatively or retrospectively, will make connections with most of the listeners and generate some understanding of some of the ideas I wish to spread. Because I deliberately strive for a kind of infectiousness, yet know the horrible consequence of mindless infection in education, as elsewhere, I must also strive to call attention to my essays as constructions, as theatre, in such a way that they provoke mindful resistance. All educational addresses, like all teaching acts, are manipulative in the sense of having designs on other people's thinking and acting. The more they parade as value-free, objective presentation of information, the more the buyer should beware.

My writing, abstracted from the occasion, will tend to frustrate readers who treat it according to the conventional genre of academic essay or journal article. It is not of that genre. I rely on considerable charges of affectivity. I do not want cool appraisal. I want images to work as powerfully as arguments. I want to tell fairly truthful stories that entertain and engage, susceptive of varying interpretations although palpably heading in a certain direction.

For this reason, I write them *poetically* as much as *transactionally*. Having settled on a set of ideas and with a sense of occasion and audience as strong as possible, I begin to write, allowing the unfolding text to influence and generate what comes next, within the constraints of the overall intention and purpose. I do not choreograph the argument beforehand nor predispose paragraphs. I know well what understandings I want to share, but without exception those ideas become modified and re-shaped in various ways by the very act of scripting them; an example of what James Britton has called 'shaping at the point of utterance'.

I suspect that my writing about education is less censored by the author than most texts in the field, so that it is likely to be open at times to charges of indulgence, over-generalisation, inaccuracy, rashness and a kind of auto-eroticism where the author's pleasure in the latest punchy phrase or idea generates a too rich mixture which does not know where to stop. I am aware that metaphors are to some readers like chocolate fudge and that from time to time the calorific valency of my writing could be prohibitive. Dispensed orally from the platform where they are evanescent, dissipated and alleviated, they may be effective, but taken intensively as writing they may be too much. This is not said as an apologia. It is simply to explain what I see to be the nature and style of my work, and to suggest that it needs to be read in a certain way to be best appreciated.

The Sources

The years 1972-73 were a watershed in my career. These were the years which I spent in study at the English as Mother-Tongue

Department of the University of London, Institute of Education, looking in particular at how teachers learn, with a specific focus on teachers within an English department at an Inner London school. The study came after ten years of work as an English teacher and consultant with the Education Department of South Australia.

In London, Nancy Martin and Harold Rosen were my chief supervisors, teachers and critics. I owe them much for introducing me to a plethora of mind-blowing, habit-shattering texts and for their superb teaching, but it is for one simple but profound attitude that I am most in their debt. They, and their colleagues, treated me as if I had a mind and they encouraged me to use it. Whether or not other teachers in my past had done this, it was my perception and experience that this was happening for the first time. I was being allowed to think my thoughts. The challenge was to get *my* ideas straight. I was not being tested on the ideas of my teachers and the texts they presented, but on what I made of what they said in relation to my own experience and ideas.

After nearly thirty years in education, I began to find my own voice. Tentatively at first, but with growing confidence, I began to break free from the kind of academic writing which tended to paste together strips of other people's words. Looking back now, if I had to boil down all I have learnt about teaching and learning into one injunction for beginning teachers, it would be this:

- *Always teach in the knowledge of the pulsating, intentional minds before you. Let that knowledge permeate everything you do.*

Once my intention had taken grip in London, my mediated conversations with great thinkers through texts changed in nature. I was not taking their thoughts and accumulating information; rather, I was using their thoughts to construct my own understanding of English teaching and learning.

Perhaps chief amongst my sources was the clinical psychologist George Kelly, as introduced originally through James Britton and his book *Language and Learning*[1]. Kelly's theory of personal constructs inspired the research design for my dissertation. The constructivist view of learning, owing much also to Vygotsky [2], which I clarified for myself in 1973 has stayed with me, not unmodified, ever since and lends, I hope, an integrity and a continuity to my educational thinking. What I say about teachers' learning in 1984 (Chapter 15) is more detailed, less naïve and better qualified than my original research[3], but it is still underpinned by the same principles of learning.

In the realms of philosophy, Susanne Langer[4], Michael Polanyi[5] and George Gusdorf[6], were key sources; in sociology, Berger and Luckmann[7]; in linguistics, Ferdinand de Saussure[8] and Edward Sapir[9]; in the theory of English teaching, James Britton[10] and James Moffett[11]; in culture, history and politics, Raymond Williams[12]; in literature, Lionel Trilling[13] and Barbara Hardy[14].

These were chief amongst the 'London' sources in 1972-73. Since then, of course, there have been many further influences, not least my professional colleagues in Australia, particularly the many teachers who have provided frank, constructive criticism from the point of view of those who have to make things work in classrooms.

As time has passed, and as the reality of schooling has moved so slowly, I have become increasingly interested in the politics of education and the ways in which innovative action is contained or diverted. The early writings in this volume seem in retrospect to be unduly confident and optimistic, and too little conscious of the networks of power which operate in society. The paper, 'The English Teacher, Research and Change' (Chapter 1), represents a growing awareness of the contexts of English teaching, while 'Teaching Against The Grain' (Chapter 14) begins to unravel the ways in which a powerful, unexamined hegemony determines much of what happens in schools.

Work in English teaching took me to learning theory and considerations about how language relates to thinking. This involved consideration of curriculum and the wider societal context in which schools operate. Writers like Giroux[15], Apple[16], Connell[17] and Foucault[18], in conjunction with my work in schools, have helped me to understand a little more clearly the ways in which, unwittingly, schools and their curricula are often loaded dice.

In only a few places in this volume do I explicitly take account of the ways in which schools systematically discriminate against girls, ethnic minorities and those from low socio-economic backgrounds. I tend to write of power in relation to individual students, and not to show how individual students are differentially treated according to ethnicity, gender and class. These things I would hope to redress in future.

The Key Ideas

The learning theory which I espouse is a theory of *deliberate*, as opposed to accidental, learning. It is the generating plant for most of the ideas in this book. Put simply, the theory depicts the learner as intentional scientist forming hypotheses or hunches, trying them out, reflecting on the consequences and thereby modifying constructs on the world which become the basis for further learning:

> Yet all experience is an arch, where thro'
> Gleams that untravelled world whose margin fades
> For ever and for ever when I move
>
> (from 'Ulysses', Tennyson)

It is a simple theory which takes account of and explains principles of language learning, as well as the way in which constructs and concepts are built in all areas of the school curriculum.

Once accepted, it has explosive and iconoclastic consequences for much of our education system which has, by and large, been predicated on a behaviourist view of the world, valorising transmission, reinforcement and repetition, and emphasising the teacher's inculcation rather than the learner's construction.

This explains why much of my writing confronts deficiencies in the school system. An early tendency to blame the short-comings of teachers has been overtaken by an awareness of how *the system*, and indeed society itself, of which teachers are only a part, works, and needs to work, given the premises upon which it has evolved.

The idea of negotiating the curriculum as a means of empowering students and improving students' learning is not new, but I believe my colleagues and I in Australia have broken some new ground in testing the idea in practice and codifying some of this practice to enhance its generalisability. The book *Negotiating the Curriculum*[19] documents this work more fully.

It has been my drive to try to articulate the theory behind my practice because I experienced and knew in London the liberating effects of such theorising, and because I realise that once you have begun to articulate your own theory you can make it even more powerful by engaging critically with the theories of others. Armed with your own theory, you are less likely to be manipulated and colonised by someone else's world view.

All great class struggles or struggles for equality, as in the women's movement, it seems to me, are based on the insurrection of counter theories about how the world works. Therefore, whether one is talking about students becoming more powerful, or Aborigines, or the working classes, or women, one will need to ask how the relatively oppressed are to develop a practical theory about their own lives and the motives of their oppressors.

In schools, it is my view that teachers interested in the empowerment of their students need to become themselves demonstrably theoretical about their own practice, the way schools work, and the way students learn. Then, in addition to teaching students the content of subjects, they will be able *deliberately* to teach them how to make theories about their practice and their context. This idea flows through much of my writing, but it is perhaps best presented in Chapters 4 and 12. I contend that the degree to which teachers keep their theories *secret*, from themselves and from their students, is the degree to which they will be rendering themselves and their students relatively powerless.

The metaphor of the dance helps me to represent the idea that although one person, the teacher, may have formal permission to lead, the other person, the student, can and does lead as well, in ways which can be mirrored and then elaborated by an imaginative partner. Whether one is looking at one-to-one interactions (see Chapter 5) or at teachers with a whole class (see Chapter 6), it is possible to see a blend of artistry and science which is akin to the dance.

The emphasis on action research, which flows consistently through to Chapter 15, is inevitable, given the learning theory. The methods of action research are the methods of good teaching and learning at any level.

The test of a good theory, I believe, is the extent to which the theory can encompass a theory about its own inadequacy. If the theory is not predicted on its own eventual demise, it is suspect. By this criterion, the learning theory which I espouse has strengths. It does lead inevitably to the conclusion that by a process of action and reflection, the theory will itself be modified or replaced eventually. It is at once a strength and weakness of my work that, as yet, I have not found reason to replace it. Much of what I write portrays a degree of certainty which I take on because, sooner or later, despite all our knowledge about the interim nature of theories, we all have to *pre-empt* and *act*. We cannot remain forever Hamlet. Therefore, when I strongly advocate certain actions, I must do so *as if* I have found a right theory.

I hope that, taken as a whole, my work in this volume indicates a continuing capacity to re-visit and re-construe.

The Future

Since 1984 as an officer within the Commonwealth Education portfolio advising government on national education policy, I have somewhat uneasily adjusted to a professional life which has removed me from continuing and close contact with teachers of English. I am at one and the same time an 'insider' and an 'outsider'. English teaching is so much a part of all that I have met that it is impossible for me to stand completely outside my English teacher's world view, and yet I have been obliged to look at education through new lenses. Each of these lenses, whether that of the educational bureaucrat, or the politician, or the economist, raises new issues and new questions for me when I come to look again at my first love.

I see, for instance, patent insularities in some of my early thinking; an understandable and, I hope, forgivable tendency towards English-centredness and a somewhat obsessive learning lens bias.

My new work also leads me to contemplate how the scope and purpose of English teaching might change if it became oriented to the consideration and possible solution of *cultural* problems through the reading and making of texts. I suppose the 'theme' approach to texts was at its best directed towards the kind of quest for cultural literacy I would advocate, but I think we now know much more about texts and would need to be much more respectful and rigorous in our study of text as an illumination and enactment of culture. With the 'theme' approach, we too often used the text as a vehicle into social issues, and not as a significant artefact reflecting and representing aspects of the society.

It is pleasing to see how English teachers are beginning to liberate themselves from a narrow conception of the literary text. Once 'text' is conceived of as a cultural artefact, any text past or present, classic or popular, fiction or non-fiction, written, oral or filmic, can be admitted to the English classroom for legitimate and rewarding scrutiny, from the standpoint of 'Who made this? In what context? With what values? In whose interests? To what effect?' In this way, I see English teaching throwing off its long entrenched associations with a bookish capital 'C' culture. The new English will take its place in the total curriculum as a vigorous, hard-headed, socially-critical, productive field of engagement with the here-and-now through its work with texts. This might not constitute a paradigm shift in itself, but it will mean substantial change to the content and direction of English teaching.

Increasingly, new developments in scholarship, in various fields, raise questions about what lurks in wait outside the present paradigmatic walls of English teaching. In framing policy advice and in trying to shape an educational future, I have been obliged to peek over the wall in a range of disciplines. The safeness of my English teaching mind is being threatened by what I see. I have been reading and listening to people talking about the frontiers of biology, physics[20], artificial intelligence, medicine and brain science [21], and technologies, including bio-technologies. It seems that, far beyond just English teaching, we are on the brink of a monumental paradigm shift.

There seems to be a coalescence of thinking in most disciplines, a realisation that the tradition of Western thought bequeathed by Aristotle, which has served us well so far, is reductive, fragmentary and, in some quite alarming ways, wrong. The awakening thoughts that I had in 'Zen And The Art of Languaging' (Chapter 8) point in the direction I see us having to take in the future. I think we will need, along with the medical scientists and physicians, to reconstrue the brain.

I predict that, as we understand more about the left brain-right brain functions, as we feel the effects of the shattering discovery that thinking is not served by electric circuitry in the brain so much as by hormones; that the brain is a gland and not a computer; that it is not 'dry' but 'wet', we may achieve new breakthroughs in the understanding and teaching of literacy. Richard Bergland[22] is currently disturbing my equilibrium in this respect:

> The new paradigm views the brain as a complex whole, an organ that does not stand apart from the rest of the body, run by different stuff, but shares the same internal milieu as other organs. At first glance the new holistic understanding of brain hormones seems mind-boggling, too complex to either understand or to be useful in designing better forms of therapy. But we now have no choice: we must acknowledge the unity of the brain and the body, admit that brain hormones are really body hormones and recognise that hormonal therapies aimed at making the brain whole again must replace reductionistic therapies aimed at bridling its electrical currents.

It is far too early to know just how these new discoveries will affect our understandings, but it looks to me as if, for instance, we will gain new insights into the right brain (pattern/image) role in our response to story and poetry. It is already clear that the behaviourist, direct-instruction, skills-based teaching of literacy will be laid to rest once and for all. What Koestler said of the genius may be equally true of the child learning to read and write, using the inspirational leaping and connecting power of the right brain:

> Most geniuses responsible for the major mutations in the history of thought seem to have certain features in common: on the one hand scepticism, often carried to the point of iconoclasm, in their attitude towards traditional ideas, axioms, and dogmas, towards everything that is taken for granted; on the other hand, an open-mindedness that verges on naive credulity towards new concepts which seem to hold out some promise to their instinctive gropings. Out of this combination results that crucial capacity of perceiving a familiar object, situation, problem, or collection of data, in a sudden new light or new context; of seeing a branch not as part of a tree, but as a potential weapon or tool; of associating the fall of an apple not with its ripeness, but with the motion of the moon. This discovery perceives relational patterns of functional analogies where nobody saw them before.[23]

What Kuhn says about scientific revolution I believe is happening, or is about to happen, in English teaching:

> During a scientific revolution...scientists take a different attitude toward existing paradigms, and the nature of their research changes accordingly. The proliferation of competing articulations, the willingness to try anything, the expression of explicit discontent, the recourse to philosophy and debate over fundamentals – all these are the symptoms of a transition from normal to extraordinary research.[24]

Similarly, at some point in English teaching, perhaps now, we will need to put aside our long tradition of rather petty malcontent and factional skirmishes *within* the existing paradigm, and make explicit our discontent with the paradigm itself.

Richard Bergland says:

> At present the world of brain science is in the middle of such a revolution...Holism replaces reductionism in a new paradigm

that gives human thoughts qualities that are warm, soft, wet, colourful, qualitative, timeless, communal and united.

In espousing the holism that is essential to neuroendocrinology, the pathfinders...may have shown us not only a better way to think about thinking but also a better way to live.[25]

Since writing this section, I find that Constance Weaver[26] in 1985 has dealt with the emerging paradigm in relation to language development in a most comprehensive and challenging way. Weaver ranges across new thinking in Quantum Physics, Chemistry and Biology, showing how new thinking in these areas is compatible with new insights into language development. She says that the 'mechanical metaphors' of the past three centuries have formed a prison which has prevented us from understanding other aspects of our world:

> In order not to become a similar prison, the organic paradigm toward which we are moving must include mechanism, must somehow transcend the simplistic dichotomy...and demonstrate the ways in which both mechanism and organicism are simultaneously true. This, of course, is what physicists themselves have done: with the advent of relativity theory and quantum mechanics, physicists have replaced the mechanistic model of the universe with an organic model, while still acknowledging that mechanism appears to be the best explanation for many aspects of reality. The universe itself is seen as fundamentally an organic process within which mechanism operates (p. 314).

Weaver, I note with pleasure, also finds the dance metaphor apt. She writes of the universe as 'fundamentally a dance of transient forms that sparkle in and out of existence...' (p. 313).

This gives some indication of the new challenges I am finding in my present work and in my reading. English teaching, as with neuroendocrinology, has always been about better ways of thinking and better ways of living. There is no doubt that the pleasurable struggle will continue.

With these introductory words, then, I invite you, the reader, to dance...

NOTES

1. Britton, J.N. (1970) *Language and Learning*, Penguin, London.
2. Vygotsky, L.S. (1962) *Thought and Language*, MIT Press, Cambridge.
3. See Garth Boomer 'Teachers' Learning,' South Australian Institute of Teachers, 1974, for a summary account of this research.
4. Langer, Susanne (1952) *Feeling and Form*, Routledge & Kegan Paul, London.
5. Polanyi, Michael (1958) *The Study of Man*, University of Chicago Press, Chicago.
6. Gusdorf, George (1965) *Speaking*, Northwestern University Press, Evanston, Il.
7. Berger, P. and Luckmann, T. (1966) *The Social Construction of Reality*, Penguin, New York.
8. de Saussure, F. (1974) *Course in General Linguistics*, Fontana, London.
9. Sapir, E. (1925) *Language*, Harcourt Brace, London.
10. Britton, *op. cit.*
11. Moffett, J. (1968) *Teaching the Universe of Discourse*, Houghton Mifflin, Boston.
12. Williams, R. (1968) *Culture and Society*, Penguin, London.
13. Trilling, L. (1964) *The Liberal Imagination: Essays on Literature and Society*, Secker & Warburg, London.
14. Hardy, Barbara, 'Towards a Poetics of Fiction: An Approach through Narrative,' *Novel* 2:2, Feb. 1986.
15. Giroux, H. (1981), 'Hegemony, resistance and the paradox of educational reform', *Interchange, 12.*, Nos 2-3.
16. Apple, M. (ed.) (1982) *Cultural and Economic Reproduction in Education*, Routledge, London.
17. Connell, R. et al. (1982) *Making the Difference*, Allen & Unwin, Sydney.
18. Foucault, M. (1980) *Power/Knowledge: Selected Interviews and Other Writings 1972-1977*, (edited by Colin Gordon), The Harvester Press, Sussex.
19. Boomer, G. (ed.) (1982) *Negotiating the Curriculum*, Ashton Scholastic, Sydney.

20. Zukav, Gary (1986) *The Dancing Wu Li Masters: An Overview of the New Physics*, Flamingo, Suffolk.
21. Bergland, Richard (1985) *The Fabric of Mind*, Penguin, Melbourne.
22. Bergland, Richard *op. cit.* p. 82
23. Koestler, A. Quoted in *The Fabric of Mind*, op. cit. p. 85
24. Kuhn, T. Quoted in *The Fabric of Mind, op. cit.* p. 92.
25. Bergland, Richard *The Fabric of Mind*, op. cit. p. 92.
26. Weaver, Constance (1985) 'Parallels between new paradigms in science and in reading and literary theories: An essay review,' *Research in the Teaching of English*, Vol. 19, No. 3, October, pp. 298-316.

SECTION ONE
On English Teaching

1

THE ENGLISH TEACHER, RESEARCH AND CHANGE

An address to the Research strand of the Third International Conference on the Teaching of English held in Sydney in 1980. The conference has now become a four yearly event of the International Federation for the Teaching of English.

Before trying to isolate significant influences on the English teacher in the past fifteen years and to assess the impact of research on classroom practice, I shall briefly sketch the network of constraints and pressures which surround the individual teacher. Figure 1, 'The Cosmic Egg of English Teaching', is an attempt to represent the forces and counterforces which act upon the teacher of English. It also attempts to assess the strength of the various forces.

In this paper, I wish to use the analogy of ecology to indicate the subtle interaction and interdependence of the system within which teachers work. I therefore find notions such as 'autonomy', 'conformity', and 'independence' inappropriate for my analysis. The English teacher is pictured within, not necessarily *trapped* within, a web of tensions. Some of these seem to me to have a higher valency than others in terms of their power to shape what happens in schools.

The umbrella of western/national/state politics and 'ruling' ideology along with economic (therefore technological and social) structure is, in my view, the chief determiner of the 'force field' or 'egg shell' within which English teaching is contained. In harmony or tension with this 'macro' umbrella, I see an equally significant 'micro control' coming from the individual's 'political/ethical profile'. The individual's belief system, having been socially constructed, is likely to be in basic sympathy with the 'macro control' but, depending on the subtle combination of all the other factors in an individual's life, it may be in tension with this macro control at various levels and in various ways.

Many of the values and beliefs embedded in the macro structure are implicit and tend to be reproduced unobtrusively from era to era, decade to decade, as part of the 'hidden curriculum' of culture.

FIGURE 1: THE COSMIC EGG OF ENGLISH TEACHING

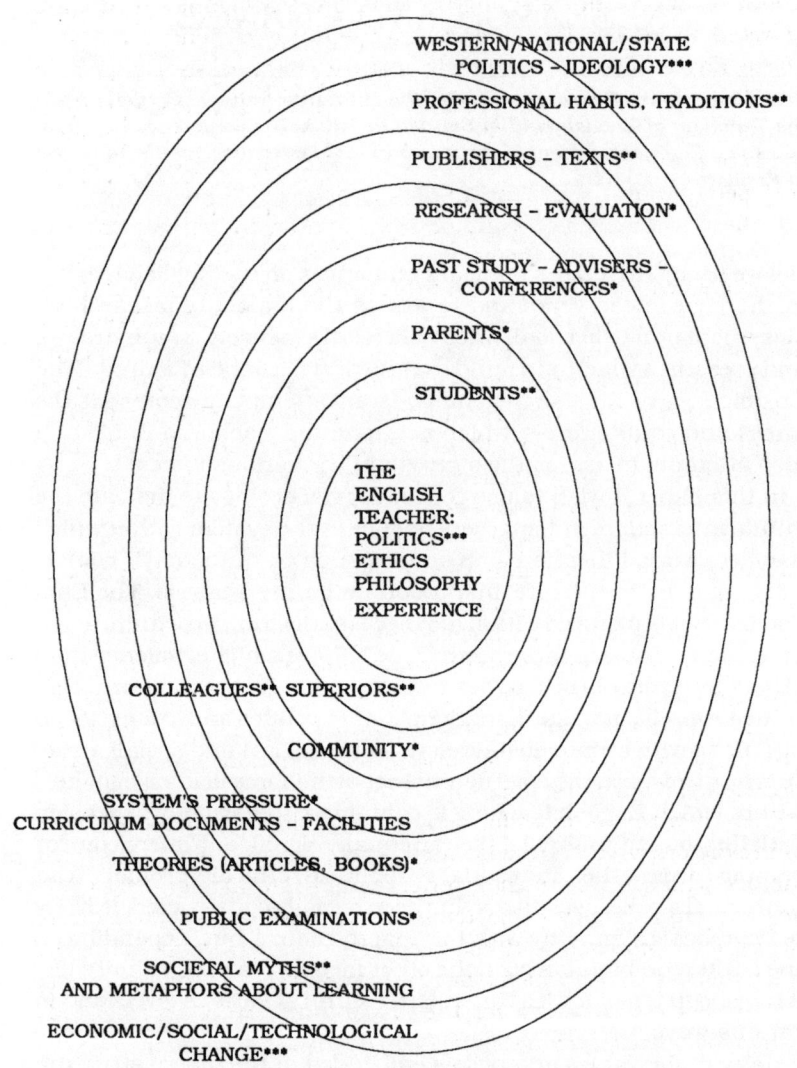

(*INDICATES POSSIBLE STRENGTH OF INFLUENCE)

A sub-set of these all-embracing 'habits' is the set of reproductions which accompany the continuing generations of teachers, more specifically English teachers. These tend to be indistinguishable from the general myths which lay-members of society perpetuate about teachers and teaching because the significant 'stories' are enacted as models for them during their stay at school. Many of these myths are well and truly institutionalised and 'reified' in public examinations, which represent established values, standards, and views of 'worthwhileness', and in textbooks, commercially or institutionally produced, which enshrine various contents and pedagogies. I see these influences as second-order forces.

If these are seen as essentially conservative influences, then in possible tension with them I would see the solutions continually being generated at the level of praxis. Each moment of the life of classrooms is likely to pose a problem requiring a creative solution. Teachers deal with these problems by calling on their personal and professional resources, usually in tension or collaboration with their students. Slightly less immediately, they may seek out help, directly or indirectly, from their teaching colleagues. The accumulated effect of solutions generated at the level of praxis may be to create a teacher consciousness which conflicts with aspects of the institutionalised pedagogies.

I therefore rate the influence of students and colleagues as 'second-order' variables along with textbooks and examinations.

At a third-order level I have rated the influence of a teacher's professional training (pre-service or in-service), of the system (through curriculum guides, advisers and conferences), of new theories and research, of the community (employers, pressure groups, parents) and of 'superiors' in education (faculty heads, principals, inspectors, etc.).

There is plenty of room for debate about the relative significance of the factors which I have isolated. There are also, no doubt, other factors which teachers themselves would rate as significant. My assessment is largely subjective, but I can call upon some aspects of my own research and the research of others to support the relatively low status which I ascribe to research and advisory work. This is not an argument for the discontinuation of research. My conception of research is that it is a crucial component in the various conversations of teachers, and of society, aspects of which conversations will eventually become part of the established mythos and thereby exert considerable influence *indirectly* on the course of education.

Having established my 'ecological' map of the English teacher in context, I have a means of reading the past fifteen years of English teaching. My analysis will not yield the truth but it may help us towards a more subtle understanding of our history and our likely futures.

I shall proceed by writing notes on some of the factors I have isolated before dwelling more fully on research and change.

Western/National/State Politics and Ideology

I would contend that although we get some changes in direction and emphasis in education according to which political party is in power, the overall effect of party-political change is fairly cosmetic, at least in Australia where politics tends to be prefigured by western philosophy, the economics of the USA and the desires of multinational pressure groups. Certain shared values tend to prevail across political parties – a roughly Christian ethic, the belief in parliamentary democracy, the rights of 'free' speech, etc. When a Liberal government holds sway in Australia, we see the metaphors of commerce, individual enterprise, competition and choice creeping into education. With a Labor government, there comes an emphasis on egalitarianism, social welfare and worker participation, but economic constraints do not usually allow great advances.

Such overriding western ideals as technological 'progress', profit and productivity, efficient use of time and resource, reward for effort, pride in achievement, obedience, loyalty, rationality and justice, as defined by the employers rather than the employed, permeate education. Those teachers who march to the beat of a radically different drummer are either subtly contained or openly repressed.

Because the ruling ideologies have changed little in the past fifty years, it is difficult to see much change in the ideals which are either explicitly or implicitly upheld in schools, but there have been some interesting changes in mood which seem to have an economic and party-political base.

I would characterise the period 1966-1970 in Australian English teaching as a breaking free from the hardened boundaries of English in terms of content and style. There was a grass-roots reaction against the imperialist policies which led to the idiocy of Vietnam.

A new idealism and belief in the individual's capacity for growth arose as an antidote to the inhuman atrocities of the war. Eventually, in Australia, this led to a change of government.

English teaching reflected this questioning of society. The thematic approach, the moves towards exploiting literature to illuminate current social issues, the proliferation of courses offering choice, the undermining of public examination restrictions, all fitted the English teacher's growing disillusionment with the old order. The cheerful economic situation meant that the 'back to basics' push was fairly feeble. Money for education was beginning to flow. Advisers were unheard of in 1966. By 1970 all states in Australia were beginning to develop advisory networks. Creative techniques were invented to provide multiple sets of books, thereby breaking the stranglehold of the 'set' course. It was a time of liberalism.

Looking back, I think it was a time when the house of English was redecorated and a few additions were built on. Despite the appearance of change there were, however, no fundamental structural changes. The architects and home owners just became a little more flamboyant and daring. New gadgets and new ways of doing things evolved. Open-space classrooms, individualised work-sheets, cartoon-packed textbooks, electives and excursions came into their own. Alternative courses also took hold. 'Catering for individual differences' was a popular slogan.

From 1970-74, money flowed even more generously. Innovation was economically supported as soon as the Labor Government took power, almost as if it were a good thing in itself. Schools (and English teachers) were encouraged, almost bullied into inviting community participation in education. The National Committee on the Teaching of English was established, along with a number of other national committees, to do some future-gazing and to recommend on the needs of the profession. After the 'flush' of breaking free, there was, at least at the 'conference going' level, a desire for knowledge, research, a sound conceptual base.

As Whitlam changed our national stance on foreign policy, English teachers also began to look outside. Visitors from America and England to various conferences helped to create the belief that there could be some international policies on English teaching.

Since 1975 a good number of fires have been put out or voluntarily died. A change of government; a down-turn in the economy; unemployment; and we find ourselves in the present state of fear and guilt. We are being urged to go back, to conserve, to play safe, to tighten up, to cut down and to take control at the very time when we are beginning to understand our craft better; indeed, at a time of national ferment about language in education. We fear and doubt the things we almost did during the outbreak. We are guilty because we half-believe the myths that children cannot get jobs because of their spelling. *Language One* (a popular English textbook in Astralia in the late 1970s and early 1980s) is a political document, beautifully symbolising that the ruling ideologies of law and order have been re-asserted after some minor aberrations.

Professional Habits and Societal Myths

Perhaps the best way to represent some of the tensions between professional habit and exploration in the last fifteen years is to pose some of the polarities.

Habit	*Possibility*
Using only acknowledged, 'good' literature.	Using any literature, including 'pop' literature, which will 'connect'.
Never giving full marks.	Giving no grading at all and simply responding.
Correcting every error.	Replacing teacher correction by student editing.
Using comprehension texts and language exercise books to teach 'grammar'.	Using no exercise books and working on actual scripts.
Seeing poems, plays and novels as the core of English.	Re-conceiving English as language study and development.
Getting students to write essays about writing.	Encouraging students to be authors in their own right.
Streaming classes according to ability.	Not streaming at all.
Teachers programming the work for students.	Students and teachers programming together.
Keeping the identity of English secure.	Discovering new ways of dividing knowledge (Humanities, Integrated Studies, etc.).

Speaking and writing correctly at all times.	Developing flexibility in language codes and registers; replacing 'correctness' with the notion of 'appropriateness.'
Running a quiet orderly classroom.	Allowing for group discussion, debate and interchange.

Teachers in defining themselves within some of these polarities are forced to take account of 'societal myths' about English teaching and learning. Here are a few of which I am strongly aware:

- Learning language is like building a house. You need a good basic foundation and then gradually, brick by brick, you can build the walls. Eventually it will be a good place to live in. (How can you write a sentence until you know how to build up all the parts?
- Children learn by practice (drill) and imitation with reward for correctness and penalty for error. (If their spelling is not corrected, they will develop bad habits – bad spelling today; heroin tomorrow.)
- English teachers should help children to speak properly and correctly and to write properly and correctly so that they can get a good job ('better job than we parents had').
- English teachers should put 'good books' in front of children, not books which deal with controversial social, sexual and religious issues.
- To pass English you have to know your facts and quotations and be able to write in sentences.
- Bad speech is a sign of slovenliness and bad citizenship.

It is, of course, dangerous to imply that all members of the community lean strongly towards these myths. My experience is that people are more than ready to alter their myths if the professionals convince them that they are wrong or misleading. Teachers, however, seem more than ready to cite societal myths for their own purpose. ('We'd like to do it, but the parents wouldn't like it.')

I am presently depressed because so many of my colleagues seem to be knuckling under to the perceived myths of society. We could, I believe, with effectiveness:

...take arms against a sea of troubles –
And by opposing end them.

Publishers

The year 1966 was the beginning of the end of centrally-prescribed texts for English at the secondary level. Few were bold enough to suggest total school-based curriculum then, but there was a strong groundswell of discontent with the pre-emptive central course, soon to be followed by rebellion even at prescription by the Faculty Head. Ironically, it seems that as the centre relinquished its hold on the content and spirit of English courses, the publishers moved in to provide the crutch, or the manacles, for the unskilled, the uncertain and the lazy.

The course book (or various euphemisms for it 'source books', 'collections', 'explorations') have always been a part of mainstream English teaching. It would be most interesting to test the relative influence of ruling ideology and research on the contents. My personal view is that there has ben a clearly observable dialectic of textbooks in which the 'habit' books have done battle with the new wave (and research-oriented) texts. A brief examination of texts which have attempted to hold the middle ground over the past fifteen years gives some indication of the dialectics.

1966:	*English in Australian Schools*	Ridout and McGregor
	Using Better English	Allsopp and Hunt
1968:	*Reflections**	Clements, Dixon, Stratta
	*Themes and Responses**	Delves and Tickell
	*Voices**	Summerfield
1970:	*Sandals in One Hand**	Boomer and Hood
	Personal English Programme	Rousch
	*Patchwork**	Carozzi
1972:	*Connexions**	Penguin Series
	*The Bad Deeds Gang**	Hannan and Tickell
	*Language in Use**	Doughty et al.
	English Today	Allsopp, Hunt et al.
1974:	*Mastering Words* (revival)	R.D. Walshe
	Catalyst	Esta de Fossard
	Your Move	Neil Fuller
1976:	*Smile On The Face of The Tiger*	Sadler, Hayller, Powell
	*English for Life**	Davis and Spicer
	Roll Over Shakespeare	Hayller, Powell, Sadler

22 *Metaphors and Meanings*

1978   *Language and Communications** Forsyth and Wood
to   *Language 1*   Sadler, Hayller, Powell
1980 *Inform**   Howard

The asterisk indicates books which I consider to be attempts to take account of certain emerging theories. *Reflections*, for instance, owes much to the work and thinking which inspired the Dartmouth conference. *Patchwork* attempted to bring Holbrook's work on literature and new insights into the reading process together in a textbook for the less able. *Connexions* was pushing the boundaries of English towards sociology in the name of relevance. *Language in Use* grew out of the work of Michael Halliday and his team and is therefore directly related to a branch of linguistics. *English for Life* attempts to apply aspects of socio-linguistics, and is related in this attempt to *Language and Communication*. Counterpoised against these are the habitual exercise-type books, variously dressed, or the 'bob-each-way' books which go for the safe ground.

Clearly in 1980 the *Language I, II, III, IV* series is top of the popularity poll, registering a dismal 'base' in the litmus test of English teachers.

Not so clearly indicated on my list is the larger battle between language and literature for the central ground, the 'core' of English. Many of those opposed to course books and disillusioned after the surfeit of source books are spending their money on 'primary sources', novels, poetry, plays. This tendency might be seen as a parallel 'back to the basics' move by the literature push. Conversely, it might be seen as a radical and informed move by those who see all textbooks as patronising of teachers' heads and essentially toxic in effect.

Research and The English Teacher

I have spent much of the past five years talking with secondary English teachers who were seeking promotion to the position of Faculty Head. It is one of my aims in these conversations to assess the extent to which the teacher has read significant new works relevant to English teaching. I also seek to engage the teacher in professional debate about current political and theoretical issues in English teaching. Given that these are teachers of some years' experience who are considered to be competent in their craft, it seems reasonable for me to generalise cautiously about English teaching and research on the basis of these interviews (approximately 150 in number). These are my findings:

- It is rare for a teacher to be able to engage in detailed debate about the significance of advances in our understanding of language learning.
- Teachers may have heard of Britton, Barnes, Moffett and Halliday but few have read them (apart from the odd quotations). Fewer still have the ability to discuss in detail the implications of the work of these people for English teaching.
- While many have been exposed to language theory in their pre-service education, it seems that most have not retained what they did in such a way that it can inform and shape their classroom practice. Attempts to revive memories usually result in vague references.
- When challenged to become engaged in consideration of theories and research, most teachers will unashamedly, some aggressively, say that they are essentially practitioners and question the usefulness of theorists.
- Teachers are able to talk reasonably fluently on topics and slogans which have currency (Language Across the Curriculum; 'Remedial' Reading; Streaming; Course Books; 'Back to Basics'). Their talk is informed by praxis and discussion with colleagues, rather than by reading or attendance at courses.
- Central curriculum guides are not well known in most schools. They may have been read superficially but they do not provide a continuing reference point.
- There are outstanding examples of teachers with a well-articulated personal theory of English teaching, but, by and large, teachers are operating, effectively or not, on implicit notions.

These findings do no necessarily mean that I see English teachers negatively. My personal view is that English teachers will not be liberated and capable of finding cracks in their cosmic egg until they have developed a personally articulated set of principles and theories to justify, explain and inform what they do. This can happen without any reference to outside theorists. Some of the best teachers I know have got their act together by tenaciously examining their own practice and reflecting upon it *without* the aid of advisers, theorists and philosophers. On the other hand, I think even these teachers would benefit from the challenge of engaging with minds which bring a new perspective to the craft.

My findings do not lead to the conclusion that researchers and theorists have little effect on English teaching. Researchers are part of the ecological system and therefore everything they do must change the balance in some way. From my evidence, however, I do not see many direct relationships between researchers and teachers. More diffusely, indirectly and mysteriously, the work of the theorists must have its effect on teachers, and conversely the work of teachers must similarly contribute to the shaping of research. Perhaps our main task, now as always, is to speculate on ways of bringing teachers and researchers into more direct partnership.

I have said that the theorists must affect English teaching. A brief analysis of the last fifteen years may help to justify my confidence. My comments on the textbook industry suggest one way in which theory comes to have a considerable influence on practice. But there seems to be a more subtle and probably more powerful dissemination process at work.

Perhaps I can explain it best by comparing researchers and theorists with story-tellers. How do some yarns eventually become part of the mythos of a culture? How do stories spread? Why do some stories die?

The way I see the last fifteen years is that, as a profession, English teachers in varying degrees and sometimes in partisan factions have come under the spell of certain powerful weavers of tales. It is not the details of the research, the ins and outs of the plot, which remain with teachers; it is the ruling metaphors or frames of mind, the ideas, which have somehow caught their imagination and inspired them to be better teachers than they are. The story-tellers are, of course, not just theorists and researchers. Politicians, principals, religious leaders, playwrights and teachers themselves can all claim the conch shell if their story is generative or compelling enough.

What catches fire depends on the present state of the 'eco' system of ideas and practice. It also depends on the ethical/political profile, the established frame of mind of those who listen to the story. Theory does not catch on because it is true, rather, because it vibrates positively and sympathetically with the growing intuitions and beliefs of the teacher. Research which threatens the deep-seated constructs of a teacher will be rejected or not heard.

My hypothesis, then, is that the most influential figures in English teaching in the realm we have designated as 'research and theory' are the metaphor-makers. Let me name my team of top metaphor-makers in the past fifteen years of English teaching: Noam Chomsky (the metaphor of the language generator); Lem Semenovich Vygotsky (the metaphor of dialectical language and thought); Susanne Langer (the metaphor of mind as symbol maker); George Mead (the metaphor of the social construction of reality); Basil Bernstein (the metaphors of boundary and control). These people tell stories in their own right but most have come to influence English teachers through superb intermediaries, story-tellers like James Britton, Frank Smith, Kenneth Goodman, John Dixon, David Holbrook, Harold Rosen, James Moffett, Lawrence Stenhouse, and Douglas Barnes, to name some of the word-spinners who have set my mind afire. These tend to be wise generalists who can translate for teachers. Some of these metaphor-makers and story-tellers are also map-makers offering to English teachers ways of analysing the territory of English teaching. Some of the most influential maps in the past fifteen years have come from Britton, Barnes, Moffett, Halliday and Tough.

Then there are some story-tellers themselves and some technicians who go on to invent tools for teachers which are a kind of do-it-yourself kit. Used well, these tools lead teachers to re-construe both their theory and their practice because of what the tool leads them to see. Striking examples are the Miscue Inventory which arose out of the Goodmans' work; the Barnes/Schemilt technique of analysing teaching style; *Breakthrough to Literacy* and *Language in Use*, the 'tools' which accompanied Halliday's work; and anthologies such as *Voices*, by Geoffrey Summerfield, which exemplified a new understanding of the relationship between poetry and culture.

People like Harold Rosen, Nancy Martin and Lawrence Stenhouse have captured imaginations with their vision of teachers as story-tellers. One of the most exciting advances of the past ten years has been the growth in 'action-research' – teachers recording, documenting and reflecting on the life of their own classrooms. Slowly and significantly this will change the balance of story-telling power. Metaphors are being exchanged and evaluated: 'It's a fine metaphor, Professor Bernstein, but it doesn't fit my classroom as neatly as you seem to suggest.'

Maybe I am too close to this work because of my specialist involvement, and this may lead me to be unduly optimistic about the new growth of teacher power. It is certainly a nice dream.

I am daunted but not depressed by the enormity of trying to put some tabs on the last fifteen years. It is good for me to try to tell the story. If I delude myself that there has been a discernible, if slow, march of mind, that there has been a lift in consciousness, then I must plead that I need thus to delude myself in order to stay with the cause.

In order to convince myself that we have 'come a long way', I have isolated four areas in which, for the better, I think English teaching will never be the same again. Whether they know the sources of the stories or not, teachers owe a debt to some seminal thinkers and researchers.

Language and Learning

The notion of language as resource for personal growth, popularised by John Dixon in *Growth Through English*, is bound up with a conception of the way in which the human mind works. George Kelly inspired James Britton with his conception of the human being as born scientist, hypothesising about the world and acting on these hypotheses. Chomsky, discredited as he may be on some scores, revolutionised our understanding of how language is acquired. The mind induces deep principles and generates infinite patterns. Vygotsky, with a similar conception of mind, helped us to see the links between language and thinking. Bruner and the cognitivist psychologists are pushing this work further each year, all the time clarifying the role of the various media of symbolic representation in human learning.

If people like Kelly, Chomsky, Vygotsky, and Bruner are the metaphor-makers in this realm, Frank Smith, Kenneth Goodman, James Britton, James Moffett, John Dixon and Douglas Barnes have been the popular story-tellers. Roger Brown, Courtney Cazden, Carol Chomsky, Gordon Wells and many others have also contributed lovely stories about language development which confirm the overriding conception of the scientific mind.

At the level of the English classroom these stories have been realised in changed pedagogy. Directly or indirectly through the work of people such as Britton and Barnes, enlightened English teachers are providing more time and opportunity for student talk and interim formulation of thought in writing. So-called discovery or research methods relate to language and learning theories. Rather than telling or giving the rules, many more teachers in 1980, compared with 1966, are challenging students to solve their own problems, individually or in collaboration with their colleagues, and to discover underlying principles.

Of course, there have been some counter-productive misconceptions and misapplications of these theories. A loose understanding of 'learning through language' has sometimes led to over-indulgent languishing in the *process* with no worthwhile territory to explore and no mind-expanding problem to solve.

Fiction and Culture

This is an area where I am a little less sure about the effects on classroom practice. I am also a little less sure where the original metaphors have been forged. I am sure, however, that just as a clearer conception of language is emerging, so there is an emerging new picture of literature as a fundamental human activity. The very metaphor of storying which informs this paper is an indication of what I mean. The anthropologists and people like Susanne Langer have helped us to break the narrow bonds of Literature defined with a capital L. Whenever human beings begin to construct an image of life, a fiction, then they are using the 'literary' function of language.

Just as archaeology can help us to read a culture through its artefacts, so the unearthing of a culture's literature, not just its 'museum' pieces, can help us to re-construct the texture of daily life. Leavis's view of literature and culture was a forerunner to new theories of literature and society but it lacked the generosity of including all literature. Raymond Williams and the Marxist literary critics such as Goldmann and Lukacs have help us reconstrue the extent and role of literature. Williams, in particular, has reminded us of the huge reservoir of working class literature which has previously been excluded from histories of literature and, of course, from classrooms.

And so, people like Harold Rosen and Raymond Williams have encouraged us to extend the range of literature read and made in classrooms. Rosen and networks of Inner London teachers have reminded us of the multicultural mix of classrooms and the need therefore to have an *inclusive* rather than exclusive view of literature.

At its best this influence on English teaching has led to less precious teaching of literature, more vigorous making of literature, and more intensive mining of literature to unearth cultural and political meaning as well as plot.

Function and Form

During the seventies in Australia, particularly since the arrival of Michael Halliday to our shores, there has been an increasingly loud call for English teachers to take language, both in form and function, seriously. It is not just a resource, it is a rule-governed symbol system. Halliday, perhaps more than any other story-teller, forces us to see language as part of a total 'context of situation'. He pictures human beings learning language in social interaction within the context of culture. The power of his conception of language, compared with that of other linguists, is the concerted emphasis on *meaning*. Taken from its context of situation and studies clinically, language is meaningless.

Halliday, with James Britton, is obviously a rare teacher as well as being a world authority on language. Teachers who study with him emerge taking language seriously and with strategies for translating the theory into the practice of English teaching.

It is a pity that many people see Halliday's view as opposed to that of Britton. Certainly Halliday reminds us, in contrast to Britton's emphasis on language as resource, of the importance of teaching *about* language, but his overarching metaphors are not sharply in conflict with Britton's.

At the classroom level, Halliday's work is being realised in approaches to language which emphasise study of *all* the functions of language, not just literature, and study of language in *use*, not as an isolated exercise.

Perhaps the most exciting results of Halliday's influence can be seen in those classrooms where children are becoming their own researchers into the language of the community and the classroom. Study of the language, in this way, inevitably leads children to consider the appropriateness of language to situation, the falsity of the notions of 'correctness', and the effect of relative status of participants on language exchange.

In this way, children are being given power through understanding how meanings are framed and exchanged in society.

Class and Control

While Basil Bernstein has been discredited or misunderstood, depending on your point of view, with respect to the early work on restricted and elaborated codes, there is no doubt that he has been one of our most exciting and influential metaphor-makers. Directly or indirectly he has led English teachers in Australia to look closely at the way in which language is used to control, to exclude and to sort. He has forced us to consider the 'middle classness' of schools and the effect which this has on the language and learning of those who have learnt alternative values and styles of meaning-exchange. The term 'hidden curriculum' takes on new meaning when examined in the light of Bernstein's work on the framing of knowledge. The very way we divide and package knowledge becomes a powerful weapon of control and imperialism in the realm of values.

My own work on 'negotiating the curriculum' is directly related to Bernstein's writing about the differential aspects of *explicit* as opposed to *implicit* control. Control and styles of using power have always been pre-occupations of English teachers, but Bernstein has helped to clarify the issues and to discredit the once popular view of the under-achieving child as deficient language user (as opposed to the view of the school as inadequate language environment).

English teachers, through the work of Bernstein and others such as Rosen, Shuy, and Halliday, are now more aware of the cultural bigotry of traditional schooling, and the more enlightened are painfully working away at their ingrained linguistic and cultural prejudices.

The problem which Bernstein poses to English teachers is how to give children access to power. In order to teach this, they must be able to demonstrate that they themselves know some of the secrets of access to power. They must be able to demonstrate their own ability to struggle and to question.

This brings me to a point where it is appropriate to stop. Teachers who are their own researchers will not be cowed by acknowledged theorists. They will tenaciously require those who talk profoundly or obscurely to yield their secrets. Once yielded, these secrets will be tested in practice. Here we have the challenge of investigating ways in which teachers can have greater access to power. This will involve exploration of present blockages, impediments and restrictions.

The last fifteen years prove to me that English teachers *are* being affected by theory and research. What worries me is whether we English teachers are significantly more able to shape, control and reject the subtle influences which come at us. How well do we know our cosmic egg?

2

STRUGGLING IN ENGLISH[1]

The inaugural address by Garth, as president of the Australian Association for the Teaching of English. It was presented at the A.A.T.E. annual conference in Melbourne, in 1981.

Teachers teach most profoundly what they are at the core. The lasting lesson is the demonstration of the self as it handles its authority and those under its authority. At the same time this 'self' demonstrates how it in turn responds to those in authority over it. It demonstrates how to deal with problems and crises, how to treat those who do not know, how to laugh or not laugh, and indeed, how to demonstrate. The self of the *English* teacher demonstrates how to make and take meanings, what to attend to in literature and life, how to make linguistic and life choices, how to be an English teacher and what English is.

Most of these demonstrations are not deliberate. These 'chunked' pervasive symbolic demonstrations can be contrasted with the deliberate demonstrative 'events' in school, the more atomistic lessons of the curriculum where the teacher can usually articulate what is being taught. I shall call these profound demonstrations 'chunks' because they develop as patterns in the context of continuing living, somewhat like a painting or a story or a poem. They are complex personalised networks of concepts, beliefs and symbols which are continually being enacted socially. Because they are recursive, redundant, persistent and tautologous in nature, they are probably assimilated and understood as non-deliberately as they are being demonstrated. They are not dinned into the consciousness of the learner but globally apprehended. By contrast it is much harder to 'read' and connect the more ephemeral parts of the formal English curriculum, just as it is difficult to understand sentences or words out of context.

Cognitive psychologists, aware of the need for learning brains to find 'cognitive footholds', have developed theories and strategies for *deliberate* 'chunking' – for the organisation of demonstrations so that the new territory is pre-structured and arranged to allow the 'known' of the learner to engage or relate to the unknowns in the territory. Bruner's 'Man: A Course of Study' is a classic example of such chunking.

English teachers in the late sixties and seventies, possibly without articulate 'chunking' theories, developed the thematic approach as a way of better demonstrating the coherences and conjunctions of literature and life.

At a meta level, each cognitive psychologist, and each composing English teacher, is demonstrating what he or she believes about human brains and human society. If the chunking is designed to inculcate specific, common learnings across all learners, if, in other words, the teacher has quite specific designs on the learner's head, we are not far removed from the reinforcement theories of the early behaviourists. We have simply found fancier ways of doing it. We still demonstrate that brains can be programmed.

If, on the other hand, the teacher's chunking, deliberate or unwitting, rests on a larger core 'chunked' belief that what learners learn from pre-structured external chunks is determined by their own efforts and their own prior chunking, then the teacher will have demonstrated that learning is a personal struggle for personal meaning and that the brain is a tenacious actor upon the world. There can never be totally common learnings. Brains under one regime, if the regime persisted across all teachers, could be expected gradually to convince themselves to 'shut up' and receive. Brains under the other regime would learn to keep struggling towards sense.

Here I wish to demonstrate a deliberately basic chunk of myself, a belief that the deep core of the curriculum, through all levels of education and all subjects, should be 'struggling'. This will be my contribution to the current debates about 'transition education'. I will address, in particular, the special contribution which English can make to this core of struggling.

In order to teach struggling, by my beginning assumption, English teachers must themselves be *bona fide* strugglers, preferably with a theory of their own and other people's struggling. To be a high level struggler, one would need to include in this theory a persistent struggle to overthrow one's own theory.

I will ask you to imagine, as I proceed, what would happen in schools if each teacher deliberately chunked what he or she knows about struggling and then deliberately taught children how to do it, pervasively, in a continuing demonstration of the self at work. What would happen if to teach and to learn were seen to be synonymous with the verb 'to struggle'?

I realise that beyond or beneath the construct of struggling there are probably more powerful values which drive and direct. Struggle towards what and with what intentions? A capitalist will readily salute my injunction to struggle, as long as it means struggle towards profit for the eventual bosses and struggle to work more productively (and to keep a job) for the workers. The Christian may teach struggling towards purity and Christ; the Marxist, struggling towards the revolution. The liberal may teach individual, self-interested struggling; the socialist, struggling together.

I hope that I teach struggling to make sense, to understand, and then to act individually or collectively in accordance with the understanding. I hope I also teach struggling judiciously against the forces which constrain and contain my will to act according to principle. Because I continually question my own values and struggles (when I discover them), I also teach how to struggle against certainty. While I might sometimes dream of the millennium when everyone is like me (an eventual nightmare), I am actually committed to a society where all people struggle whether with me or against me. For this to occur, everyone would need to be a deliberate struggler.

When I first publicly suggested struggling as the core of education, a gently cynical friend said that he had an image of a can of worms, struggling in a container. Clearly I reject that image. I mean *intentional* struggling, constructive struggling, concerned struggling, inspired by a kind of educational Darwinism[2].

But even if none of my teaching colleagues shared this meaning and yet all tenaciously and deliberately taught t*heir* version of struggling, I believe we would have something of an educational revolution. As it is, so many, having given up the struggle, teach acquiescence, correctness, ritual, subordination, *fear* and how to fail – the ingredients of retro-revolution, disastrous in terms of universal psycho-social evolution and, specifically, disastrous in terms of so-called 'transition' from school to post-school life in the eighties.

The aims, goals and structures, the very cogs of education which have remained largely unchanged since the industrial revolution, creak and rattle as panicky 'basic' mechanics apply the once-good oil. The mass-produced species will not survive.

In the curriculum, we tend to be atomistic at the subject level and at the lesson level. We do not, by and large, 'chunk' powerful ideas and human strategies. Instead we seem to work on the principle of 'cumulative fragmentalism'[3]. The learner may one day make sense. This is inefficient and outmoded pedagogy. Ultimately, I am suggesting we will have to chunk knowledge in radically different ways well beyond the present experiments with social education and environmental studies. These are still underpinned by some notion of common *content*. The underlying metaphor is still inert bodies of knowledge.

I am contemplating a future curriculum chunked first according to *process* and then directed towards gutsy content and issues. Imagine 'The School of Struggling' which offers the following 'subjects':

- **Chunking** (the making of theories, ideologies and beliefs)
- **Tool Making and Using** (analysing, applying, constructing)
- **Symbol Making** (semiology, storying, 'arting', making music, making marks)
- **Working Together** (group work, patterns of organisation, decision making)
- **Nurturing** (sexual reproduction, caring, planting, fertilizing, tending, feeding)
- **Decoding** (interpreting cultures, literatures, media, societies, human behaviours, political parties, languages, dialects, etc.)
- **Exchanging** (buying, selling, bartering and sharing)
- **Amplifying** (transporting, reckoning, communicating, computing, exploring).

Here are eight subjects for the twenty-first century all to be informed by the theory or value of struggling and all, I suggest, basic to the survival and evolution of the species. Present 'disciplines' would illuminate each of these new subjects where appropriate. English, for example, would be particularly strong in chunking, symbol-making and decoding.

My secondary school daughter says that she would love to go to such a school. Maybe it is just her anticipation of novelty, but there seems also to be an excitement about the implicit dynamism and futurism in this scenario, in contrast with the 'setness' and past orientation of the traditional subjects she now studies.

You will note that these subjects are strongly directed towards living and acting in the world, that they relate fundamentally to those things which characterise and empower the human race, and that they do not distinguish between vocational and non-vocational pursuits, nor between the 'academic' and the 'practical'.

Because such radical re-framing of knowledge is some time away, I shall not pursue the vision further here. Instead, I wish to focus on the present subject English to see what we might be getting on with on the way.

At its worst in the past, English has been, to be punny, a kind of 'Angle-ish' – a game where teachers try to get students hooked on good literature; a contest in which the 'educated imagination' of the teacher tries to lure, overtly or covertly, the unformed imaginations of the schools of 'finny prey'. I suggest we are evolving towards something which I shall call 'Strugglish', where the emphasis is upon tenacious collaborative forging of meaning, contradiction, question and opposition to those who try to impose a governing imagination. Indeed the best English teaching I know is fully fledged 'Strugglish'.

The tension in schools today, to put it crudely, is between the anglers and the strugglers; between 'the psychological/political policemen' (as Harold Rosen recently put it) and the space fighters who run the gauntlet of 'hostility and threat'. Rosen in a brilliant account of present English teaching⁴ sees schools:

> [not as] battle grounds where major collisions between alternative views are fought out and a few heroes go to their doom. In most there is a never ending series of small but important skirmishes and incursions. They arise because so many teachers cannot fail, to some extent at least, 'to suspect the work the system asks them to do' and to confront its contradictions and tensions.

Rosen is at pains to acknowledge the countless 'little heroes' who struggle everyday in schools to win spaces for their students' cultures and minds⁵. I think it is with some pride that he quotes Gerald Grace who carried out a careful study of sixteen urban comprehensive schools with respect to their ideology and control:

> English teachers represented a complete spectrum of ideological positions in education, from the Arnoldian stance to the Marxist. If they differed significantly from other groups of teachers it was not in respect of a thorough-going radicalism designed to subvert

the conventions of English usage, but as a group they contained more teachers who exhibited 'radical doubt' and critical reflection about the curriculum...in certain schools their members showed *a distinctive awareness of recent theoretical criticisms of the assumptions of traditional curricula and of the dilemmas and possibilities which these posed* (Rosen's italics).[6]

Rosen acknowledges that we are in danger of being crushed by the I.S.A. (the Ideological State Apparatus, as described by Louis Althusser), but he refuses to accept the bleakest determinism of the academic far left. Acknowledging that many conservative educational commentators are gleefully recording the demise of the so-called 'social democracy' and 'progressive-ism' of the late sixties and early seventies, he graphically depicts the alternative:

> In hard times it is Gradgrind and Squeers who cast the longest shadows and all the schemes which in the past confined, stultified and inhibited the language learning of school students are being dusted down, refurbished; old discredited practices come with modern labels. Cross out *Graded English Exercises* and call it *Graded Language Development* (p. 5).

And yet:

> ...Bleak House...for all its high walls cannot shut out messages from outside which will be loud or muted according to the strength or weakness of the forces for change in the community. In English teaching we have been able to register this pulse in very specific ways (p. 17).

I now want to come to a brief consideration, in very general terms, of what is pulsing outside the walls of schools, before closing on the specific struggles of English.

In opening, I spoke of what the individual teacher demonstrates 'at the core'. It is possible and generative, I think, to take a similar view of western society since the industrial revolution. I am indebted to Alvaro Ascui for much of the following analysis[7]. In a recent unpublished paper, Ascui applies Kellian construct theory, originally designed for individual clinical psychology, to society itself. He 'chunks' the dominant ideas of our culture and, in Kelly's terms, begins to analyse where the very slots of our ideologies are being rattled. This, if you like, is the macro struggle within which schools, and English teachers, can – or rather, must – do their bit.

Looming over all is the superordinate construct, Life-Death. Death has been seen as the opposite of life. All things bright and beautiful are aligned with life. There is a stigma, a social taboo, attached to death. All the lesser societal constructs are emotionally charged with the power of the ruling construct. Death stalks the negative poles of all our constructs.

Ascui defines three constructs at the next level: 'progress-decay' (with 'civilisation-primitiveness' and 'growth-decrease' subordinate to it); 'activity-passivity' (with 'work-idleness', 'male-female', 'ruler-subject' subordinate); and 'order-chaos' (with 'man-nature', 'part-whole' and 'reason-emotion' subordinate). He then proceeds to link these constructs with the 'isms' of western society such as 'scientific determinism', 'productivism', 'utilitarianism', 'sexism', 'authoritarianism', 'anthropocentrism', 'reductionism' and 'rationalism'.

It is at this level that we can see specific societal struggles which indicate how, in Ascui's terms, the dominant paradigm is being threatened. He depicts a system in crisis, a system where we must all struggle to evolve new 'psycho-social-constructs' in order to survive.

Each one of the 'isms' is being threatened at its base. For example, the simplistic, emotionally charged distinction between work and idleness is a stereotype now being challenged by the fact of millions of jobless. The exploitation of those previously construed into passive roles (women, servants, the workers, third world countries) is being attacked and weakened on many fronts. In separating humanity from nature (order from chaos), we have in many ways alienated ourselves from our environment. At the conservationist and alternative life-style fronts, anthropocentrism is being eroded. The territories once colonised by rationalism are giving way to a more unified view, reluctantly admitting the powers and forces of emotion.

These and many other struggles illustrate the present contested nature of social and cultural reproduction. The extent to which schools acknowledge and educate for and about this contest will depend on the ability of teachers to struggle against the mind-paralysing lobotomies of the established institution and its codes, not to mention the inertia of their own personal constructs. There is a massive transition problem for schools; it is no less than a challenge to educate for transition to a new society, *against* the ruling constructs of yesterday.

In turning to the special struggles of the English teacher, I can add little more to Harold Rosen's analysis which I shall now briefly summarise as imperatives for the eighties.

We must struggle to relinquish some of our authority by admitting the children's experience. We must allow the voices of living cultures into our classrooms. We must supplement the hitherto 'thin gruel of culture we administer with Bumble's spoon'. We must admit and foster constructive contradiction. We must break down the discontinuity of school and community:

> This is the most thorough-going strategy of *control*, an elaborated methodology which leaves huge oppressive silences, a muffling and gagging of all those disturbing voices which might otherwise be heard in schools.[8]

We must learn to listen to the insidious silent 'musak' of the institution, to see the invisible procedures and criteria, 'the very grounds of authority's legitimation'. Then, in the classroom, we must introduce 'disruptive' literature with compelling themes to illuminate, not reflect, culture. We must remove books from that arcane realm of the 'interposed screen of interrogation and privileged interpretation'[9].

We must not relinquish what we have learnt in the past twenty years about reading and writing and how it is best taught. We must stand up against the bigoted and misinformed who think that:

> ...language is essentially something to be cured, cleansed and purged of deformities rather than extended, enriched, developed.[10]

Daunting as it may sound, we will only make headway as opposition, 'whether it be about the choice of literature, the significance of West Indian dialect, how children learn to read, the learning of English as a second language, the significance of spelling, English for industry and commerce, or anything else'[11].

Moving on from Rosen's gritty optimism (for he believes that many English teachers will carry on the struggle), I want to finish with some remarks about the 'strugglish' teacher in interaction with the struggling learner.

In a recent monograph[12], Don Novick records the opinions of teachers and students in a South Australian comprehensive secondary school. I have extracted three pieces which will help me to focus on key issues.

At on point in an interview Bob Brand (in his fourth year of high school) says: 'I have mucked it up that much now I might as well muck it up the rest of the way'[13]. Here we have an example of what Frank Smith has called 'the time bomb in the classroom'[14]. It is almost impossible to stop the brain from learning and Bob will continue to learn. He is likely to struggle in school to continue his experiment of mucking it up. He will learn from his teachers, amongst other things, how teachers respond to kids who muck up. He will learn the same from the institution. There are many points at which the English teacher could encourage some real dialogue. If people like Peter Medway[15] are right, the best way for starters is to admit his experience. He is far from speechless about that:

> If I want to work I can work, and work really hard, but like last term I was a good student. I was really plugging away and really working, and then I had two weeks' holiday and something happened to me during those two weeks but I am not too sure what it was. When I came back, oh shit, my whole outlook changed. It's just something within me. I don't know what it is. See, I am an easy sort of person and I don't care what I do from day to day as long as I have got something to occupy my mind and that. I like to work, you know. I like to keep moving all the time. Like yesterday I sat down from half-past nine, ten o'clock, to about quarter to five trying to get a lawn mower to work. I pulled the whole thing apart, the carbie, the head, the works. Reassembled it all back together again. I started it up, beauty, she's working mate, ace, then all of a sudden there was a bang and that was it. It's not getting enough juice across so I have got to find out what's wrong in there and I will clean it. I have got to go home tonight and clean out all the lines.[16]

Reflecting on his experience of interviewing and observing, Novick concludes:

> Nobody I interviewed expected 'too much'. Nobody expected very much at all. The pupils and teacher seemed to accommodate each other. Each expected minimum compliance from the other. No more. In general, that expectation was satisfied.[17]

Bob Brand perseveres with his lawn-mower. It is a problematic chunk of his life. He expects to master it. (If only that tenacity could be turned on to other problematic chunks in the curriculum.) After many years of observing in classrooms at both primary and secondary level, I also find that schools rarely expect 'too much'. As a consequence, there is not too much to struggle for. The stragglers, the ones most in need of the chance to become strugglers, are, ironically, often 'remediated' by being given *'successful experiences'* on lock-step exercises and games. Thin gruel, indeed. A formula for keeping them weedy.

Teachers cannot relinquish their official and experiential superiority over students. But they can construe themselves as fellow strugglers. If they believe this, then that is what they will teach. They will show students where they stand and stand together with them.

NOTES

1. In writing this paper I must acknowledge at least two important debts: one to George Kelly and his theory of personal constructs, and one to Douglas Hofstadter for the notion of 'chunking'.
2. George Kelly's term 'constructive alternativism' gets close to what I mean.
3. See Kelly, G. (1955) *The Psychology of Personal Constructs*, Norton, New York.
4. Rosen, H. (1981) *Neither Bleak House Nor Liberty Hall: English in the Curriculum*, University of London Institute of Education.
5. c.f. Novick, p. 69: 'within the rules and regulations and less tractable and more enduring superstructure of taken for granted beliefs, an immense scope for individual and collective action is provided. The school at all levels continually adapts to what it registers in the environment and imposes on it. Like a person walking or pedalling a bicycle, adjustments in the school are small and constant: each change is simultaneously a result of previous acts and causes new acts. The school keeps going, balancing, counter-balancing, never arriving, and is as mindful of its progress and process as it chooses to be.' [Note 12]
6. Grace, G. (1978) *Teachers, Ideology and Control*, Routledge and Kegan Paul, p. 7.
7. Ascui, A.F. (1980) 'The Concept of Psycho-Social Constructs and Future Research in the Behavioural Sciences', mimeo, Western Australian Institute of Technology.
8. Rosen, *op.cit.* p. 8

9. *Ibid.*
10. *Ibid.*
11. *Ibid.*
12. Novick, D. (1981) *Portraits from an Institution – A Study of Secondary Schooling*, Education Department of South Australia.
13. *Ibid.*
14. Smith, F. (1981) 'Demonstrations, Engagement and Sensitivity', *Language Arts*, 58, 1, pp. 103-112.
15. Medway, Peter (1980) *Finding a Language*, Chameleon Books.
16. Novick, *op. cit.*
17. *Ibid.*

3

COMING OF AGE IN DRAMA; OR, THE IMPORTANCE OF BEING ORDINARY

This address was given to the annual conference of the National Association for Drama in Education, in Brisbane, 1980.

Background

It will become clear during this paper that I am an outside educator asking drama teachers to let me in. Or, conversely, I am an outside educator urging drama teachers to come outside. It will also become clear that I *assume* about the past of drama in education, *romance* about its present, and *hazard* into the future riding on sketchy evidence and powered by high-octane intuition. I mean what I say but it is hardly likely to be true.

By accident, in 1977, I became chairman of the R-12 Drama Curriculum Committee of the Education Department of South Australia after a decade of work in English and general curriculum development. Neither academically nor by experience was I qualified for the job. For this allows me to pollute certainty wherever I come across it in the world of drama, simply by being ignorantly unbelieving or disarmingly uninformed. This is an asset if, like me, you consider certainty to be the most noxious enemy of education. It is also an asset because it induces people to inform, contradict and demonstrate in order to cure my ignorance and agnosticism. Drama teachers have, in this way, let me see them. And so as an infidel cohabiting with drama teachers, I have had the privilege of being a part of the drama movement, while still remaining apart.

A book *Images of Life: Guidelines for Drama R-12*[1] represents the culmination of four years' work in South Australia. It has been four years of mingled torment and joy for all of us who helped make it. Networks of teachers in all regions of the state have worked with curriculum committee members thrashing out principles, turning principles into practice, disagreeing, confirming, discarding, enacting and reflecting. The outcome will not be palatable to all who read it and in five years' time it will no doubt be unsatisfying even to those who wrote it. Nevertheless we can be forgiven a moment of pride. We have done it and we offer it to drama teachers in Australia as a sign that we have come of age. It is something for others to hit up against; something defined that will help further definition.

This brief background has been necessary in order to clarify the peculiar perspective that I am about to offer. As a system's curriculum developer and 'change agent', I intend to offer a critique of drama in education, a possible conceptualisation and a vision for tomorrow.

Adolescence (1969-1980)

When I went to Teachers College I was compelled to do 'Speech and Drama I'. The reasoning behind this compulsion was that all teachers ought to be able to speak well. Some faith was also placed in the folk-lore that all teaching is akin to acting. Drama, where it existed in secondary schools, tended to be part of English (one-act plays in Junior School and Shakespeare as literary text at senior levels). Speech Night provided an opportunity for some teachers to live vicariously through student performance. At Primary level, the odd teacher put on the odd play and poetry was an excuse for choral rendition. This was the early sixties. It is not clear in retrospect whether this was the dotage of the old drama or the infancy of the new.

It seems that back in England, at this time, there was a renaissance. Creative drama, child drama, improvised drama, group drama, the 'play' way was coming into its own, particularly at the primary level. It seemed to go along with new movements in the teaching of English where 'organic', creative aspects were being emphasised. Thematic approaches were gaining currency. Relevance and child-centredness began to dominate over 'chalk and talk', at least at the philosophical level.

I can remember David Adland's visit to Australia in 1969 and so arbitrarily I shall set this year as the beginning of the 'New Drama's' adolescence in this country. It coincides with the beginning of the golden years of funding which lasted into the mid-seventies. It also coincides with the explosion of the teacher-training institutions and the expansion within them of flourishing drama departments. It was the beginning of an era of optimism, of alternative approaches, of diminished public examination, of colourful textbooks and 'options'.

Adland was received with some excitement as he demonstrated the amazing ability of children to work collaboratively in groups to improvise upon a theme. 'Group' drama spread feverishly and faddishly in junior secondary English classes, one-act plays became taboo, public performance became de-valued. Shelter sheds, outdoor spaces, 'double pre-fabs', even corridors served as venues for drama. Other big names followed Adland to Australia; drama in education along with the arts generally in Australia gained in respectability. Specialist lobbies began to pressure education systems to provide specialist spaces for drama. The first in South Australia was an old library converted after Commonwealth funds had provided a new resource centre. With facilities for blacking out, carpet on the floor and a functional lighting board, it became a rallying point, a sign and a stimulus.

Special drama spaces need special drama teachers. The CAEs began to provide such specialists and drama was away. By the mid-seventies in South Australia there were over a hundred specialist drama teachers; all new secondary schools had a drama space and many of the older schools managed creditable conversions of existing spaces. New primary schools, too, were provided with a well-designed 'activity' room.

In the schools, drama teaching was not quite 'headless chookery' but it tended to be a little frantic. Enormous energy was expended. The attrition rate was high. Drama teachers were young, visionary, innovative, but not always wise. They still had only immigrant status on most staffs and often failed to understand the language of schools.

Drama, like any adolescent, had an ambiguous identity. Sometimes it was flamboyant, sometimes shy and shamefaced (especially when timetable debates were on). It was at once a prima donna and a fringe dweller blacked out on the boundary of the school. It wanted to be part of the main course curriculum yet it enjoyed being the spice. It was creative, volatile, spasmodic, moody. It was a time of guruism. Drama teachers 'tried on' a variety of cloaks. Even CAE departments varied markedly in allegiance and style. Courtney; Slade; Heathcote; Adland; Way, and so on – each term, it seemed, saw a new star in the spotlight. And the stars would have been less than pleased in most cases with what they had inspired.

Dorothy Heathcote, without the universal questions and political commitment, becomes the bullying autocrat; the aspiring young Adland plays a monotone of group work, re-cycling experience in the service of the conservation of ignorance; latent Oliviers use children to flesh out their fantasies. In one school you might well have seen the great tambourine act with a circus of performing kids; in another the whole school might have been caught up in an epidemic of the Michael Edgley follies preparing the greatest show on earth for the gratification of the Principal. The smart operators, popular with other teachers because their classes are not noisy, may have learnt to rely on cunning stunts in mime requiring tongue-tied discipline. Too often, out of fear and a desire to be liked, the drama teacher might have been seen treading the boards as the entertainer, entrepreneur of the five finger exercise and the games that drama people play; the hors-d'oeuvres approach; titbits and titillation; nibbles for beginners.

Just as there were many teaching styles concomitant with this adolescence, so were there many ways of offering drama. Let me name a few to make the point.

- *The Old Dull Stream.* This is a course based on the understanding that drama is non-cognitive – that is, non-academic – and therefore may be offered to the less able streams who are not taking two foreign languages. However, it is not significant enough to offer to all such children. Therefore it should be seen as an alternative to other 'non-academic' subjects such as art, craft or typing.
- *The Weekly Matinee.* Heads down and bums up all week make Jack and Jill dull children. Therefore, an injection of physical education, for bodies, and drama, for feelings, is necessary. One or two lessons a week is enough. In drama this is usually a course which is popular to begin with but is in danger of running out of ideas. At worst it will be seen as a bludge, a rave, a relief or an entertainment. At best it will offer a small oasis of sweetness and light.
- *The Russian Roulette.* This is drama by chance. If you happen to have an English teacher who has not yet been shamed into feeling 'de-skilled' by specialist drama teachers, you may have some drama offered from time to time, even if it's only 'push the desks back and act out this scene from the text'.
- *The Transient Flare.* This may be born out of club or elective activity. The school may be lucky enough to have a brilliant poor person's Peter Brook on the staff, an ex-professional in mime, or

puppetry or dance or film-making. Over time the school curriculum may be altered to include a bona-fide course in this specialism. It is brilliant until the teacher is transferred.

Running these courses, usually without a faculty to belong to or reluctantly adopted by the Head of the English Department, were some very courageous people. Some went under; some have survived to tell much truer tales than mine. They were most prone to labelling because they threatened to be uncontained and labelling is a great container. Some drama teachers were forced to be the misunderstood martyr; others were resident witchdoctors practising some mysterious rites in their blackened rooms; some were the tolerated radicals or trend-setters; some were considered to be ostentatiously different. The ones with greatest respect were those who could keep discipline, work miracles with 'dumb' kids, and put on one or two really good shows during the year. It also helped if you coached a sporting team.

I have caricatured the adolescence of drama in order to highlight some problems:

- drama was in need of an identity, a conceptualisation of its role in the school
- drama was a curriculum experiment, tolerated but not belonging
- drama teachers were so bound up with themselves and their emerging craft that they did not see clearly what was happening
- drama teachers wore the label of 'special' and so allowed themselves to be contained.

Being different is not easy to sustain.

The Importance of Being Ordinary

Drama, dance, consumer studies, wine-making, and cosmetics are clearly different from English literature, Pure Mathematics, Chemistry and Foreign Languages. The former group is where you get your frills in the curriculum. These are subjects relatively uncommon in schools, though they relate strongly to everyday life. The latter group comprises subjects most common in the curriculum but less commonly seen in the texture of daily life.

I do not need to go into detail about current economic and political pressures being put on schools. Those in schools know that the 'tightening up' process involves 'cutting down' in the curriculum. What is considered not to be 'basic' is at risk. There is therefore a very

clear survival argument behind my contention that drama must become common or ordinary. Some of the surface attributes of ordinariness in education are:
- being able to show tangible outcomes
- being examinable
- being offered as a full course at the senior level
- being teachable at the lower levels by non-specialists
- being accepted as important by parents and teachers
- being accepted as important by the community
- being cognitive (i.e. to do with thinking).

Clearly drama during its adolescence has been anything but ordinary. Coming of age, as I see it, is to approach more closely to ordinariness. The 'ordinary' subjects have an established mythology about why they are essential; they are legitimated by central curriculum documents and set examinations; they have widely recognisable contents and products; they have sequence; and they have public demand. This ordinariness may be in some respects a sham but there is no doubt about its protective qualities. At a Machiavellian level, I believe that drama should begin to take on some of the attributes of ordinariness, if this can be done without destroying its essence.

At a deeper level, educationally and philosophically, drama has to discover that it is indeed ordinary, and that sham is not necessary in the quest to be common. I now wish to establish this deep-level ordinariness.

'Adolescent' drama had an immature conception of itself. Drama was justified sometimes on the grounds of social development (learning to get along and work together); sometimes on the grounds of educating for mental health and imagination (learning to understand oneself, to create, to discover and to feel); sometimes on the grounds of drama for art's sake (learning to be cultured citizens). The tendency was to justify drama because of what it did that was *different* from other subjects. It was also customary to define the territory of drama either by reference to the natural play of the young or to the distillation of drama as fully-fledged theatre. On the one hand, drama was loosely construed, romanticised and condoned as a good thing because it was 'natural'; on the other it was prematurely shaped into a tight discipline, sequenced and aimed at the holy grail of theatre. It is important to note as well that educational drama was defined *within education* and not *within society*. In trying to name and place drama, educators looked to what had previously been done in drama in schools. And so drama remains, even now, precariously perched on an inadequate conceptual base. Symbolically, drama can be found dwelling uncomfortably on the fringes of the school.

In the quest for deep-level ordinariness, I start from a fundamental question: 'What is it to be human?' What separates human beings from the animals? With Susanne Langer, I am satisfied with the answer: 'Mind', that is, the capacity to represent experience symbolically, to manipulate these symbols and thereby to create possible new worlds. Imagination makes us human.

My next question is: 'How do human beings learn to manipulate symbol systems?' I am satisfied by the view that we learn this through the observation of others manipulating symbols and through social interaction, which leads us to hypothesize, to test and to reflect. This is indeed basic. It encourages me to modestly formulate seven conditions for human life on earth. Without these conditions, mind will not function.

Seven Conditions For Human Life On Earth

- Being able to observe other human beings interacting.
- Being able to imagine what it might be like to be able to do something that they are doing and wanting to do it.
- Being able to ask questions (not necessarily verbally) of someone who can do it.
- Having the opportunity to rehearse it mentally and in action through trial and error.
- Having the opportunity to seek interim evaluations from someone who can do it.
- Having the opportunity to put it to the test in order to evaluate it.
- Having the opportunity to dwell on it and to celebrate.

I have not reached this simple formulation easily. At another time, I could justify and defend it. For the purposes of this paper I seek your indulgence in temporarily considering it to be valid. It provides a powerful means of understanding human endeavour. As an educator, it takes me out of the blinkered world of education and into a space where I can view human beings, including myself, anthropologically, culturally, psychologically and socially. It becomes a set of seven conditions for human learning and so it underpins my educational philosophy, my curriculum theory and my theory of teaching. Each subject in the curriculum, if I am right, must provide for those seven conditions if children are to be initiated into what that school offers. Each subject, if I am right, no matter how we divide knowledge, depends on the learner's imagination. Without imagination, the child can be trained but not educated. At the pioneering edges of civilisation's collective mind, it is imagination which enables the next leap whether it be in philosophy, science, music or engineering. Imagination is the essential, 'ordinary', common ingredient. Drama teachers therefore share a common conceptual base with all teachers.

It is now logically appropriate to consider the media which human beings have developed in order to represent the world symbolically. What are the culturally important media through which human beings have exercised their imagination, transformed, transmitted and exchanged meaning? Gesture, dance, art (making marks), music (making patterned sound), enactment and speech are the most primitive, but even the tools, artefacts and products of a culture become symbols carrying meaning. Over time human beings have extended their symbol systems through the invention of mathematical systems, print, film, computers, lasers and so on. Each one of these symbol systems can be manipulated to help us better know and control 'the world'. One's power to amplify one's meaning, to influence and to mediate the influences of others depends on one's ability to perform skilfully in culturally important media. Knowledge is sterile unless it can be transformed and transmitted through media. Knowing beyond rote fact cannot be gained in the first place other than through the manipulation of symbols. Scientific knowledge is built up through language, mathematics, art, photography, diagrams and even enactment (if experiments are seen as intentional improvisations in new scenarios). Historical knowledge is similarly constructed, and so on.

This analysis enables us to conceive of drama (enactment) as one of the culturally significant media necessary for the development and advancement of human society. Schools having defined what knowledge they consider to be significant should, according to this conceptualisation, decide which media will be used to impart, develop and extend that knowledge. At the same time as they teach content, they must teach the manipulation of culturally significant symbol systems. But schools do not share my conceptualisation. Judging by their present operation, they tend to be gravely monotonous, putting their mainstream money on languaging and mathematics. Other media tend to be seen, with some exceptions in some schools, as optional extras. Even in the teaching of language and mathematics, it could be argued that children are more competent in the receptive mode than in the productive mode. (Sadly, it seems to be a feature of schools not to allow children too much control of the media, perhaps because they reflect society.)

However, this is deviating from the argument. The fact is that drama is not presently considered to be a *basic* learning medium in schools. If it is to become basic, then we must establish that it is essential to human learning. There are several compelling lines which can now be taken. In the first place drama is arguably the richest medium apart from life itself for learning the nuances of the culture. It is the most primitive, the least abstracted and the most complex of all media in that it is most nearly a virtual image of life. Art, language, dance and music are attentuated, stylised and selective by comparison. Drama is an *inclusive* medium, being a subtle, complicated, harmonic blend of sound, voice, gesture and movement, appropriating where necessary music, light, costume, art and any other media which may enrich the 'image of life'. In Halliday's terms, enactment is a layered text which realises the 'social semiotic' at many levels. It represents three-dimensionally the subtlety of a culture's network of meaning-exchange. To operate through the medium of enactment is to pay attention to life simultaneously at a number of levels. It is a higher level of realisation of culture than language in that it includes within itself the semiotics which language represents only at the semantic and lexicogrammatical level. In language exchange, the context of situation may be taken for granted or implied. In enactment, the context of situation is deliberately represented along with the meaning. Therefore, in order to create a dramatic composition it is necessary to make explicit, in order to select and stylise, the non-linguistic cultural meanings implicit in social intercourse. To compose dramatically is to re-construct life. The medium of drama enables, indeed forces, us to hold life up close in order to 'read the world'. Before human beings made their mark in more lasting ways, drama provided the demonstrations, the text, of the myths which served cultural literacy. Whether viewed phylogenetically or ontogenetically, drama is clearly a primitive, basic medium of human learning. The life of early civilisations, and the life of the pre-school infant, are steeped in drama. If, as Vygotsky says, outer, synpractic speech eventually goes underground to become inner speech which is inextricably bound to thinking, early physical enactments may go underground to become the chief servant of imagination which is the very essence of mind.

If this case for ordinariness stands, then schools which deny children the medium of enactment are seriously impeding their learning.

Another way to view enactment is to look at it as Halliday[2] looks at language – that is, functionally. The most dangerous conception of drama in education is, to my mind, the view that drama is merely an art form. This is a view that focusses narrowly on one function of enactment in society. It is as lop-sided as to view language merely as literature. Perhaps it is because enactment is so much part of the texture of everyday life that we only recognise it when it is withdrawn and framed in a theatre.

Taking an anthropological view, how has enactment evolved in the service of human endeavour? What functions has it come to serve? I believe Halliday's analysis of linguistic functions apply equally to enactment:

Instrumental: satisfying material needs ('I want').
Regulating: controlling the behaviour of others ('Do as I tell you').
Interactional: getting along with other people ('me and you').
Personal: identifying and expressing the self ('here I come').
Heuristic: exploring the world around and inside one ('tell me why').
Imaginative: creating a world of one's own ('let's pretend').
Informative: communicating new information ('I've got something to tell you').

Drama, like any other medium, can be and is manipulated artistically to create. But right before our eyes, every day, enactment functions to sustain society. We signal through mime the need for a drink; we create the image of disapproval to control; we take on roles to facilitate collaboration; we rehearse an important interview; we demonstrate new understandings and skills for the benefit of

3 *Coming of Age in Drama* 51

others; not to mention the dramatic life of mind, the rich internalisation of the ways of the world, so accessible to 'action replays', editing and re-formulation.

Schools are riddled with drama already, and yet ironically most teachers are unaware of the enormous resources which surround them just waiting to be pressed more deliberately and formally into the service of learning. In a survey of Junior Primary Schools in South Australia only five reported that they were doing any drama! Story telling, dressing up, playing shops, making cubby-holes and the like were not construed as 'drama'. 'Drama' was evidently that rarified thing which specialists do in drama rooms.

One further argument for ordinariness is the fact that the composing process of enactment is a classic demonstration of the human mind at work. It is therefore a superb medium for helping children to reflect on human learning and to develop their own deliberate learning strategies. In the composition of an enactment the seven conditions which I have formulated are seen to apply – observation of life leads to the 'imaging' of life, an idea which is shaped and modified through exploration and question, and eventually tried in performance. The learning process in other media and in other subjects is basically the same but it is less observable.

To summarise, drama will come of age when it breaks through the crack in the present conceptual egg in which it is contained. Conceived of functionally as a culturally vital medium, it can offer itself to schools on a quite different scale with quite different arguments. No longer a frill, it can aspire, with articulate righteousness, to become the ordinary base of the common curriculum. Our adolescent years have 'something to expiate; / a pettiness' (D.H. Lawrence).

Drama and The Future

Inspired by this liberated view of itself, the drama network in South Australia has written guidelines which will revolutionise drama in education if they are followed. Unfortunately (or fortunately, depending on your view) most curriculum developers pull levers with no one at the other end. We hope to avoid the usual pitfalls of transmission, by inviting teachers, according to our own learning principles, to imagine what it might be like to be this new kind of teacher and then to enact aspects of the role to see how it works. Then, through the documentation of praxis by teachers all over the state, we hope to build up a picture of the new reality, which will help ordinariness to prevail.

In ten years' time you may call me back to testify or to recant. These are some of the major tenets of our guidelines:

- Drama, or enactment, is a medium for exploring, understanding and transforming the world and ourselves.
- Drama is therefore a means of learning across all subject areas; it is a way of exploring territory or content.
- Drama as theatre has been used to shape culturally important myths. This material and the special medium of theatre can become content or knowledge in its own right in the curriculum. The secondary school, especially the senior secondary school, is seen as the appropriate place for such courses.
- Enactment in its various forms can also be a product which expresses understanding and offers a symbolic representation of life. Therefore, in education it can be an educational outcome or 'product' in any area of the curriculum.
- Drama can be conceived of as having three modes: the expressive, the performance and the spectator modes. Where drama is taught as a subject in its own right the course should reflect an appropriate balance between these modes.
- Drama in education is *ordinary*. It can be and should be part of the repertoire of every teacher.
- Drama specialists should not be used in primary school to withdraw drama classes but, rather, to assist general practitioners to use drama in the service of learning.
- Drama specialists at secondary level should similarly act as a resource to all teachers, besides being bona fide teachers of drama as a subject.
- The skills of manipulating the medium of drama should be learnt in used, where the function of the drama is clear and the skills are needed in order to make the meaning.
- Drama wherever it is employed must serve worthwhile *meaning*. Drama should be used to explore challenging content which raises culturally important issues and problems.
- Courses in drama should be consistent with the stated learning theory. This implies a curriculum theory which calls for the deliberate planning of the curriculum process, from challenge or problem through to performance, testing and evaluation.

And so to the vision of the 'drama' teacher 'come of age'. This teacher may not be recognised as a drama teacher because he or she may be a primary school general practitioner or a teacher of history and health education at the secondary level. The work of the teacher will be supported by central curriculum documents which outdo even mathematics statements in their rigour and their authority. The teacher will be accountable by producing end products which are available for scrutiny. These may or may not be in the medium of drama. They will, however, demonstrate what has been learnt. Drama will be justified above all because of its capacity to stretch children's thinking.

When drama is a subject in its own right, the teacher will be able to talk articulately and convincingly about content, skills, processes, products and evaluation, *and* theorise about his or her own practice.

Through the strength of argument and the politics of ordinariness, drama will be offered as a full subject or, where this is not possible, extra lessons will be allocated to other subjects so that the drama teacher can collaborate to use drama as a means of enriching and extending the learning in, say, History.

Students in drama will not be subjected to one-off drama lessons; out-of-context games; sequenced skills instruction in isolation; or protocols which bear resemblance to hypnotherapy.

Programming for drama will be done in collaboration with the students so that they know from period to period, from week to week, where they are heading and why they are doing what they are doing.

The ordinary teacher will draw on the resources and ideas of the students. Spurious motivation and stimulation will be a thing of the past. The discipline of the classroom will be the discipline born of tension as children work towards a quality product. The emphasis will be on making, reflecting, connecting, and acting on the world.

NOTES

1. R-12 Drama Curriculum Committee, *Images of Life: Guidelines for Drama R-12*, Education Department of South Australia, 1981.
2. Halliday, M.A.K., *Language as Social Semiotic*, Edward Arnold, 1978 pp. 19-20.

4

THE POLITICS OF DRAMA TEACHING

This was an address to drama teachers at the annual conference of the National Association for Drama in Education in Adelaide, in 1983. By this time, Garth was Director of Wattle Park Teachers Centre but still retained a close interest in drama curriculum development.

Students require an education in curriculum as in sentiments in order to discover what they assumed – with the complicity of their teachers – was nature, was in fact culture; what was given is no more than a way of taking.

(Adapted from Richard Howard in the preface to Roland Barthes, *S/Z: An essay*, Hill and Wang, New York, 1974.)

But schools declare themselves as surely as people do. And children learn to read the implicit meanings more quickly and thoroughly than they learn many prescribed tasks. 'What does the place say to me?,' they ask and look for the answer in every intonation of the institution. In finding the answer they also discover what it is possible for them to say.

(Connie and Harold Rosen, *The Language of Primary School Children*, Penguin, Harmondsworth, 1973, p. 21.)

In drama classrooms throughout this country children are being taught the politics of their teachers. By politics I mean the teachers' beliefs about desired power relationships between people and about how power can be used in a community of people. By politics I also mean *enacted* politics, not *espoused* politics; the living example of the teacher in situ as the curriculum unfolds in the school.

The micro-community of the drama class is also subject, of course, to the politics taught by the school which through every artefact on display, ever word written in reports, every rule made, every person praised, every textbook chosen, speaks profoundly to the students about what is valued here, how one is expected to live here, what one is allowed to say here, and who makes what decisions here. Because such political messages come to the students through the very pores of the school body, they are profoundly militant. They make war and peace selectively and rarely operate 'in uniform'. Congruent values are subtly stroked; incongruent values may be attacked with a battery of weapons ranging from corporal assault through to the less visible withholding of affection or the persistent generation of uncomfortableness.

Where the drama teachers' politics, as defined, are largely incongruent with the politics of the school, it is likely that students will experience various kinds of confusion about political messages. The drama teacher, subject to the same militant school politics as the students, will, if not continually vigilant, carry school-political contamination (from his or her own point of view) into the classroom; for example, simply by reluctantly complying with a school requirement that homework be regularly set. The teacher will be tacitly demonstrating compliance with a misguided authority if the issue is not explicitly discussed with students, or openly confronting the fact of strategic compromise for survival if the issue is explicitly raised. In the latter case the teacher will be demonstrating, in the eyes of many teachers, some form of professional disloyalty.

This brings us quickly to questions of personal integrity, authenticity and honesty. It also leads one to reflect on what I have termed elsewhere the 'complicity of tact' in schools[1], the phenomenon of keeping secrets for the so-called good of others. 'They are not yet ready to handle it' or 'It would cause more trouble than it's worth' or 'The parents wouldn't like it' or 'One day [as with Father Christmas] they will understand'. In all cases of secrecy, 'not saying' is a political act, confirming the people who do not have this information in the belief that what they already know is sufficient, maybe even true. If information is the fuel of power it is an act of subjugation. It secures the power of those who have the secret.

What I have to say here applies to any teaching at any level. However, I am convinced that drama, because of its potent 'life' connections, illustrates the politics of teaching more dramatically than any other subject. It should be clear from my preamble that I am about to address questions of *knowing, controlling, telling* and *acting* in drama teaching. It will be my contention that many drama teachers are unwitting agents of oppression, perpetrating each day acts of covert terrorism out of habit.

I wish to question some habits of drama teaching in order to unmask the politics of habit and to diagnose the likely toxic effect of strategies which *power at* students rather than *empower* them.

This will lead me also to look closely at the politics of surprise which goes to the very heart of drama teaching.

Habits and Contexts

I shall assume that the easy targets of criticism are well-known to you and that you share, without explication, an understanding of the sapping narcosis which attends persistent tambourine bearing ('Circus, Circus'); teacher direction of class plays ('Help *me* realise *my* fantasies'); a staple diet of student-generated improvisations ('Trap them where they are); a regime of mime last week, puppets this week and voice production next week ('Who killed Cock Robin?'); or 'doing' periods and the plays of the 'greats' for examination purposes ('Distancing, dissection and dessication'). Habitually employed, such routines leave students feeling that knowledge and power reside elsewhere. These have long been part of drama teaching's contribution to containment of the citizenry and progressive socialisation into acquiescence.

I shall assume also that the school makes many potentially harmful things non-negotiable for the teacher, but I will not treat the politics and ideology of such contexts as 40-minute lessons, classes of 30, assessment by grading, using drama as a 'sink' (or drain) subject, or giving drama to a specialist at primary level (a particularly effective way of painting it into a corner).

I take it for granted that every teacher of drama is to varying degrees at war with such contexts and that students are also implicated in the struggle. My focus will be on the curriculum *text* which is jointly made by teachers and students within the context of school and society. What happens when the door closes on the drama room or space and the action begins? How is the script written? What in the fullest sense does drama in school *mean*? What lessons are learned?

As a test case I shall present an hypothetical drama teacher who is as rhetorically committed to the empowerment of students as Dorothy Heathcote and who has gone well beyond the cruder forms of *training* through drama.

The Script

Let us eavesdrop on a unit of work with a Year Ten drama class of twenty 15-year-olds.

The teacher brings into the class a video recording of a television programme exploring the bone-marrow disease commonly known as Gargoylism which eventually proves fatal for children but not until they have become horribly grotesque, malformed and brain-damaged. The programme explores the traumas of two sets of parents as they battle with doctors to save their children through a process of bone-marrow transplants from relatives. Eventually one child dies and one survives with a reasonable chance of a normal life. At the end of the programme we see doctors at the overloaded hospital having to decide which of two new patients with terminal illnesses will be admitted to undergo the possibly life-saving operation. The one omitted is likely to die while waiting.

The class discussion following this programme is intense. Issues such as euthanasia, the cost to the community, the right to abortion (the disease can be detected in the embryo), the ethical and emotional strain on parents and doctors, etc., are canvassed. At a certain point, the teacher says she would like them as a class to work up their own dramatic exploration of some of these issues over the next few weeks with a view to showing it to another Year Ten class.

Before the lesson ends, they decide fairly amicably to develop an improvisation around the basic situation delineated at the end of the programme. A choice must be made between two parents. The stakes are life and death. The teacher undertakes to come up with a suggested plan of action for the next lesson.

In the next lesson, the class agrees to the teacher's plan that one group form to improvise being the relatives of one patient, while another is to become the relatives of the other patient. There is also to be a group of doctors and medical staff and a group of 'concerned' citizens (a minister, a politician, a reporter, etc.). The teacher takes on the role of chief surgeon and the task is for participants in each group to develop a character, to begin discussion, and to prepare for preliminary discussion with the chief surgeon.

In the next lesson, each group in turn has an improvised session where it confronts the chief surgeon who, in each case, manages to throw in unforeseen complications and counter arguments. In a debriefing session the whole class reflects on the emerging plot, comments on ways of proceeding, and suggests improvements on the improvisation to date.

From here, on the next day the teacher organises the students to re-group to marshal further arguments. However, instead of them meeting the surgeon again, they find that they are to meet another group, though unprepared for it. The teacher has thrown this in as a means of further stretching them and to widen their appreciation of other perspectives on the dilemma.

This proves to be a lively session. In the de-briefing for the day they discuss good points and points of potential growth as well as considering where to go from here. They decide they need some time to write some embryonic scripts in terms of issues, stances and unfolding action rather than specific lines.

After the script writing, they go back over two scenes (with the chief surgeon and with another group). They then face the difficulty of how to round off their presentation to make it cohere for the spectator class. With some teacher prompting, it is resolved that they will all attend a formal meeting of interested parties at which the chief surgeon will hear the pros and cons and made a decision. The improvisation will end with the chief surgeon's summing up and decision.

Because none of the groups has really grappled with the wider political/economic restrictions on the hospital, the teacher decides privately that the chief surgeon will refuse to operate on either patient, as a public protest, until the government makes more funds and resources available. This, she knows, will create a rich base for further class discussion of forms of protest, leading nicely into the next experience she has arranged – a class viewing of the film *Ghandi*.

The improvisation is eventually polished for performance. It is very well received by the spectator class and there is excellent spontaneous discussion (theatre-in-education style) after the presentation.

The teacher is well satisfied that students have come to grips with issues of power, control, decision-making and vested interest. She feels that this experience has raised political awareness and complicated simplistic views about how decisions are made. She herself, as a female chief surgeon, has modelled assertiveness against constraining authorities.

This teacher is highly regarded by students and fellow staff members, though considered to be a bit radical and 'bolshy' in the themes she has students consider. Many other drama teachers covet her ability to take risks and to trust in the power of students to work up their own scripts. The principal values her because she allows him to demonstrate publicly, through her students, that his is a school where students can stand up and put on a show. Drama is not some kind of mystical dark-room ritual in this school.

Having admitted that such teaching goes well beyond present 'par-for-the-course' teaching in our secondary schools, in terms of allowing student initiative, I wish to look at the politics of her enactment of the curriculum: at the *texture* and *intentions* of the text.

Analysis of the Script

Two crucial questions in any analysis of a political 'text' are 'Who wrote the script?' and 'Whose interests are being served?'. Within the hospital script, it is true that the students develop much of the script in collaboration with each other, but the parameters of the plot and the territory to be explored have been pre-empted by the teacher who has made a crucial shaping decision in introducing the video-tape. The teacher administers their labours and, with their consent, organises the mechanics both of the classroom meta-script (managing the time allocation, the movement and the activity sequences) and the emerging class 'hospital' script (controlling group focus, patterns of interaction and key aspects of plot resolution). Student decisions are made largely about issues to be raised and attitudes to be presented within the offering they have agreed to prepare with (or for?) the teacher.

Indeed much of the meta-script is submerged because we do not have direct access to the teacher's intentions. Why did she choose the Gargoyle video? What skills, knowledge and attitudes, precisely, was she hoping to promote? How much of the script seen in retrospect had she already imagined? Did she have some form of evaluation in mind? What criteria did she have for any evaluation? What degree of deviance from her imagination of the script was she willing to tolerate? There are clues within the unfolding classroom drama which suggest that she did indeed have a powerfully conceived script in mind. She may be been surprised by some of the inventions of the students within the play, but by and large one gets the feeling that things happened as planned. The teacher wrote the script and the students agreeably fleshed it out.

The question 'In whose interests?' is harder to answer. The teacher would no doubt answer along these lines: 'In the interests of the students' articulateness, awareness and capacity to plan, and of fostering their growing ability to work together tenaciously towards a goal'. Furthermore, they were obviously interested. Co-operation was high. There was little resistance.

But what teacher interests are also being served? In the first place the teacher has professional interests, connected with being a good drama teacher, with professional kudos. Then there are her interests in control, public approval and the excitement of seeing what the students will make of it all. She seems to have had quite a good time, taking on the starring role, throwing in plot complications and appropriating the last words. Maybe it was in her interests as a lover of acting to be in the limelight. Another way to ask the question is: 'Who wanted to do it in the first place?' Clearly, the students came to accept what the teacher wanted. They are gently manipulated into the act: the contract to pretend. 'You pretend to be other than students and I'll pretend to be other than teacher'. And yet within the pretence, the teacher continues to be in charge, in role. The pretence is not in the direction of playing at being powerful. It is playing at being trapped. The simulation mirrors the entrapment of the classroom outside the pretence. By seemingly divesting herself of the teacher role, the teacher intensifies her power.

Surprise

Another litmus test for power is to ask: 'Who knows what is going to happen?' The ones being most surprised are the ones with least control over their own destiny. The more one is subject to surprise, the more vulnerable one is.

The drama teacher would conceivably produce the following evidence. The students knew the following:

- they were to explore a shared theme known to them
- they were to perform the outcomes to another class
- the teacher would help to organise them
- they were responsible for developing their own parts.

At the curriculum planning level, then, they knew what was required and in the play within the plan knew what they had to explore. They agreed to do this.

But what did the drama teacher know which was unknown to the students? She knew:

- why she was doing this work
- why she chose this particular set of teaching strategies
- how she would organise each lesson (in advance of students)
- how she would evaluate its success

- how she would intervene to push the students' thinking
- what she hoped the students would learn about.

She had information and clear intentions which enabled her to teach *deliberately, systematically, productively* and *reflectively*. The daily consequences of her plan in action empowered her to adjust and move forward to the resolution.

By contrast, the students could not be deliberate learners because they did not know what they were supposed to learn about. They knew what they were supposed to do and how but they did not know, in the fullest sense, why. They only knew part of what the teacher had in mind. They were therefore 'surprised' each day by the teacher's revelation of what they were to do and, within that, they were further surprised by the unpredictable turns of the teacher – in and out of role.

It should be noted that such surprise is so much part of school that students do not perceive it as surprise. Whereas with their peers they shared the vulnerability of unpredictability, with their teacher in and out of role they were relatively vulnerable to premeditated teacher shifts. It is interesting to contemplate what would have happened if the teacher had suddenly been taken ill and had handed over to another supervising teacher. Without the teacher's devices, left to their own devices, would they have resolved the plot in ways which would have surprised their teacher?

Certainly the students had intentions within the pretence – to explore and resolve a conflict with a view to performance. Outside the pretence they had no clear learning intentions other than to act in collusion with the teacher to see if the task could be done. They pretended to be students. After the act they could see and talk about what they had 'surprisingly' learned from the experience. Experience thus acted upon them rather than vice versa. Because the students did not know what they were intending to learn, the consequences of their in-role drama could not be potent for them (as the teacher's were for her). They could reflect upon the consequences of the mechanics of their plotting and acting, because the intention to perform was explicit, but they could not reflect in a *focussed* way on the *content* of what they were exploring. The teacher, secure in the knowledge that they were, perhaps *despite* themselves, exploring gutsy political and ethical issues, was content with the content. The students, because this was not explicitly on their agenda, were, ironically, contentedly 'dis-contented'.

The teacher might contend that she could not predict how the students would handle their improvisations and how they would develop the issues. She was thus put in a position of having to react, as pedagogue, to student 'surprises'. While she knew the broad plot, the details could not be predicted. But this is little more than the surprise teachers of any subject anywhere have to cope with as students make variable responses in variable ways to the set curriculum. Teachers *expect* to be 'surprised' in this sense so that it is not really very surprising, merely temporarily annoying, diverting, stimulating or challenging. Habitually, the teacher's job is to take what comes and shape it, with varying degrees of latitude, towards prefigured ends. These moments are mere hiccups in the balance of power.

The balance of surprise would have changed had the students negotiated the teacher into the role of giver of information and demonstration as commissioned by them. You cannot learn your lines for such a classroom. You must improvise from a position of some vulnerability and certain fallibility.

Secrets

This drama teacher, allegedly committed to the empowerment of her students, critical of existing power relationships in society and in the school and powerful in her own teaching, is out of habit and some delusion, I would say, teaching dependence and powerlessness. This is because she has not confronted the fact that in addition to experience and status she holds secrets which constitute power and could constitute increased power for others, if shared, particularly with those who live in schools. Or, if she has reached the point of knowing the power of her secrets, she has decided that there is as yet no point in, or no good to be derived from, telling them to her students. Perhaps it is because she feels that they would not comprehend. Or it may be that she operates on the false analogy that you do not need to know about car engines to drive a car.

It is habitual for teachers to write curriculum scripts. It is not habitual for teachers to question the politics of habit.

Here is a partial list of information which the teacher could have decided to give her students.

- Why she chose to introduce the 'Gargoyle' video.
- What she had in mind as a way of exploring it further.

- What she hoped students would be learning about and doing in this unit. (Not *what* they would learn, which can only be foreseen by rat psychologists and animal trainers.)
- Why she considered this important.
- What role she was going to play and the kinds of things she intended to do.
- The relevant parts of her learning or teaching theory upon which she based her plans.
- Her predictions, with reasons, as to why this unit of work would succeed as a learning experience.
- The criteria by which she would evaluate the curriculum unit itself and the individual performance of students (how they would be tested).
- The degree of negotiability she would allow in framing the script and the performances (what decision could be made by students).

She must know all this to write the curriculum script. Perhaps she has not admitted some of these secrets even to herself but, when she has, she can then make them available to the students in terms that they can understand.

If the students remain in the dark about all this, the curriculum will seem to them to be somehow *given, impermeable,* maybe even *magic* if the teacher is as charismatic as this one. It will not be considered by students to be pertinent matter for them. It is the teacher's 'show business', not theirs.

Teachers who do not take students behind their curriculum set to show how it is done, have:

either not thought about it

- *or* consider curriculum production and management issues are of no real concern to the workers
- *or* are unwilling to spend the time and energy which would then need to be expended each time a new 'script' was to be introduced
- *or* think that the students would reject such intimacy as a tactless breaking of the established rules and roles of teaching and learning

> *or* do not want to be an alienating Brecht with respect to their own theatre
>
> *or* would find it threatening...

The list could go on, for the fact is that few teachers *do* take this step. My own informal research has yielded a full crop of 'Yes, buts...' whenever coming clean about the curriculum and the school is suggested. These 'Yes, buts' are not to be sneered at. They are significant, real and perceived aspects of the teacher's contestation for room and power in the school.

It seems, however, that *theoretically* most can see that students who are illiterate with respect to the school and the curriculum (who cannot 'read' the place in which they operate as students) are gravely at risk and likely to be 'done in' by schooling. And yet, it is considered a radical and dangerous step to break the complicity (or is it conspiracy?) of tact where the successful pick up the passwords according to privilege and chance. It is almost taboo to *tell* students how the place works, how the curriculum is constructed, and how to negotiate for reward. In whose interests is this information withheld?

By choosing not to tell, not to make their own teaching explicitly problematic for students, or by being naively unaware of the possibility of telling, teachers are teaching a politics which condones information capital and privilege, cultural discrimination against the young, and the division of mental labour.

Trust

Returning to our hypothetical drama teacher, we need to correct some tendencies to score easy points. In a mediated exchange a few years ago, I got the impression from Dorothy Heathcote that the key to good drama teaching is the TRUST which students have in their teacher.

This teacher has the trust of her students. If over time the students learn through experience and consequences that the teacher cares about them and is working in their interests then there is no need, says Dorothy Heathcote, to get into convolutions of negotiation and explanation. Our hypothetical drama teacher would argue that she should not be judged on the basis of one unit: that because of her genuine *intention* to empower, this will permeate the curriculum in subtle ways and eventually take hold without the need for self-conscious dwelling on it. She might also argue that one must always move the students gradually from their learned helplessness in most classrooms to new regimes where they can progressively take up more power and responsibility. Rebellion and rejection too often accompany sudden shifts in the teaching roles. My present stance is to reject these counter arguments.

For me, TRUST is a worrisome concept. I am continually on my guard against those in power over me, no matter how 'good' they are, and I require continual demonstration and negotiation to confirm that I am not being manipulated against my own interest. Indeed, the more trustworthy the authority, the more I need to be alert. 'Trustworthy' people are often warm hosts to the invisible bad habits of society. In my own teaching these days, I deliberately seek to alienate my students from my teaching performance by showing them what I am about. I wish to rouse their suspicions about what I say and do, so that I will be tested before swallowing. I always try to teach the meta-text along with the text. This is my contribution to the breaking of the reproduction of dependence that the schooling industry usually achieves.

In these resolves I continually fall short, catching myself out in compromise, contradiction and insidious bad habits. While striving to set up a collaboration of equals, I accept that as teacher I have 'unequal' power. For this reason, the contradictions of my classroom are more pleasing than the harmonies. They indicate that my authority is questionable.

Struggling and Penetrating

Returning to the drama teacher *constructed* in this paper, I need to draw attention to the fact that this is *my construct* cited for my own purposes. Real teachers would tell a far more complex story of subtle changes in power and influence as students exercise their capacities to resist and to charm teachers in their own interests. They would also, no doubt, set their script-writing in a context which includes far more complex industrial, ethical and physical constraints than I have sketched out in my convenient hypothesis.

Nevertheless, I have tried to suggest how it is that all of us, no matter how finely tuned our consciousness, will teach with variable integrity, authenticity and consistency:

> ...ideologies are not abstract ideas merely 'held in the heads of people'. As recent European social theorists remind us, they are constituted by our whole array of commonsense practices and

meanings that are lived out as we go about our daily lives. Furthermore, they may be internally inconsistent. These common-sense practices and meanings are often 'deeply contradictory, shot through with [both] ideological elements [and] elements of good sense'. Thus side by side with beliefs and actions that maintain the dominance of powerful classes and groups, there will be elements of serious (though perhaps incomplete) understanding, elements that see the differential benefits and penetrate close to the core of an unequal reality.[2]

We are at once opponents and agents of the hegemony of schools. Our students also vacillate from subversion of some parts of our regime to reinforcement of some of our comfortable habits. Just as we teachers are engaged in a continuing struggle to penetrate social reality, so should our students be encouraged to struggle and penetrate.

In drama classrooms throughout the country, children are being taught the politics of their teachers, the politics of the school and the politics of the nation. Drama teaching can, and should, be a powerful vehicle for helping students to penetrate and interpret what is happening to them.

NOTES

1. See 'Reading the Whole Curriculum', this volume.
2. Apple, Michael V., 'Analyzing Determinations: Understanding and Evaluating the Production of Social Outcomes in Schools', *Curriculum Inquiry*, 10, 1, 1980, p. 61.

5

LITERACY, POWER, AND THE COMMUNITY

A public lecture delivered at Murdoch University, during a short period when Garth was invited to Murdoch as a visiting scholar in 1984. The audience comprised academics, English teachers and educational administrators.

Let me begin this broad exploration of the nominated territory by naming some signposts which I deem to be pointing towards powerful ideas:

- Demonstration
- Secrets and Surprises
- Building Structure
- Dancing
- Chunking
- Running Commentary
- QWERTY
- Syntonicity
- Inner Tennis
- Social Penetration

At this point I shall stop for a moment and ask you, now that you have access to an albeit cryptic set of organisers, to jot down or mentally contemplate how my signposts might be used to illuminate the theme of 'literacy, power and the community'.

I ask you to do this not as a quaint whim of mine but as a logical extension of a key principle of reading and writing. You are about to be confronted with my text. Your task, since I presume you wish to try to understand me, is to 'read' what I am about to present. A few moments ago this was a secret. Less than a few moments ago it was slightly less secret. To gain power over my text, you need to activate and mobilise what you already know and begin a process of predicting and checking your hypotheses as I progressively reveal my script. This is at once a process for you of generous indwelling in my head and critical alienation from it. We are about to enter into an intellectual courtship where, on principle, I shall try not to use magic.

Now that you have increased your power by getting some kind of bead on me, I shall begin weaving. My goal after exploration will be to find some keys which might help schools and the community to unlock doors to powerful literacy and to increased power through literacy.

Exploration

I am sure that we know more than we can tell. Therefore, it is dangerous to assess people purely on what they can say. I also believe we know more than we can do. Thus, to judge people merely on what they can do is also a form of reductionism. Many ideals and acts are in rehearsal or waiting in the wings. We know, for instance, that before the very young reach out and grasp for the first time, there is a stage when at a subliminal level the requisite muscles for the performance are orchestrated in a nonproductive inner simulation. Link this, if you like, to swimming with one foot on the bottom, or riding a bike while someone holds the seat. *Making out* is a forerunner to *making changes*.

How do we come to know the inner script which we can initially neither tell nor show? I don't know, but this is what I imagine. We see other people doing things which we begin to imagine ourselves doing with pleasure or effect. Before the imagining takes hold, the surrounding deeds are a kind of unacknowledged cultural amniotic. As soon as we begin to imagine ourselves doing these things, they become a *demonstration* for us. The stronger the intention to become what has been imagined, the more intensely will the demonstrations be cased. And so an internal image of the *whole* act, a *chunk* of culture, as opposed to atomic bits, takes hold in the mind and body. This becomes a powerful idea, a blue-print, the beginning of a building.

What sets us imagining doing these things? We are not just voyeurs on the culture. The culture through the agency of other human beings deliberately acts on us. The culture has designs on us; the major design is to enculturate. Those more sophisticated than us expect us to become like them, at least until their sophistication corrupts them into a form of cultural private enterprise. Adults interact with the young and treat them *as if they already know*. When out of the beginning babel of sounds a chance conjunction produces something approximating 'Ma Ma', an exaggerated celebration occurs. The child's accident is accorded immense status. It is extended, repeated, named, and, in many cases, documented. The child has learnt a hitherto cultural secret.

The dance has begun. And the child leads more often than the adult. At the first signs of a new child's step, however, the adult enters into the dance and shows variations upon the theme, demonstrating new possibilities, and naming what is happening, weaving around the new act with new words.

As the act takes shape, a running commentary emerges, a metalanguage which brings into consciousness what seemed at first to come naturally. A kind of grammar of the act merges only when or *after* the process of producing a version of the whole game has begun.

This running commentary is rudimentary theory, the description, at least, of practice which begins also to build in evaluations of the act. It is an early narrative about how one part of the world works; or perhaps a primitive scientific explanation.

Here is a three-year-old producing an 'action replay' running commentary on a chunk of experience. The commentary takes place after the act during a pre-sleep monologue:

> We have a swing
> O Pee Doodle
> Fell off the swing (to the tune of *Humpty Dumpty*)...clumsy
> Why you crying, don't cry, hosh, don't prosh will you?
> Don't cry.

This relates to an incident of that day when a young child fell off a swing, hit her had, and was comforted by her mother, all of this observed by the monologist. Note that the commentary uses very powerful learning strategies for drawing purchase on and power over that event:

- an analogy between the injured child and Humpty Dumpty whose story is known;
- a dramatisation involving imitation is performed, requiring the dramatist to indwell in or empathise with the rescuing mother;
- an evaluation is made from the point of view of the observer.

The infant ethnographer triangulates. With three 'fixes', she ties down the experience and makes it her own. She powers into the past day with the militant stories/theories she has so far accumulated.

Note that she loads her inquiry with affectivity. Listening to the actual performance, one is struck by the clear change of emotion in the indwelling. The observer takes on the embodied anguish of the recollected participants.

In the jargon of the clinical psychologists she is engaged in *syntonic* learning. Hers is not just a mental enmeshment. She imprints the event on her whole being, body and mind. The complexities are caught factually and fictionally, transactionally and poetically.

Short of actually suffering a fall from a swing, she gives herself the next best thing, a rich, vicarious 'Clayton's' experience (the experience you have when you're not having an experience!). And this allows her to penetrate further into the cultural flux. What might have been a fleeting and elusive experience is held, named, and placed in her developing frames of mind. She has noted as well as noticed. If she then proceeded for the rest of her life to view accidents through these frames, frozen and held because they seem adequate, she would be a victim of what I shall call the QWERTY syndrome.

It is time to reveal one of my inspirational sources. Seymour Papert in his book *Mind-Storms: Children, Computers and Powerful Ideas* (1980) has this to say about QWERTY:

> The top row of alphabetic keys of the standard typewriter reads QWERTY. For me this symbolises the way in which technology can all too often serve not as a force of progress but for keeping things stuck. The QWERTY arrangement has no rational explanation, only a historical one. It was introduced in response to a problem in the early days of the typewriter. The keys used to jam. The idea was to minimise the collision problem by separating those keys that followed one another frequently. Just a few years later, general improvements in the technology removed the jamming problem but QWERTY stuck. Once adopted, it resulted in many millions of typewriters and a method (indeed a full blown curriculum) for learning typing. The social cost of change (for example putting the most used keys together on the keyboard) mounted with a vested interest created by the fact that so many fingers now knew how to follow the QWERTY keyboard, QWERTY has stayed on despite the existence of other more 'rational' systems. On the other hand if you talk to people about the QWERTY arrangement, they will justify it by 'objective' criteria. They will tell you that it 'optimises this' or 'minimises that'.

Although these justifications have no rational foundation, they illustrate a process, a social process, of myth construction that allows us to build a justification for primitivity into the system.

In terms of *further penetration* of social and cultural reality, the three year old's brilliant three-year-old frames will, if fixed, become blunter and blunter instruments, a flatter battery, if you like. QWERTY is the anodyne of painful cultural and personal struggle. It would render us extinct in the long run.

From my initial signposts, only *inner tennis* remains to be incorporated as an illuminative device. With collusion both Seymour Papert and I have read, with profit, Timothy Gallwey's book *Inner Tennis* (1976). Gallwey conceives the inner learner as having two selves: an analytic, verbal self and a more holistic, intuitive one. He believes that at different times different selves need to be in control and that an important part of learning is to teach each self when to take over and when to leave it to the other. He is not far removed, I think, from Polanyi's notions of focal and global awareness. Sometimes we must apprehend our goal and rely on automated behaviours to work in a kind of gestalt towards the desired end. At times we need to refocus on a faulty segment or a problematic technique. This applies to reading, writing, tennis, and teaching.

While tacit, ineffable knowledge may be the vanguard of the mind, the capacity to move towards ever new frontiers depends on securing the conquered domains with explanatory language. By structuring ways of talking about our past accomplishments, we increase our power to go beyond.

I am now ready to shine some of these ideas on schools and society to see what happens to our children as they are initiated into literacy.

Looking at Schooling

Schools and the community are quite limited by what their language allows them to note. In talking about how we use language to mean things, we are, even at the level of our outstanding linguists, still comparatively primitive. Our capacity to become more powerfully literate as a society depends on our capacity to develop better ways to explain to and to show others what we do when we read and write.

I suspect we are better equipped to describe how to hit a forehand than how to place a full stop in a sentence. I suspect also that in education we are chronically word-bound in our attempts to enculturate. Verbal explanation almost certainly needs to be preceded by the learner being allowed to watch and commission further demonstration. By deliberately structuring the opportunity to eavesdrop on authentic examples of the act to be mastered, we may enhance that rich and complex imprinting of the image that is, I suggest, a necessary precursor to accomplishment.

Our present verbal explanations of how language works are fairly crude myths compared with that of which we cannot speak but surely know has to happen before new learnings take hold. Instead of acknowledging them as a kind of virtuous lying, however, we tend to reify and deify our present verbal constructs into manuals and then put these at the heart of curricula for literacy. We attribute exaggerated status to what are relatively crude observations that we have made about reading and writing and, QWERTY-like, we develop justification for our myths. After all, like QWERTY, they work. Children, by and large, learn to read and write under a regime dominated by our myths but, I suggest, they only do this *by discovering for themselves secrets that either we know and do not tell or know and cannot tell.* They may, nevertheless, be 'magicked' into believing that the teachers' medicine did the trick.

Ironically, I fear, as the community becomes better informed about what schools do with reading and writing, it will be polluted by the school QWERTY and learn to abandon the powerful folk wisdom or intuition that has so brilliantly enabled it to teach talking without the aid of schools. Indeed, there is evidence that parents in assisting reading and writing instruction at home abandon the common sense that accompanied their teaching of talk in favor of school-type protocols.

I do not wish to become too romantic about homespun methods, nor do I wish to suggest that all schools and teachers are in the grip of QWERTY. But I do think improvement in literacy is being impeded by the equivalent of 'Father Christmas' explanations which we give to the young. At school and at home, we are in danger of cutting them off from their own and our sources of power by suggesting that power resides in our relatively weak codified verbal constructs rather than in our *powerful ideas, images* and a *complex 'feel'* for what we do. Furthermore, we unwittingly tend to withhold the major fuel of power – *information.* Or rather, we give *academic* information as opposed to *procedural* information that tends to be so taken for granted by us that we no longer consider it important.

Thus we are likely to teach 'full stops' by introducing the notion of a complete sentence with an obligatory finite verb. We present this 'lie', when it would be better quality information to take the top off our own heads and think aloud for the learner about how we do it. In such an approach, the learner might be told how the sophisticated writer uses a kind of rhythmic feel to bring periodicity into the text. The explanation might be along the lines of 'I kind of read it aloud in my head and hear when it's time for a full stop'. Lacking the certainty of a textbook explanation, it is paradoxically better quality information, more assimilable and more practical.

At another level for another purpose (for example, for a scholar wishing to learn more about linguistics rather than for a person learning to write), the academic information may be pertinent and powerful information. I doubt, however, whether it has, at any level, much to do with literacy.

Remember my emphasis. I am arguing that the verbal tying down of experience or applied skills by the learner is essential as scaffolding for further building, but it must be the *learner's scaffolding*, not a transplanted scaffolding offered by someone else, even if that scaffolding is an authentic personal working model for the well-intentioned interventionist. When the enlightened teacher offers a sample of his or her own authentic inner running commentary of how full stops are orchestrated, the spirit should be 'this is the kind of running commentary you might find useful', rather than 'this is the running commentary that you should adopt'. Of course, if the running commentary offered is an attentuated definitional explanation offered on page 44 of a language exercise text, then its constructive potency for the learner is likely to be very low indeed. In terms of assisting personal power, I suggest that it will be positively toxic.

Perhaps the formula might be this: 'The more cryptically exact the information, the less useful it will be'. Consider, for instance, the destructive power of a precise, scientifically valid set of instructions on bike riding.

What we show and do for the learner is richer information than what we say, but what we say can be very useful if it is an authentic account of our present running commentary. Or, perhaps better still, our *re-creation* of the kind of running commentary we remember as being a useful aid to breakthrough when we were at the stage of 'building' that the learner is now experiencing. *A pre-disciplinary account* which is nevertheless consistent with principles underpinning more sophisticated formulations is advocated. In helping learners, the richest demonstrations will include windows on both action *and* reflection on that action, on both practice and theory. ('This is what I'm doing, and this is how I think I'm doing it.')

I was struck by the teaching style of my son's hockey coach during the half-time break recently. He provided selected commentaries on separate 'plays', analysing what happened and offering new vision or possibilities of what could have happened if a better theory had been practised. He was telling a story about the game hoping, no doubt, that some of it would be internalised and incorporated into the sets of different stories presently buzzing in the heads of his charges. He accompanied his verbal construct with simulated moves and dramatic gestures. In commenting on certain technical flaws, he advised players to keep remembering what it would be like when they could do 'it'. 'Keep working at it and it will come', he said. He also promised further demonstration and focus on that technique at training. He was 'dancing' for them, showing them inside the head of a thinking, accomplished hockey player. I reflected on how generously he was giving them access to 'know-how' and how attentive the learners were. They were imagining themselves being better.

I am sure you have begun to imagine the kind of school and community that I would advocate in the interests of literacy and increased personal power. Let me briefly remind you by contrast how QWERTY strangles many of our schools today.

The literacy game equivalent to the 'stuck keyboard' are notions that language skills are put together like building blocks to make language, that training in the part must precede practice of the whole, that repetition and imitation is the way to mastery. A whole education industry built on the factory metaphor has grown around these myths. The allocation of patchwork subject time-slots encourages compartmentalisation, and the decontextualisation of learning is ensured through the use of algorithmic exercises. The publishing industry reinforces the myths and parents also reinforce QWERTY although they can be forgiven for thinking that schools know what they are doing. Teachers are trained not to be outstanding practitioners of reading and writing, highly articulate about how they do it, but rather, at best, to be pseudo-linguists capable of being spectators on other people's reading and writing. They are asked to come to terms with other people's theories rather than their own.

The game is rigged to keep children from the secrets of reading and writing. Indeed, teachers-to-be and teachers-in-service are seduced by QWERTY away from any common sense they may have had, to the point that they are likely to disavow or forget their own deep secrets (as opposed to the 'official' explanations). If teachers are alienated from their own early secrets, they will teach similar alienation to their children. We need nothing short of a smashing of present school and university structures and a reconstruction according to new principles, if we are to break the present vicious circle, replacing disconnected learning with syntonicity.

Let me use some of my own recent research to indicate how huge a challenge this is[1].

I have gathered rich data from a Year Ten English classroom where a teacher, who understands and believes much of what I am saying in this paper, is attempting to empower her students to extend their literacy. Indeed, she knows that asking children to read a novel when they cannot read the school (and the teacher within the school and the subject within the subject offerings and the present unit of work within the subject) is a peculiarly sterile and frustrating task. She therefore sets out deliberately to give important information about how schools work, how teachers work, how English works, and how various literacy forms work. She is teaching students to read their world as much as she teaches them to read a novel. Reading the novel contributes to a better reading of the world.

She is infinitely patient in thinking aloud for students about the unit of work, aspects of the novel, how to handle assignments, and how to organise time. She is providing multiple commentaries at a number of levels. Her 'subject', rather than English, might better be termed 'learning to live in schools and the community (using literature as a medium)'.

I am interested in comparing the teacher's stories and designs with the students' stories and designs. I have records of the teacher early in a unit of work explaining in detail what will happen in this lesson and the next. These I put alongside post-lesson commentaries by those students who indicate that they did not listen or remember and that they have little idea of what will come next, apart from some fairly crude predictions based on teachers in general rather than on this teacher. They clearly do not see a need to develop a detailed predictive apparatus for the curriculum. They have been socialised into being programmed, and they therefore choose not to take note of the considerable flow of secrets offered by the teacher. It is not culturally expected in education that students will become literate about the curriculum (able, that is, to read it and write it). So even when the teacher immerses them in demonstrations of reading the school, they persist in seeing this as irrelevant.

One of the teacher's aims is to help her students become designers and planners of their own work. For two weeks she struggled to get her 'story' of the programme to mesh with the intentions and designs of the students. Eventually, she achieved a dramatic breakthrough when various groups became involved in planning a presentation of performance poetry. The moment they began working in groups to this end, the quality and volume of student discourse about coming events changed. Suddenly, they were able to articulate in great detail what they intended, the constraints on that intention, and the likely time sequence of their work.

'Syntonically', they were learning what it is to be a programmer. They still remain relatively speechless about what their teacher has in mind for them, but I predict that as they become theorisers about themselves as planners they will gradually begin, with encouragement, to indwell in the teacher's problems as curriculum planner. They will become progressively more literate about programming as they practise it themselves and pay attention to the teacher's deliberate demonstrations of programming.

At other levels the teacher is explicitly making available techniques for handling school assignments, showing for instance how to embed quotations in an essay on poetry or how to find illustrations for a theme. She has also herself written on one of the topics set, explaining how she did it. The students tell me that this is the first time in ten years that any teacher has thus exposed his or her own writing to them.

And yet, significantly, immersed in an empowering, information-giving culture, the students still claim that they are not doing much 'work' and not learning anything new. The dreaded QWERTY has fashioned their minds to conceive of learning in terms of assessments in the 'Marks Book', homework exercises completed, and the absence of enjoyment. Ten years of schooling have to be unlearnt if what this teacher is doing is to be construed as valuable by the students. They have to relearn what learning is.

Working within the school are many forces antipathetic to this English teacher's intention. Students who actively begin to read the curriculum demand to know 'why' and to suggest alternative constructions. This is subversive of QWERTY and of teachers framed by QWERTY. It puts pressure on teachers to know why they teach the way they do and to reveal this to their clients. In other words, it threatens to undermine the comfortable control and power which comes from keeping one's plans secret and being able to surprise.

Surprising things might happen if the students started to read the game with the intent of sharing in the shaping of it.

So What?

Here, in great brevity, is a summary of the points I have found myself making in the course of composing this text.

- School assessments, whether of performance in reading or writing or ability to write or talk about reading or writing, should be seen as a limited indication of what the student knows. The implication for teaching is that students' heads should always be overestimated.
- An empowering school and community will arrange for a good deal of penalty-free pretending, making-believe, and rehearsing.
- Schools and communities will also arrange for accomplished adults to demonstrate what is considered important for students to be able to do and to talk abut how they do it.
- Schools and communities will value imagination and 'feel', arranging for students to get on the inside of ideas and forms and protocols, by means of playing a version of the whole game from the earliest time.
- Schools and communities will encourage students to develop commentaries on their accomplishments by modelling themselves as commentators.
- Schools will neither allow literacy to develop solely through osmosis and doing it, nor solely through catechistic injunctions and exercise. They will develop a sensitive balance between holistic artistry and specifically focussed crafting.
- Teachers and parents need to become reacquainted with the predisciplinary personal building structures they themselves used as tools of penetration into early (and later) acts of literacy, so that they can collaborate with young children as they in turn construct their own devices.

- Teachers and parents need to pass on to the young the very best version of what they do and how they do it in all areas which affect the young, not just literacy. We learn to read the world by being privileged to eavesdrop on or interact with those who read it better than ourselves.

NOTE
1. The research is described in detail in the following essay.

REFERENCES

Gallwey, T. (1976) *Inner Tennis*, New York: Random House.

Papert, S. (1980) *Mindstorms: Children, Computers and Powerful Ideas*, New York: Basic Books

6

ENGLISH TEACHING: ART AND SCIENCE

An address given as keynote speaker at the annual conference of the USA National Council for the Teaching of English, in Detroit, 1984

The Curriculum Text

Mrs Bell, a teacher of ten years' experience in the one school, has begun a unit of work at Timbertown High School with her Year Ten (15 year olds) English class of twenty-one. The school is in a predominantly working class area but is essentially an academic institution. The setting is a second floor semi-enclosed classroom in a former open-space section of the school built to accommodate eight such classes. Noise drifts in around partitions and through concertina dividers from classes next door. We cannot take in everything and everyone and so we concentrate on Tammy, a vivacious Greek-Australian, Guiseppe known as Joseph, of Italian descent, the infinitely self-effacing AuKim, newly arrived from Vietnam, and Brenton, the ocker Australian who carries a cricket bat with him everywhere like a wand to ward off evil, occasionally using it as a mock machine gun on his enemies. Progressively over a two month period we will get to know each member of the class, as, like a negative becoming positive in developing fluid, they emerge and are particularised in our awareness. They have been with the teacher for only five weeks. They are to read the Ruth Park novel, *Playing Beatie Bow*, the story of a present day Sydney girl, Abigail, who is taken back one hundred years in time to live with her ancestors in the early settlement region of Sydney Rocks. The experience helps her to understand her confused adolescence and to come to terms with her parents' separation.

Early in the unit of work we find Mrs Bell reading the third chapter, pausing to show pictures from a book on colonial Sydney. After some reading, she stops to negotiate with the class about how the rest of the book is to be read. Tammy suggests they read in groups, not friendship groups but groups that will be 'best for you'. Homework is to find quotations in the early chapters which relate to Abigail's 'inner conflict'.

The next lesson is two days on. The entry to the class is ragged and noisy. Mrs Bell pauses patiently for attention. Joseph is not eager to begin. When Mrs Bell announces that she is pregnant, Brenton raises a laugh by asking 'How far gone?' They all edge forward to clarify the details of when she will be leaving. Mrs Bell lets them know exactly when she will take leave (five months hence).

Groups are given contract sheets to fill in, indicating to the teacher how they intend to carry out the reading assignment and what time line they will use. Brenton repeatedly seeks teacher attention as Mrs Bell circulates, answering questions of clarification about the contract and the task. Eventually they begin to read, some silently, some in groups. Brenton can be overheard telling Joseph about 'midwives'. 'In olden days they had grannies who helped people have kids'. AuKim and LaiAnh read alone with immense concentration, and Tammy chatters volubly, postponing the task.

Later in the lesson, as requested by Mrs Bell, they negotiate themselves into new friendship or 'convenience' groups and each group receives a worksheet which asks them to establish what is meant by 'self-awareness', 'inner conflict' and 'in search of inner self' in relation to the novel. It is suggested that they brainstorm personal examples and then report to the class. After this they are each to prepare a reading/performance or presentation of a poem which reveals one of these themes, explaining how it relates to the novel. The instruction reads:

> Decide how the group will go about this. In what way can the group support each other? How will you present the poems and your reactions? Decide on group and individual tasks.

Brenton wants to work individually, but seeing all the others in groups, he approaches two very conscientious workers, Cain and Phillip, who quite patently do not want him. Reluctantly, however, they grant him entry.

Mrs Bell is busy explaining 'inner conflict', clarifying time lines and answering 'commissions' from students, especially from the irrepressible Brenton who sends out frequent mock radio messages: 'Calling Mrs Bell, Calling Mrs Bell...' Eavesdropping on Joseph's group, we discover them talking about shoplifting and smoking, while from another group of girls we overhear: 'Sodium's Na'. The previous lesson in science has carried over. Glen companionably wanders across to tell Tammy's group to be quiet and stays to yarn. Joseph yawns, takes out his watch, shakes it, and announces that it has had a cardiac arrest.

When it comes to silent or group reading time, Brenton paces the room like a caged tiger, asserting that he has finished. Mrs Bell, with great patience, suggests a range of extension novels which she has brought along for this very purpose, and, causing our eyebrows to lift slightly, Brenton eventually settles down ostentatiously with *Dr Zhivago*.

After six pages Brenton re-enters a group and announces that Abigail is a 'schizophrenic antidisestablishmentarian'.

We note, by the way, that each lesson begins with very explicit recapitulation by Mrs Bell about what has happened, along with reminders about where the work is heading and how it is to be organised.

After the weekend, the teacher brings in a good range of poetry anthologies and talks with the whole class about how to use the library to find more poetry. Before long, after leafing through the anthologies, most of them containing poems by children of about their own age, they begin to read pieces to each other. 'Listen to this one', or 'I've found one'.

Joseph's group discusses cricket until Glen interrupts. He has found a poem about a drag race between rival gangs. Joseph laughs. Glen suggests a group poem about 'The Street Machine' and they begin tossing in lines. The effort falters; Chris announces that he's going to write about 'The Lifestyle of a Rice Bubble', while Michael and Glen take out a motor magazine and look at the pictures. Eventually, they pause to hear Chris's poem. Mrs Bell approaches and they all give the impression of serious work. Without destroying the rice bubble initiative, she reminds them of the need to find poems about inner conflict. She directs them back to the task sheet. She suggests that they might find a whole range of ways to present their work dramatically.

A couple of lessons on, Mrs Bell takes two groups who seem to be making little headway and suggests that she provide a model of how to analyse a poem and find aspects of its themes. 'What do you think?' she asks and, with little enthusiasm it seems, they agree. She reads the poem 'At Sixteen' and they jot down 'what the poem is about'; except for Joseph, who can't find his paper.

While other groups argue and negotiate about how to perform their poems, Mrs Bell is still at work on her modelling exercise. Now she is at the point of reading them her own piece on 'At Sixteen', showing them how she interweaves quotation and commentary.

At another table Brenton and his two conscientious colleagues are preparing a poster, the centre of which is a huge brain around which they attach poems on inner conflict. Brenton announces that this was his idea. The other two repudiate the claim.

A joint decision that their work will be video-taped galvanises formerly tardy groups. It takes three more lessons to complete the performances which contain some real surprises. Brenton, for instance, performs passionately and well the role of a drug addict and wins acclaim from those who usually find him a pain. The camera is forgotten. The Vietnamese girls, still shy, get through their parts, while Joseph and Glen take the acting award with a fine piece on racial discrimination. Each performance is followed by constructive evaluation from Mrs Bell and the class.

Two events serve as end points. In one lesson the whole class reflects on what they have learnt, and a couple of weeks later they sit rapt and fascinated watching the video replay of their achievements.

A Student Perspective

Throughout the enactment of this particular English curriculum text, we have had the privilege of talking at the end of each lesson to Tammy, AuKim and Joseph about what happened, what they thought of what happened, and what they thought might happen next.

In the early interviews with the students we note an almost total lack of empathy with the teacher as teacher. They do not perceive that what she is doing is premeditated and constantly re-worked in the light of their response to her planning. When asked to predict what Mrs Bell will do next, they are at first working simply on their general knowledge of 'what English teachers do': 'She's getting us to underline things, so probably at the end she'll get us to write that up and then write an essay on it', says Tammy.

While they begin with a very poor understanding of why they are doing what they are doing, despite Mrs Bell's persistent and patient re-iteration at the beginning of each lesson and during lessons, they are aware that English this year is different: 'We are going deeper into things this year', says Joseph.

Some way into the unit, such self-consciousness emerges in the interviews. Tammy, reflecting upon a group-work session, shows a grasp of some things we might wish more teachers to appreciate: 'It was good. If we didn't understand, we'd share it around the group. When we got really stuck, we called her over and figured it out. Once you're in groups, you don't feel scared about whether it's right or wrong, you can just say it.'

All of them do not perceive that they have *worked*. 'We didn't do too much work. Writing work. It was all reading and getting into groups. Talking. We didn't get much work done.' Clearly work is acquainted with writing.

While they are inarticulate about Mrs Bell's and their own intentions early in the unit, towards the end they are highly articulate, expansive and detailed in heir prediction about what is going to happen. Indeed, their remarks take on very similar qualities to the monologue planning texts of Mrs Bell herself. They become, over time, co-planners of the curriculum. 'Tuesday we're probably going to go back into our reading groups – a lesson of that. Wednesday we don't have English. Thursday we've got a double lesson, so I think one lesson we're going to be performing and it will probably run into the next lesson and then Friday – the next two lessons we'll probably rehearse – and perform it again. And the week after that, earlier than expected, we'll probably show the play.'

They also show themselves to be aware of each other in more than superficial ways.

'How do you explain Brenton?' the interviewer says.

'He wants attention,' says Tammy.

'Mm,' says Joseph.

'He's got problems,' says Tammy. 'You know, home and all that. Personal problems. Doesn't get enough love and attention at home.'

They do much better empathising with Brenton than they do with Mrs. Bell. Despite her openness about herself and her own experience in class discussion, an occlusion operates. She is a teacher. 'I don't think teachers worry about many things,' says Tammy. They find it almost impossible to talk about what she might have felt or thought about a lesson.

'But don't you try to read your teacher's mind?' says the interviewer.

'Only when there's a test coming up,' says Joseph.

When it is all over, they interestingly contradict themselves. They have not worked and yet they say they have learnt 'bulk about poems', gained confidence which will help them get a job, survived the test of performing to their peers ('It will be much easier next time'), and furthermore they understand that they have been allowed to work through some of the darker areas of adolescence. 'It helps you to get feelings out of your head.'

Inside the Teacher's Mind

We have seen the unfolding drama. We have heard the spectator/participant comments of some students. Now we are allowed the unique experience of eavesdropping on the mind of the teacher in her initial composing, during the enactment of the curriculum unit, and in reflection on the work done. She has tried to capture the life of her mind by speaking a running commentary monologue of her thoughts into a hand-held tape recorder. In the essentially privatised world of education, educational writers have been prone to stigmatise and stereotype teachers, reducing them to types and styles; speculating, often patronisingly, about intentions and designs. But we are to come close to a direct window on the mind of the practitioner at work. We who have been teachers, too, recognise it as authentic. This archaeological exercise reminds us of treasures we tend to bury and forget; things we know but do not speak of when we write about the art and science of our own teaching; perhaps so taken-for-granted that we de-value them.

In the incubating stages, Mrs Bell loosely construes the unit. Her preference is to use the novel *The Outsiders* by Ruth Park because 'it works well with Year 10s'.

She wants to set up group collaboration on writing and she is keen to introduce extension reading. She is not happy yet with their contribution to class discussion. She hopes that in groups she can structure things so that they feel comfortable to exchange ideas.

Following the flow sometime later, we are reminded that schools are complex contexts: 'Well, *The Outsiders* is not available. In fact, I'm sixth on the list in application for it. Its popularity is spreading alike with teachers and students. *Romeo and Juliet* looks as though it couldn't be arranged in time, so *Playing Beatie Bow* it is.'

She begins to spark ideas off herself. 'I'd like some to take a literary criticism type approach...I think some get enjoyment out of using their skills as writers, their skills of honing down their thoughts. I can certainly remember at Year 10 level myself starting to feel that come together in the pure enjoyment of it...but it also lends itself really well to an exploration of the historical aspects of the novel and the idea of time travel which is an element of this story and I think we could look into that particularly because of its Australian setting, although it wouldn't have to be confined to Australia...'

From this consideration she moves on to think about stream-of-consciousness writing in journals and this leads her to the idea which from our vantage point we know finally takes the central ground: 'I think poetry is another area. I think I'd do that before we get into writing at the end of the novel. Poetry that takes up one of the themes of the book, of growing personal awareness of the inner conflict that the girl is going through...It's an area that Year 10s are into themselves... Last year we started a poem called *At Sixteen* and there was lots of response to that poem...and then I invited them to find poems that they thought expressed conflict... I also suggested that they might like to write poems... That was really good... So I would really like to capture some of that again this year. The poetry would be something that we could do. Yes...that is something I will do for sure.'

Then she plunges deep into the experience of the novel, exploring its themes and symbols, testing the limits of its territory and its relevance to the students.

She dwells for some time on the problems of the Vietnamese students who will need extra help.

We leave her first monologue at the point where she will now write up the curriculum unit, along with some structures for them to work within: 'a framework for them to choose their own sorts of work and set their own questions...'

As the work begins, we listen to her contemplating some of the surprise turns in the plot: 'There was a group who opted to read with me who were not weak students who might be looking for help and guidance. In fact, those chose not to work with me. Those who did are quite confident readers who said they enjoyed discussing their reading and reflecting on the novel as they went along...'

She is critical of her ambiguous or unclear wording on the task sheets and acknowledges the confusion, 'although they came up with some good ideas in groups'.

Within the commentary on the content and process of the lessons are embedded observations on the students: 'Brenton went and sat himself with Cain and Phillip much to their displeasure but he stood his ground.' Also: 'Kim and Anh showed their usual reluctance to join a group. I don't know whether it's because they don't want to join a group or because of their shyness; they think perhaps they're not welcome. And I suggested to them that Tammy and Elvira's group would make them welcome having asked them if it was OK with them. They're very friendly and Kim and Anh came over quietly. But I was impressed by the way the other girls made them welcome and they seemed to settle in quite well there.'

Since Brenton has already forced us to attend to him, it is worth following what Mrs Bell thinks about him: 'I put some pressure on him early in the piece of work, an unfinished piece...and his comment to me was: "Oh, what are you bothering for; nobody else does"...I think Brenton interrupts and does his usual thing with the cricket bat...to make his presence felt. That's his way of making contact. It doesn't particularly worry me.'

Quite extensively she expands upon her theories of teaching the novel, particularly dwelling on the perspectives she brings as an historian. She also reflects upon the quality of student work: 'There's still not as much commitment to the work as I'd hoped...especially from being able to work in groups. I feel it's been a bit slow this week. There's always that time factor. There's so much we could do in relation to the novel...but I feel a bit restricted by time. This week I hope that the interest in poetry will really get going...' A week later she is more satisfied: 'The week finished on quite a high note... People seemed to be really getting into the poetry. Tammy's group has quite an exciting notion of threading their poems into a play. However, a couple of groups seem a bit baffled by the open-ended nature of the task.'

In explaining her decision to take two groups aside for some intensive 'modelling', she enters into some detailed theorising: 'I'll be trying to show them by example, by getting to do things I would do in coming to grips with the poem... Obviously I'd already chosen it because I feel that it is suitable...but later we can go back with a better awareness to their choices... So I'm trying to show them how I would work, create a structure that they can take back and apply...and also show them a bit of the excitement of coming to terms with a poem they at first may not have a positive reaction to... The excitement of working through until you feel you've come to grips with the poem... And I'll actually write with them...'

Her relief and pleasure shows as she comments on what eventually happens: 'Cain and Brenton and Phillip did their performance today. I think the class was half embarrassed...about Brenton's approach to his work, his passionate delivery... They were obviously interested in achieving a level of finished product that Brenton usually would not pay attention to...'

'Diane's confidence in front of the camera was amazing. I heard Linda say "How could she do it?" and I must admit I share Linda's awe...but it was a marvellous impassioned reading...'

'Joseph's little cameo-role theme of the beer drinking man watching TV, I thought was excellent and yet despite all this he doesn't want to work in English... But the group made him commit himself to the task and it was a real high point.'

Looking back on the transcript of her incubation, she expressed satisfaction that, while the specifics changed, she achieved some of her broad intentions. With evident pleasure she recounts to herself what the class achieved, without overlooking the shortcomings: 'They worked well together, they worked effectively.'

The Science and The Art

In thinking about how I should present to you my ideas about the science and art of English teaching, indeed all teaching, I have had many false starts. I knew I must ground my remarks. My privileged association with Mrs Bell gave me such grounding to the point where it hurts. Again and again I have come back to my data, layer upon layer of complex insights into Mrs Bell and her work. The more I have looked, the more awestruck I have become at the immensity of her achievement and the more angry I have become at myself and many other well-intentioned English educators who in the past have stood up at conferences and confidently sailed into learned analyses about English teachers and English teaching with varying degrees of meta-immunity from the territory. So often I have cleverly drawn maps without experiencing the terrain. This time, I must assail the teacher reducers and teacher bashers (often sadly teachers themselves) with a demonstration that would illustrate the relative bankruptcy of any one academic discipline in terms of the common wealth of teachers.

Mrs Bell is a da Vinci and a Galileo. In order to practise her craft at Timbertown High School in 1984, she needs a brilliant generic promiscuity. She must mix psychology, history, literature, politics, sociology, linguistics, economics, art, science, philosophy, poetics and aesthetics with passion and dispassion, with pragmatism and vision.

Aware that I had collected riches and treasures about English teaching that I had never found before, I knew nevertheless how inadequate my portrayal of Mrs Bell to you would still be.

Mrs Bell told me how inadequate her spoken monologues were in capturing what she really did when she composed. Even as we spoke about her teaching, she kept catching herself out in half-truths or inadequate representations of what she did and how she did it. She tended to depict herself as not having a learning theory and yet, as she talked, she realised, perhaps for the first time, the degree to which she deliberately and systematically operates on a coherent theory of teaching: 'In retrospect, I realise that I've read many things that must have influenced me and I have actually written down my views about learning. When I teach I'm not conscious of these things, but as we sit here and talk, I realise that it is all there as a kind of fuel to my teaching...'

So now, with the proviso that Mrs Bell herself doubts her own veracity as a story-teller, that I captured only a fraction of the interaction in my lesson notes, that truth is always tangential, I will try in this part of my address to analyse some of what Mrs Bell does, and in so doing I hope that, through one example, I might celebrate the Universal English Teacher. The picture I paint is one of infinite embeddedness. The teaching moment is set within the teaching sequence, set within a particular classroom of a particular school in a particular socio-political context at a particular moment of history. The participants can cause infinite variations from moment to moment, each coming from a distinct and complex setting, and each interpreting the moment differently.

I have sought appropriate analogies to capture what Mrs Bell does. I considered the circus performer keeping a range of plates spinning on a pole. Then I thought of the script writer turned drama director.

Finally, I concluded that teaching is like nothing else.

Taking Mrs Bell's teaching apart is akin to dissecting a poem, but let me see if, in order to sharpen our appreciation, I can analyse just ten aspects of her repertoire, and then put her back together again.

She is:

Indweller, Imaginer, Psychologist.

Mrs Bell illustrates that one cannot teach without imagining, and imagining means being able to see events unfolding in contexts as well as being able to create a version of what it might be like in someone else's mind, particularly in the minds of learners. The transcripts show the complex construing that goes on when a teacher incubates on a possible unit of work.

Mrs Bell conjures up last year's class and holds it alongside this year's class, balancing similarities and differences. She imagines what is possible with this group, this year, fielding in her mind how the whole class might respond while keeping a delicate hold on how different individuals might respond to the chosen novel.

She has to become a Vietnamese refugee, an unloved adolescent boy, a teenager in 1984, a poor reader and a high flier.

As a base for these imaginings, it seems that she needs first to become again herself at fifteen. This is her touchstone: 'How did I feel about these things when I was their age?'

In order to teach Brenton and AuKim, she must progressively feel with them their confusion and their pleasures. She needs to build in herself an image of their present understandings in order to know when and how to teach them. She knows that only in those parts where she shares their dreams can she profitably teach.

Experimenter/Theoretician/Scientist

So alienating has been Mrs Bell's undergraduate experience with 'theory' that, like many of her colleagues, she does not consider herself a theoretician. 'Theory' tends to be for those who theorise but do not teach. Yet the transcripts reveal a tenaciously theorising mind at work, operating deliberately and concertedly on established principles and procedures. Teaching may be an inexact science but it is nonetheless a science, in the sense that it cannot operate without the setting up of predictions about likely consequences in certain contexts. Just because there are multiple variables does not deny the need for science, the systematic pressing of present knowledge into new territory.

Let me list some of the principles and assumptions which help form Mrs Bell's science. As she says, these things are so 'naturalised' for her that she is most of the time not conscious that they form part of her composing and enactment 'generating plant'.

- *Collaboration:* She knows that being in the company of others who are thinking aloud about how to do things and interacting with those people is a way to cognitive gain, both about the 'stuff' being explored and about how other people think and learn.

- *Modelling/Demonstration:* She knows that demonstration at the point of confusion is potent, if the learner really wants to overcome the confusion.
- *Extended Responses:* Transcripts reveal that, independent of Roger Brown, Ruth Weir and many other experts on language acquisition, Mrs Bell learnt from her experience as a mother with her first child the subtleties of the complex linguistic dance which goes on between the learning child and adults. She realised for herself the power of the extended response which gives learners rich data upon which to base new forays into the world through language. Having deeply internalised this understanding, she operates on this with great patience, skill and empathy with her fifteen year old students.
- *Performance and Production:* She knows that skills are learnt and consolidated through application in tasks which have consequences. She also knows that the intention to perform or produce unlocks tacit powers (to use Polanyi's term).
- *Answering Questions:* Just as demonstration is important, so is question answering at the point of confusion. Mrs Bell deliberately experiments in this sequence of work with allowing them to experience confusion and to make mistakes. This is the mark of a confident and established theoretician. She knows that this will lead to her being *commissioned* to teach: 'I set out to be even bolder in letting the kids take the wrong direction. I stood back more and let the questions come...'
- *Transformation:* Mrs Bell has not read Jerome Bruner on the theory of transformation (that each time we transform present understandings from one medium to another we increase our present understandings), and yet she *knows* the theory. The students read the novel. They then talk about the novel, through the medium of poetry. They then transform what they know into drama and into illustrations and posters. They write scripts and they read scripts. The series of transformations intensifies the learning. Mrs Bell is quite deliberate in her planning for this to occur.
- *Intention/Negotiation:* Mrs Bell has evolved over many years a very clear stance on the power of student intention as opposed to teacher coercion. She admits that she could have forced the class to be more superficially efficient in getting through the work. She

could also have imposed a tighter, less-negotiable structure. Instead, she provided firm parameters within which she negotiated groupings, task allocations, and the form and content of assignments. She kept throwing the responsibility of choice and time management back onto the class. The result was a sequence where the class was slow to begin and floundering for a week or so. Gradually, as intentions and ownership took hold, the momentum gathered until in many ways the class took over. Her theories about withholding are linked with her strategies for empowerment. She has a very subtle understanding of the de-powering effects of premature instruction and direction.

An examination of Mrs Bell's composing shows that in this sequence she also deliberately thinks aloud for students (linked with her theory of empowerment); that she insists on student self-evaluation for the same reason; and that she consistently requires prediction both about the outcomes of the novel and about the emerging shape of the unit of work.

As a scientist/teacher she is experimenting on a number of fronts in this sequence of work. Perhaps the most interesting exploration is her attempt to give them insight into her curriculum construction and to teach them how to construct their own curriculum. The subtext of this curriculum story deals with what it is to be a teacher and a learner. As an experimenter, Mrs Bell is constantly construing and reconstruing in the light of her observations about what happens.

Technician/Designer

In her pre-teaching monologues, Mrs Bell is somewhat like a painter before a blank canvas, looking at what she wishes to paint; using figurative hands to frame it in various ways in her mind and contemplating how to place it on the canvas. But this is a too static depiction of what she does. *Her* canvas is one which, she knows, will continually re-cast itself of its own volition. In designing her unit, she knows that she must take into account the counter-designs of the students. There is artistry in her imagining, but the excitement of the vision is shaped and constrained by a wide range of technical and practical considerations.

Mrs Bell has to take into account the nature of the classrooms, the availability of resources and materials, the time available (including the intervention of Sports Day and Easter), the school's assessment and reporting requirements and the present capabilities of the class.

She has to consider questions of sequence, balance, and pace.

Implicit in any art or science is technology and skill in the manipulation of media. Mrs Bell deploys oral, written, dramatic and visual media in a subtle blend to give colour, variety and changing tensions to her creation.

Knower/Believer

What does Mrs Bell know in order to practise her art and science in this sequence of work? An inadequate shopping list will give some idea. She knows about:

- Australian literature, Ruth Park as a novelist, and this novel in particular
- Australian history as it affects this novel
- a range of poetry dealing with adolescent emotions similar to those in the novel
- the various levels of work that might be expected of her 15-year-old students
- the eventual requirements of examiners in English in terms of what constitutes a good literary-critical essay
- the kind of diet that the class has had in the past and will have in the future
- the rationale of process writing.

To such knowledge, combined with her theories, she brings strong beliefs, the product of her particular socialisation.

She believes that:

- her job is to extend horizons so that students can move beyond their present world view
- teachers should 'come clean' on as many levels as possible
- students' questions should be treated seriously
- schools generally are repressive, secretive and confining
- self esteem is the cornerstone of learning
- too many English teachers do not teach that which they hope students will learn
- society should be based on sharing and collaboration.

Both art and science advance through theory from a base of knowledge under the direction of beliefs.

Controller/Shaper/Sculptor

Let us not be romantic. Mrs Bell is in control. She has to be. What we have not observed closely is the superb peripheral vision that allows her to move around the classroom settling pockets of unrest, unsettling ghettoes of idleness and provoking those who are sitting on their assets. There is a weaponry of gentle inquiry and reminder which she brings to this task. Most of the time she is one step ahead. She knows that Joseph, Glen and Michael are talking motor-bikes rather than inner conflict. They think they are getting away with it. She knows that there is value in the talk and allows it to develop a productive head of steam. She then delicately intervenes to re-direct the energy towards the formal task.

One way to look at what happens is to see it as a kind of physics of the classroom in which the law of conservation of energy operates, except that classrooms leak. Without vigilance, entropy will occur; the class resolve will wind down. Mrs Bell is an anti-entropic agent redirecting and focussing energy. She also feeds energy by contributing her knowledge and ideas.

I had also thought to use the analogy of teacher as sculptor but clearly this is to deny the co-sculpting of students. In fact, we see Mrs Bell early in the piece sculpting while the students are reluctant helpers or voyeurs. Then, gradually, the students take the basic clay shape and push it in directions unforeseen. At the end Mrs Bell is admiring *their work*.

Coach/Demonstrator/Teacher

Mrs Bell works with great commitment on an apprenticeship model. She deplores the way in which some of her colleagues expect students to pick up competencies by themselves. (The kind of teacher who puts encouraging or discouraging remarks on essays but never shows how to write an essay.)

She believes that it is her job to teach, to show, to explain. The students recognise and appreciate this. They know that they are going deep and that Mrs Bell will help them when they are lost.

Mrs Bell's talent lies in that subtle apprehension of when to tell and when to remain silent. She gets her cues from the students. When they genuinely ask, she teaches her heart out. If they don't ask and she feels strongly that they need her teaching and don't know it, she will impose herself but only if she judges that the students are confused and will therefore pay attention to her demonstration. She must be assured that retrospectively they will appreciate what she has done.

In this sequence of work, she takes aside a small group to instruct them on how to read a poem, extract its themes and relate these to the novel. She does this by giving a very generous window on herself at work. She thinks for them, writes for them and comments in detail on why and how she does it.

She is a coach who can do it. She is an empress who wears clothes!

Metaphysicist/Illuminator/Commentator

Mrs Bell knows and shares my own interest in experimenting with teaching students to become theorisers about the teaching of their teachers and about their own learning. The slogan I use is 'making the information and the theory available to the students'. If teachers are *deliberate* teachers, consciously operating on principles and clearly aware of why they use certain strategies to serve their intentions, *then* they can, if they wish, tell all of this to their students and invite them to see if it works. In this way, teachers can enlist the aid of students as laboratory assistants in the ongoing experiment.

We observe Mrs Bell explaining repetitiously why she is doing certain things, how she sees it working and what she thinks will be the benefits to them.

My recording of the students' comments show that early in the sequence they simply do not listen to this. Her explanatory spiels are treated almost like the opening credits for a film. Or perhaps more accurately, because schools generally do not require students to know why they are doing what they do, the explanations and the philosophising go unregarded as a kind of noise or insignificant foreplay.

Significantly, later in the sequence the teacher's persistence is paying off. Students can not only indicate in detail what is happing and why. They have clear goals that they are deliberately trying to reach. They can also comment on the learning advantages and disadvantages of group work and performance.

I am reminded of the story of the interns who met each week with specialists to examine x-ray prints. At first the bewildered interns watched without comprehension as the specialist discussed shadows the learners could not see. Eventually, they came to see what the specialists saw.

Politician/Battler

Behind the scenes of this teaching set, the politics of the school and the education system are fought out. Mrs Bell in many ways teaches against the grain of the school and, sadly, of the English faculty itself.

Allowing group work and a degree of student decision-making is considered at the very least a mild form of insanity. Noise is first sign of the dreaded disease 'lack of control'. People whisper pityingly behind hands about the unfortunates who cannot keep their classes quiet.

Mrs Bell has had painful crises of nerve when all the overt and covert signals of the school have said 'Go back, you're going the wrong way'. But, armed with her theory and her implacable desire to be congruent with her beliefs, she has persevered. Her greatest allies are her students and the parents of her students who know her commitment, her dedication and her record of *delivering* what she promises.

Her main protection is her articulate theory of education. With faulty heads, the school principal or outside questioners, she is strong in knowing why she teaches as she does. Opposition tends to wilt if it argues from dogma and entrenchment rather than from rationality and understanding.

Mrs Bell has won room to move but it has taken her ten years. Recently she has become better at recruiting allies on the staff.

Provider/Servant

We have already discussed Mrs Bell as formal demonstrator and question answerer. Her role as giver goes deeper than the more overt manifestations. Between lessons she searches for books on early Sydney, finds and provides additional poetry anthologies, puts students in touch with extension novels and writes copious responses on written offerings.

This is a servant role, largely unappreciated by the students. If students are to get on with the work, teachers must re-cast their role. For instance, because time was short at the end of the sequence, Mrs Bell sensibly became an executive officer for the class committee: 'We heard from each group, quickly, and then I undertook the task to write that up into a summary, which I will photocopy and give back to them.'

Connoisseur/Reflector/Critic

Mrs Bell's pre-teaching monologue, the reflections during the sequence and her retrospective comments, show clearly the role of the English teacher as savourer and mixer. This is the teacher as gourmet, checking for the right mix, testing effect and affect, worrying about unpalatable diversions and taking pleasure in things coming out well.

Hers is an artistic focus. Keeping her sights on the desired finished unit, she zooms in to sample what Brenton is doing, or stands back to contemplate the total dynamics of the group or class. Knowing that the class cannot help her to achieve the proper aesthetic blend if they are unaware of her criteria for valuing, she tells them as a reflective critic what she is making of their work and how she feels about the quality of their involvement and their products.

Her lessons are packed with valuing, almost always positive but with suggestions and prompts: 'You could perhaps take one more step...' or 'If you wanted to improve it, maybe you could...'

Mrs Bell is not coy about her role as judge but her judgement is always in the direction of making her students better judges. To this end, she makes her criteria explicit and does not get into the trickery and sadism we sometimes find in schools where teachers keep the password secret.

Behind her connoisseurship is a theory of empowerment. Miss Jean Brodie has no place in her scheme of things.

Conclusion

Putting this all back together again, we are left with the teacher as artist. Her art is to deploy all these roles, and more, flexibly and simultaneously, sometimes with one thing in front of her consciousness but always with the tonal background of every other item in her repertoire.

She is *poly-attentive*. With one part of her mind's-eye on the imagined outcomes, she must read with feeling and sensitivity from the novel, while sensing whether she has engaged the class, knowing how much time she has left and remaining ready to break off for explanation at any time according to a judgement of whether this is necessary or whether it would intrude on the spell of the story. In James Britton's terms, she must have both a global and piecemeal awareness of what is happening. The technician, the scientist and the artist work together.

Frustrating as it may be for teacher educators, I doubt whether we can teach the 'feel' that Mrs Bell has learnt. We can only create the conditions and promote the frame of mind that will allow it to come. I have only been able to construct some fairly crude signposts which point roughly in the direction of that 'feel'.

When we ask contemporary artists to explain themselves, they refer us back to their work. They are reluctant to translate their effort into words. 'If I could tell you what it meant', said Isodora Duncan, 'there would be no point in dancing it.'

In the end, I cannot translate Mrs Bell for you. As Frost says: 'Poetry is what is lost in the translation.'

Perhaps we can illuminate Mrs Bell's work by noting the difference between synchronised music played by musicians obedient to a strict conductor, and music interweaving rhythm patterns played by improvisors, with their own downbeats. Certain African musicians carry on five simultaneous rhythms, the melody and four percussion parts. Three rhythms are common in pre-literate music: melody, handclapping and tapping the feet; the individual performs all three simultaneously, though not in synchronisation.

I suspect that something pre-literate, passionate and primitive pulses behind the civilised surfaces of Mrs Bell's teaching. Analogies with dance, music and sculpture help us to get closer to what she does. But they are inadequate. It is left for me simply to celebrate her achievement – hoping, of course, that we will all recognise in Mrs Bell the wonder of ourselves...

7

LITERATURE AND ENGLISH TEACHING: OPENING UP THE TERRITORY

A 'pre-reading' on the topic Language, Literature and Human Values for an invitational seminar on Language, Schooling and Society in East Lansing, Michigan, USA, 1984.

At East Lansing[1] we will have a few days in which to use some fine English teaching resources (our own heads) to consolidate what we know and maybe to push out some new frontiers in the field of literature teaching. This job is not just for ourselves. Throughout the seminar we need to keep in mind the thousands of English teachers at work in our member nations and elsewhere. When we report to them through the seminar publication, I would like to feel that our work is seen as useful, challenging and supportive.

We cannot tell whether in the 1980s we will help to lead the profession into a Dartmouth-like revolution, but there is excitement in knowing that if we work and talk hard we could make a significant contribution to worldwide conversation about the teaching of English.

Even from a small knowledge of some of the participants, I know that our eventual writing will be speculative, suggestive and questioning rather than definitive and sure. Constructive critiques and contradiction may be more evident than harmony and consensus; though it would be nice to agree on some things.

It is my task here to begin to open up the territory, and to suggest some of the issues that may emerge.

In Australia at present, there is an urgent and profound curriculum struggle around the question: 'What might be the form of a democratic curriculum?' In response to several years now of the past Government's pressures for 'choice and diversity' in curriculum, the new Government's portmanteau phrase is 'participation and equity'. Questions of access to cultural wealth arise and, indeed, there is a strong drive to re-define what is culturally significant and 'rich'. Many who have seen the working classes, the immigrants, the aborigines and girls being further disadvantaged under 'choice and diversity' ideals, are calling for the formulation of a common curriculum which would be offered to all students still under compulsion (to age 15 in Australia). There seems to be in this quarter a new valuing of a future Australian society that coheres through shared understandings of the culture. Others who fear the colonising powers of a dominant culture oppose the common curriculum and suggest various strategies of specialist provision for the presently less powerful groups. For instance, there is a strong lobby for single-sex schools in order to empower girls, and there is a growing advocacy for a new curriculum tailor-made especially for the working class.

Jerome Bruner said somewhere, I recall, that schools should be devoted to ensuring skilled performance in culturally significant media. We need to add to this, I think, skilled performance (and production) with respect to culturally important *content* and *issues*. Then, to show further my own prejudices, I would want to emphasise the *transforming* power of whatever is learnt. Mere cultural transmission would render us human dinosaurs in the last years of the twentieth century. And whose 'culture' are we talking about?

This is by way of suggesting very crudely a philosophical, political and educational context for our enquiries.

In what follows, I sketch out a number of topics bearing on the possible reconceptualisation of English teaching and literary education.

The Making of Literature

This is the title of a new book, published by A.A.T.E., written by Professor Ian Reid[2] It reminds us that literature is, indeed, produced and consumed. It is not magically given. It is not natural. It is socially constructed within socially shared conventions. It is culturally and historically conditioned, and it is differentially received by readers (of different cultures, ages, genders, beliefs, etc), who thus help to *make* it. Furthermore, any one text owes a debt to the whole family of texts which has come before it. In this sense it is perhaps limiting to think of *an* author who makes meaning. The text is given authority by a complex complicity of many agents.

Those with a Marxist analysis of literature might characterise it as a 'truth-production' industry where the messages and forms of popular fiction support the hegemony of a dominant ideology. In this analysis books might be seen as the products of society rather than of persons, since society has shaped the person and one cannot stand outside one's own culture.

- Have we romantically over-valued the disruptive, critical function of literature and under-played its role as a palliative and a subtle instrument of containment and oppression?
- Have we enshrined in our teaching of literature the cult of the person? The muse-inspired magician? Is this a toxic notion?
- How well do we teach an understanding of 'inter-textuality', the relationship of any one text to a network of other texts?
- Does our teaching of literature reflect an understanding of how literature is made?
- Do our students make literature themselves?
- Is literature a form of power-play and, if so, do we need deliberately to teach children how to resist it?

The Boundaries of Literature

Can we begin with an agreement that literature is made by people of all ages and all cultures, assuming that we can agree on what we mean by 'literature'? Ian Reid, in the book referred to above, is finding it almost impossible to come up with an exclusive definition. Indeed, his is, finally, an indecisive view. Literature is not just what is written down. It can be oral, visual and audio-visual. It can be biography or scientific tracts as well as poems, plays and novels. Do we want to be this inclusive? Or do we want to retain a definition that encompasses the notion of 'storying', the re-creation or creation of a representation of experience? That is, literature functions in society as a means of making sense of the world through spectatorship on past, present and possible future events, real or imaginary, in such a way that the representation is shaped into a form that is aesthetically pleasing? Rather badly, I am alluding to what James Britton has said much better.

My inclination is to reject the narrow focus of Literature (with a capital 'L') which has in some way been voted as good (if not classic) by certain people who act as guardians of culture and good taste. I want schools to be places where children study the fullest possible range of literature, from oral story-telling, to street theatre, to popular novels, to films and video plays.

But are there some works that have greater emancipatory power for children? Are some works richer in potential to help them read themselves and the world with greater subtlety? If the answer is 'yes', as I suspect it might be, then what distinguishes these works and how much should they dominate the curriculum (once they have been found), as opposed to other forms of literature that may be less powerful? Who is to say what these preferred works are? And can we say, with confidence, that they will be good for all?

If we do push out the boundaries of English teaching to include a wider range of literature, will English finally disappear as a subject?

Do we have the capacity to educate teachers who can deal confidently with the widest possible spectrum of literature?

The Literary Text

'Text', if we define literature to include oral literature, television and multi-media 'storying', takes on a new meaning.

Elsewhere, I have offered a provisional description: 'By "text" I do not mean simply something written. I mean anything written or enacted or experienced which is *framed* in some way that makes it amenable to analysis and comprehension.'[3]

Semiotics, though it is not a field I know well, is helping us to new understandings of how texts are shaped and how they cohere internally. It draws our attention to subtleties in genre, conventions, aesthetics and poetics. It requires to place *texts* in *contexts* and to examine the relationship between text and context.

- What are the implications for the teaching of literature in the developing field of semiotics?
- How would literary study differ if informed by semiotics?
- What are the kinds of texts that children might study at different levels?

Literature and Pedagogy – or, Literature and Curriculum Composition

Eventually all that we do and say will need to be translated by us and teachers into new forms of teaching and variations on old forms.

- What kind or kinds of literature curriculum do we advocate?

- To what ends do we teach literature? What do we hope our students might say and do and be as a result of our teaching?
- To what extend should programmes be structured by teachers, to what extent co-planned, and to what extent negotiated?
- What things might we value and how do we suggest they might be valued? (And by whom?)
- Should or can teachers be neutral with respect to texts? If not, how far should they go in suggesting interpretations?
- How far should teachers go in expressing their own values?
- What is the role of teacher as senior meaning-maker in a literature class?
- What relative balance might there be between *experiencing* literature and *analysing* it?
- What might be the balance between private *reading* and *public* sharing; between *individual* work and *group* work?
- What visions do we have of the ideal literature 'community' in classrooms?

Literary Response

Louise Rosenblatt and others[4] have much to say about 'response' to literature.

Much of the writing in Australia (e.g. *A Single Impulse*[5]) in the 80s is suggesting that we need to go much further in our schools in allowing and using the responses to and interpretations of literature by children and that we need to afford these much higher status.

People like Bill Green, however, sound warnings about over-indulgence in *engagement* and *response* to texts at the expense of critical detachment.[6]

- Are there interpretations which can be shown to be more accurate than others?
- If so, to what extent, and how, should this be demonstrated to children?
- To what extent do we educate for future disillusionment if we accept responses from children without contradiction or critique?

- Do schools indulge in 'childism' (prejudice against children) in seeking to develop and change children's responses to a more adult-like sophistication?
- Do girls respond differently from boys? If so, what should we do about it?
- What should we value in literary response, and how should we teach in order to increase its power for the reader?

Literature and Values

I have written elsewhere that when all of the surface features of our teaching are stripped away, we teach profoundly what we are, what we know, what we value and what we believe. If this is so, no matter what literature we bring into the classroom, even if we are trying to present children with a range of values and views, we will, through the process of dealing with it, give valency to our own values. Does this mean that we should stop being coy and take into the classrooms what we love, know and wish to make accessible to our students?

How do we defend the children against what we know to be our powerful views and values? Is it possible to create a Brechtian-type alienation effect in the theatre of our classrooms so that children are encouraged to read us 'against the grain'[7], to resist and to question?

- If we take in our books, can they be encouraged to fire back with *their* books?
- How can we analyse in whose interests we are teaching? (Are we favouring boys, the gifted, the rich, etc.?)
- For what kind of 'ideal' society are we striving?
- How ethnocentric, sexist, racist, childist is our curriculum?
- What is the role of the English teacher (and literature) in fighting value propaganda that emanates from the school's dominant culture? (Institutional contamination.)
- Are some text narcotic (and escapist) and therefore to be rejected in favour of books which offer keys to doors in reality?
- Have we found a place for black literature, literature in translation, multi-cultural studies?
- Should it be mandatory to study literature beyond the white-Anglo-Saxon products of western civilisation?

Literature and Literacy

We all know how, both in the beginning years and in senior secondary schools, primitive and mechanistic educators can advocate a highly technical, 'functional' approach to literacy which is based on a 'building blocks' view of language. Skills-and-drills work based on clinical sequencing and exercises on bits of language out of context is a feature of too many of our classrooms at all levels throughout the world. Beginning 'readers' are too often distorted and painful strips of language resembling no other texts outside schools.

A deferred gratification is required, it seems. 'Become literate (i.e. able to bark at nonsensical print) *first* and then *one* day you will be allowed to read real books.' No wonder that many graduates of this regime learn to hate books and reading.

It is fashionable for 'hard-nosed' educators and employers in Australia to advocate functional language courses for 'illiterate' secondary students (as opposed to literature-based courses). There is little or no evidence, however, to suggest that literacy is achieved or improved by such courses.

- What is our justification for framing 'literacy' curriculum with a literature base?
- How shall we, as a profession, confront the community and our colleagues with the bankruptcy of skills-based literacy courses?
- What values are learnt by working on language exercises?
- What are the relative claims of enjoyment and utility? Are they mutually exclusive?

Literature and Censorship

It seems in all member countries of I.F.T.E. that there are growing numbers of fundamentalist vigilantes wishing to purge our schools of unpalatable, unclean and seductive literature. Different groups have different taboos. Some wish to attack books on religious/sectarian grounds; others seek to excise violence, or sex, or 'bad language', or all three. Then there are the various attacks on Enid Blyton and Biggles.

Systems in Australia generally devolve the responsibility for book selection to schools, although one state in particular exercises central vetos. Parents do have considerable powers to have books removed because Principals tend to be very twitchy about public criticism and therefore inclined to play it safe with book selection when parents complain.

I know that N.C.T.E. and N.Z.A.T.E. have developed manifestos on the right to read. Perhaps we need to look again at these with a view to strengthening them and extending their scope.

- Where do we draw the line, or do we advocate no lines?
- Who is to judge pornography or corruptive literature?
- What constraints should be put on teachers in order to protect children?
- Can we generate a set of criteria for book selection? Should we?

Literature and Cognition

Work in cognitive psychology, brain science, and artificial intelligence is yielding evidence that suggests we have multiple intelligences and that different sectors of the brain deal with different functions and tasks.

Studies of narrative and anecdote in human cognition suggest that 'storying' is a powerful human way of knowing and understanding.[8]

- What claims can we make for literature as a promoter of thinking?
- What particular features of literature promote thinking?
- How can literature be selected, presented, studied and made to enhance thinking powers?

Literature and Desire

- How important to society are passion, love, desire and will?
- What value do we place on the emotions and sensibilities in education?
- Some commentators now speak of the sexuality of literature. Reading at its most intense is an almost sexual desire and attraction towards loved things. How are we to deal in schools with this aspect of literature?
- Are we to encourage students to satisfy desires through reading and making literature?
- What new dimensions do we need to give the old phrase 'love of literature'?

The Theory of Literature and Theory for the Teaching of Literature

The Australian Association for the Teaching of English has supported a three year project to examine the teaching of literature. Its conference in Adelaide in August 1984 celebrated the outcomes of various state projects and enquiries. I suspect, however, that we will not yet have solved the problem of an absence of a coherent theory of literature which could be taken up by teachers and pressed into service in support of a theory or theories for the *teaching* of literature.

Peter Moss[9], Bill Green, Ian Reid and others in Australia, while acknowledging the generative contributions of the so-called 'Growth model' to the teaching of literature, suggest that there is an urgent need to develop a stronger conception of literature. We cannot ignore new technologies (especially computer technologies) and the increasing accessibility of 'literature' through the mass media.

Old literary-critical approaches do not fit the new media and genres. We need to develop new ways of dealing with new forms and media.

We also need to recognise the fact that, for instance, *Jane Eyre* means different things to girls than to boys, to middle-class children than to the working classes, to adults than to adolescents.

We need to revisit our notions of literature and sociology, literature and philosophy, literature and politics, literature and psychology, literature and semiotics; we need to re-think the 'Growth Model' or the literary tradition model or any other models in the light of new understandings. We need to consider the plight of education and indeed of the world, and then perhaps we will begin to construe new ways of using literature in schools within a comprehensive theory of literature and teaching.

I have been more and more teased in writing about the future of English teaching in this paper. I suspect that we are moving to a new era when the term 'English' will have to go. My view is that the umbrella 'cultural studies' may more properly represent what we are offering to the curriculum. We are indeed about reading and making the world through reading and making literature, broadly defined. Aren't we?

NOTES

1. International Federation for the Teaching of English Seminar, East Lansing, U.S.A., November 1984; see Stephen N. Tchudi (ed), *Language, Schooling and Society*, Boynton/Cook, N.J. 1985.

2. Reid, Ian. *The Making of Literature*, A.A.T.E., 1984.

3. Garth Boomer, 'Newspapers and Cultural Literacy', paper delivered at the Newspapers in Education Conference, Sydney, Sept. 1985; published in Garth Boomer, *Changing Education: Reflections on National Issues in Australia*, Commonwealth Schools Commission, Canberra, 1987.

4. See for instance Louise Rosenblatt, 'The Literary Transaction: Evocation and Response', *Theory Into Practice* Vol. XXI No. 4, Autumn 1982, and Margaret Meek, 'Response – Begin Again', in David Mallick, Peter Moss, Ian Hansen (eds), *New Essays in the Teaching of Literature*, A.A.T.E., 1982.

5. Education Department of South Australia, 1983.

6. Green, Bill, '"Yes but..." A Single Impulse', *English in Australia*, No. 68, June 1984.

7. See 'Teaching Against the Grain', this volume.

8. See Harold Rosen, *Stories and Meanings*, N.A.T.E., 1984 for a succinct account of these matters.

9. Moss, Peter, *Writing Matters*, St. Clair Press, Sydney, 1981.

SECTION TWO
On Curriculum and Learning

8

ZEN AND THE ART OF LANGUAGING

As a Principal Education Officer, responsible for language development and drama across primary and secondary schools, Garth prepared this article in 1977 for Pivot, a journal published by the Education Department of South Australia.

> Water walking
> Walking in the middle of the river
> With straw sandals,
> The boatsman.
>
> Anon.

The boatsman walks on water. It is not a miracle. Technology, not faith, produced the boat he stands in. His sandals, too, have been fashioned in skilled home-industry. On the river he may be thinking about the top of a mountain or the petals of a flower.

Analogies pursued too avidly mislead; with constraint they may enlighten. For a while I want to look at some current attitudes to language and language teaching, with the help of some constrained analogies and Robert M. Pirsig[1].

Like him, I want to speculate about 'that strange separation of what man is from what man does' which may provide 'some clues as to what the hell has gone wrong in this twentieth century' (p. 27).

Do you believe in ghosts?

No, I say.

Why not?

Because they are un-sci-en-ti-fic... They contain no matter, and have no energy and, therefore, according to the laws of science, do not exist except in people's minds... Of course, the laws of science contain no matter and have no energy either and therefore do not exist except in people's minds. It's best to be completely scientific about the whole thing and refuse to believe in either ghosts or the laws of science. That way you're safe. That doesn't leave you very much to believe in, but that's scientific, too. (p. 32)

The 'laws' of the new linguists are just as ghostly as the prescriptions of the old grammarians. And yet, applied with care, both seem to work. Both are attempts to explain the world of words. Both are ways of looking which have become formalised and turned into manuals, often by disengaged spectators. The trouble is that some teachers have believed these manuals without caring and, like shoddy mechanics, have proceeded to fix kids with indecent haste:

They sat down to do a job and they performed it like chimpanzees. Nothing personal in it. There was no obvious reason for it... The radio was the clue. You can't really think hard about what you're doing and listen to the radio at the same time. Maybe they didn't see their job as having anything to do with hard thought, just wrench twiddling... They were really slopping things around in a hurry and not looking where they slopped them. More money that way – if you don't stop to think that it usually takes longer or comes out worse. (p.26)

In contrast, there are the 'groovy' teachers vaguely aware of the laws behind the manuals but so enchanted by the trip of 'being there' in the classroom that they find technology an intrusion. They've tried technology but now they're in another dimension:

In the other dimension (technology) he gets all screwed up and is rebuffed by it. It just won't swing for him. He tries to swing it without any rational premeditation and botches it and botches it and botches it and after so many botches gives up and just kind of puts a blanket curse on the whole nuts-and-bolts scene. He will not or cannot believe that there is anything in his world for which grooving is not the way to go. (p. 53)

And so we have the 'let it flow' school of language teaching, believers in the unconfined expression of whatever happens to be part of this day's grooving. Some care deeply; others are as irresponsible as the wrench-twiddling mechanics.

Classical vs Romantic

To put it much too simply, we are considering a dichotomy between classical understanding and romantic understanding:

> A classical understanding sees the world primarily as underlying form itself. A romantic understanding sees it primarily in terms of immediate appearance. (p. 6)

In 1977, we live in an educational world divided against itself. Unless we learn how to reconcile romantic and classical understanding, we are headed for a most uncivil civil war. Specifically, the teaching of reading, writing, speaking and listening may become a lost art (if it ever was found).

People who have never worked closely with language, and even some who have, may be misled through a false application of classical rationality into thinking that words and sentences have fixed and inviolable shapes and connections and that they have to be assembled in fixed and inviolable ways. Certainly there are generally accepted understandings of what is possible and what is not possible, but – within the conventions – language is beautifully malleable. You can shape language for your own ends. But as you shape it, in subtle ways it shapes you. It waits for the skilled user to exploit its potential for meaning. Language can be put together as an exercise, but, like a motorcycle, it is no good until it works. The *post hoc* expert observer of this language in use will find the classical underlying form and may then proceed to write a manual for future users.

Herein lies an irony. For unless you already know how a motorcycle, or language, works from practical experience, then it's most likely that you won't be able to read and apply those manuals, based on classical understanding, which purport to tell you how to do it. The phenomenon of language in use determines the theoretical system and language users need to use language more than they need theory.

Historically, the theoretical system, or current hypothesis, for language has been constantly changing to take account of the ever-changing phenomenon.

Paradoxically, the more assiduously one applies scientific method to get closer to fixed truth, the more rapidly one creates change and uncertainty as new hypotheses are generated infinitely. And yet you will find in language teaching fanatical adherents to certain dogmas, certain manuals, certain teaching formulae both classical and romantic. This is the rigour of fear and death:

> You are never dedicated to something you have complete confidence in. No one is fanatically shouting that the sun is going to

rise tomorrow. They *know* it's going to rise tomorrow. When people are fanatically dedicated to political or religious faith or any other kinds of dogmas or goals, it's always because these dogmas or goals are in doubt. (p. 146).

Perhaps, what is needed more than anything else for our English teachers and 'language developers' is the peace of mind which comes from knowing that there is no right way which spells freedom both from the classical tyranny of the manual and the romantic tyranny of the existential moment. It would ensure the 'cool' needed to reflect with care and discrimination upon the multitude of possible solutions to any teaching problem. It would allow patience and thoroughness to be applied with serenity.

This attitude applied to language itself by both teacher and student might promote a wedding between the artist's wonder about the possibilities for making meaning and the technologist's desire to assemble language to make it work:

> If you have to choose among an infinite number of ways to put it together then the relation of the machine to you, and the relation of the machine and you to the rest of the world, has to be considered, because the selection from among many choices, the art of the work, is just as dependent upon your own mind and spirit as it is upon the material of the machine. That's why you need peace of mind. (p. 160)

Blending Technology with Art

For instance: I may wish to inform the Director-General of Education in writing that South Australian children are becoming alienated from their own language, and that urgent measures are needed to re-acquaint them lovingly with the vehicle they learned to use and play with before they came to school. To convey this information, I must blend technology with art. I must bring to bear not only what I know about memorandum writing, but also what I know about the Director-General and myself and the Education Department of South Australia. I must consider a host of possible styles, tones, vocabularies. I must select my instances. Every sentence will present limitless syntactical and semantic choices.

There is no manual which deals with the real business of using language. There is no formula which will help me in my task. Depending on how deep and wide my own curiosity, tinkering and past uses of language have been, I may have internalised knowledge that will help me to make appropriate artistic decisions, more by a kind of 'gestalt', by a feeling of 'rightness' and 'quality', than from the application of scientific method. Fine tuning of the verbal equivalents of tappets and carburettors will be necessary, more by 'ear' than by rule, although an occasional reference to the rule book may be required. Above all, I will need concentration and care. Poincaré, the brilliant French mathematician, explains such selection from infinite possibilities by reference to 'the subliminal self':

> The subliminal self, Poincaré said, looks at a large number of solutions to a problem, but only the *interesting* ones break into the domain of consciousness. Mathematical solutions are selected by the subliminal self on the basis of 'mathematical beauty', of the harmony of numbers and forms, of geometric elegance... 'This is a true aesthetic feeling which all mathematicians know,' Poincaré said, 'but of which the profane are so ignorant as often to be tempted to smile.' (p. 261)

A Basis of Quality

It is this awareness of quality, argues Pirsig, unteachable and elusive, that is at the heart of good technology and good art. I want to add that I think it is also the basis of good teaching and good learning. And if Pirsig is right, we inherit the awareness of quality at birth as part of the collective consciousness, or mythos, of civilisation. But Western society has duped itself into raising classical reasoning and deduction above quality, and thereby it has perverted education and technology. We sell to our school children the notion that only the teacher, the 'expert', knows what quality is, because the teacher has learned rationally how to add up all the points and give a grade. We rarely say to children, 'Work at it until your mind is at rest and you're satisfied it has quality'.

Pirsig's protagonist did this in a writing class, withholding grades to the initial dismay of his tertiary students:

> He was pointing to no principle, no rule of good writing, no theory – but he was pointing to something, nevertheless, that was very real, whose reality they couldn't deny. The vacuum that had been created by the withholding of grades was suddenly filled with the positive goal of Quality, and the whole thing fitted together. Students, astonished, came by his office and said, 'I used to just

hate English. Now I spend more time on it than anything else.' Not just one or two. Many. The whole Quality concept was beautiful. It worked. It was that mysterious, individual, internal goal of each creative person. (p.203).

The radical turn here is the assumption that students have the ability to discern quality or the lack of it in their own work. The schools of the Western world are generally predicated on the inability of students. The confidently able student presents a threat. In requiring our students to be incompetent so that we can teach them, do we spread barbarity?

The student who never experiences the delight of pursuing quality with care may respond either by serving technology mindlessly as a 'wrench twiddler' or by fleeing from technology, out of fear and ignorance, to the arms of serendipity.

The ideal boatsman walking on water is not alienated from his craft, nor is he fearful of the river. He is at one with himself and the world, both man-made and natural. He cares for and about his craft so that he can use it with peace of mind.

Speculation leads me, prematurely and possibly crudely, to suggest that a 'quality' language programme might have some of the following features.

- A teacher, confident in uncertainty, infinitely curious about language and life, in pursuit of quality.
- Continuing intense discussion about the possibilities for saying things and the possible interpretation of things said.
- An atmosphere where language is crafted with care for useful, real purposes, and where the smallest details are not neglected.
- Consideration of the quality of what others say and write.
- The withholding of external, finite judgements.
- Time for reflection and contemplation.
- Freedom from the fear which accompanies dogma.
- Wise (that is, sparing) use of manuals.
- Self discipline.
- Delight.

Let me, in finishing, give Pirsig the final word:

The difference between a good mechanic and a bad one...is precisely this ability to *select* the good facts from the bad ones on the basis of quality. He has to *care!* This is an ability about which formal traditional scientific method has nothing to say. It's long past time to take a look at this qualitative pre-selection of facts which has been so scrupulously ignored by those who make so much of these facts after they are 'observed'. I think it will be found that a formal acknowledgement of the role of Quality in the scientific process doesn't destroy the empirical vision at all. It expands it, strengthens it and brings it far closer to actual scientific practice. (p. 275)

NOTES

1. This tentative exploration relies almost entirely on responses to *Zen and the Art of Motor Cycle Maintenance* by Robert M. Pirsig (Corgi, London, 1976), a book which happened to illuminate and partially solve some of my dilemmas about the teaching of the English language. My interpretation of Pirsig is incomplete and I am really only wading in the shallows of his philosophical ocean. Pirsig writes about the way he maintains his motor cycle as a spring board into the realm of values.

9

LANGUAGE, LEARNING AND THE HYPERACTIVE

An address to the Hyperactivity Association of South Australia in Adelaide in 1979. Garth used this occasion to bring together a good deal of his work on language and learning theory. The audience was a mixture of parents of hyperactive children and professional workers in the field.

This paper is to do with language and learning. It is supposed to be related to the problems of the hyperactive child but because, by experience, I am unqualified to speak specifically and categorically I am confined to commenting more generally and speculatively about some of my hunches with respect to what has been described as 'the conditions most likely' to promote language and learning for the hyperactive. It so happens that my major hunch is that these conditions are precisely those which I would advocate for *all* children. Tragically, I think, these conditions will be seen to be demonstrably not available to all children (not even to most) in South Australia. Optimistically we may be able to move a little closer towards them in the service of children, language and learning. Indirectly, or rather because they are generally part of normal schools, 'hyperactive' children would benefit if this could be achieved.

I do not wish to be understood to say that 'hyperactivity' is a socially (or environmentally) constructed disorder. I simply do not know how far this is true. I do wish to be understood as saying that certain changes to the context of schooling and to schools could make it more possible for the 'hyperactive' to enjoy and profit from their education.

1. The Hyperkinetic Society

Western society treats time like capital. To waste time is a cardinal business sin. The race is to the swift. Communications fly electronically across the hemispheres. Concords make discords in a war against time and space. Even our leisure is 'hyped-up' with sound spectaculars, frenetic discos, thrillers and the greatest of the land, wound up like the insides of a golf ball, aligned against each other for our intense delight on tennis courts, raceways, boxing rings and the disney-type scenarios of 'Anything Goes'.

At the risk of compounding a cliché. I turn my attention to the rat-psychology of the stimulus-mongers. On television, radio and in the magazines, the sellers hit us with the stimulus and watch us respond neurotically in the nervous hip-pocket. 'Be other than you are' imply the cosmeticians. 'Old-fashioned is sad-fashioned' whisper the designers. 'Burn, burn, burn' chant the multinational oil companies. 'Sedate' say the valium vendors. 'Drink up' shout the brewers. 'Go, go, go' belts out the rock group. 'Work harder for promotion' warns the boss. 'Make believe it's the real thing' entice the junk food preservators and colourers. 'Get a divorce', 'Have an abortion', 'Heart transplants going cheap', '1979 Cardboard replicas now available at your nearest deception centre.'

In a world geared to a dishwasher next year and a new car 'as soon as we can afford it', 'hope springs eternal in the human breast. Man never *is*, but always *to be* blest.'

The Hyperkinetic School in the Hyperkinetic Society

If you have not dismissed all of the above as caricature, you may be led like me to wonder what kinds of schools western society is breeding.

Do they reflect the pulsating society around them? Ask yourself these questions about your child's school:

- Are there quiet times where children sit and read or write or think (perchance to dream)?
- Is the day fragmented into lessons so that the child is jerked from one thing to another, or is there an easy ritual to the day?
- Are the teachers able to wait and listen when they have asked a question? (The indications are that most teachers cannot tolerate more than five seconds of silence before they intervene.)
- How much of the 'talking space' is taken up by teachers as compared with children? Do the teachers talk a lot?
- How many of the materials used by your children were pre-packaged overseas, or interstate, or several years ago? (Do they have preservatives added, and are they nutritionally sound?)

- Is there a lot of technical virtuosity and complicated scheming? (Rotating groups, diagnostic testing, language laboratories, blue groups, green groups, individual work-sheets, roneoed word games, etc.)
- Do the children do a lot of exercise work? (When you've finished page 33, do page 34, Nos. 1-8)
- Are the children told why they are doing what they are doing and do they know what is coming next? (Or are they puppets in the hands of an enterprising teacher?)
- Are the children encouraged to share and help each other, or is there overt or implicit competition via ticks and stamps and grades?
- How many teachers does your child see in one day?
- Are your children encouraged to finish what they set out to do, or is your child's day a trail of partly competed things?

I could go on with such questions. It is probably clear, from my pointed questions, where my values lie.

In a time of increasing complexity in society, I crave simplicity in schools. Simplicity that values conversations between teachers and children; simplicity that does not seek spurious 'progressive prettiness' (I sometimes feel there is a great affinity between some decorated open spaces and the sets of western movies); simplicity that allows time to talk about the way the world wags; simplicity that spurns the enticing laboratory and exercise books, preferring the humble wisdom of the teacher and the real materials of life.

This may sound romantic. It is not, however, meant to be 'soft'. I also favour a school where there is a secure toughness that emphasises finishing it and doing it well. It may also sound as if I am a refugee from technology and open-space teaching. Not so. I am a refugee from frenzy and falsity. I am a refugee from educational hustlers who want to lure teachers into being 'with it' for the sake of 'being with it'. I am also a refugee from the tension-packed traditional classroom where the martinet drilled facts and ruled by fear. There are other schools which, to varying degrees, twitch and clench from Monday to Friday. Is it any wonder if some children begin to pick up the vibrations?

2. Some Thoughts on Language and Learning

It is best to begin with my views on how we *all* learn anything. We all have human minds. My proposition is that this delicate instrument functions according to common laws and principles. My reading of psychological treatises has encompassed various theories from the behaviourists, through the gestaltists, to the so-called cognitivists. I have been led not to reject behaviourism but to see it as, at best, inadequate. As it is interpreted in schools, it is often highly toxic. I have come to adopt a view which I shall over-simplify here, that we are born into this world as scientists, predicting, hypothesising, and eventually acting on the basis of *principles* which we have induced or deduced from the data gathered by our senses.

At a very low level we can be trained, like the animals, to behave in a certain way under the influence of a certain stimulus. It is possible to imprint on the minds of children, rules, formulae and habits of response through repetition and a variety of punishment and reward strategies. Such imprinting, sometimes called 'over-learning', should not be rejected as a teaching device, but it should be recognised for what it is – learning at a low level of intellect, where the control of what is to be learnt, when it is to be learnt and how it is to be learnt lies elsewhere than with the learner. Teaching methodologies of this kind are often justified by reference to a kind of 'tools of trade' metaphor which suggests that the learner needs to practise using the 'basic' tools before he/she can begin to operate successfully on the more creative aspects of a craft: 'How can you write a story before you know how to write a sentence?' When the exercise of component skills is carried out by a learner out of context and without any appreciation of the nature of the complex, global act that may eventually be mastered, the teacher must rely either on the learner deferring gratification ('you will understand why eventually') or on the learner being satisfied with immediate external gratification for success in an intrinsically mundane task ('well done; keep it up'). This requires considerable effort by the teacher to keep the learner at the task.

Perseverance may be achieved through strong motivation such as a stimulating 'pep-talk' or through the promise of some kind of reward or penalty at the end. When such a theory is in operation, a good teacher may be assessed according to criteria such as these:

- wins the children's confidence
- sets unambiguous short-term goals

- is able to enthuse the learners
- pre-selects the learning path to be followed
- carefully structures and sequences the skills to be acquired
- encourages and demands effort
- expects perseverance
- runs an orderly classroom
- clearly indicates children's errors
- insists on correction of errors
- rewards 'trying' and correct work.

According to the teacher's expectation of a class, this theory may be seen to work in that children may learn to carry out the prescribed operations. However, an examination of the 'side effects' of such learning may not be so encouraging. The learner could be reinforcing the following attitudes towards self and towards learning:

- teacher will structure my learning path for me
- teacher will tell me when I am wrong
- I must try not to make errors
- I will wait for teacher to set my task and get me working
- learning is easy with this teacher
- I will do this because I like/fear teacher
- I cannot do it on my own (I *need* teacher).

Armed, or rather disarmed, with such a set of attitudes, the future of the child as an independent learner outside a circumscribed school environment will be bleak. Society may inherit a cautiously conforming citizen. It is argued, therefore, that while such a teaching regime may achieve low-level learning of certain operations, facts and 'strips of words', it is inadequate and positively harmful if it constitutes the child's sole exposure to learning.

A more powerful learning theory which considers the full range of human learning will absorb the simplistic theory outlined above and go beyond, to take account of the feats of intellect which distinguish human beings from animals – the capacity to abstract; to conceptualise; to symbolise (that is, language, film, dance, music, all as instruments of learning, communication and artistic expression).

The book *Language and English* (Education Department of South Australia, 1977) explores a range of assumptions about learning through language. Implicit in these assumptions is a learning theory which rests on the following axioms:

- deliberate learning arises from the learner's intention to solve a problem
- the search for answers involves the learner in inquiry, hypothesising, testing and reflection on consequences
- human beings represent the world to themselves symbolically in order to make sense of the past, to predict the future, and to communicate to others not immediately present
- learning involves relating and assimilating new facts, experiences, or ideas into the learner's present 'map' of the world, thereby changing it
- understanding is achieved through talking, writing, listening, reading and making, culminating in successful application of principles in an original task (beyond language one would add mathematics, drawing, photography, film, music, enactment, observing, imagining, modelling, etc., as means by which understanding can be reached)
- it is largely through language that we achieve progressively more subtle concepts
- learning cannot be achieved by transmission of information from teacher to learner; it involves active interpretation and application by the learner.

Given these axioms, it is acknowledged that each learner will have an individual *style* of making sense. It is possible, however, to isolate the following phases in the learning process, not as discrete lock-step sequences but as complex, interacting stages which seem to be essential in any deliberate act of learning.

I Recognising the Problematic

The learner comes into new territory and is confronted with the unknown.

II Intending to Learn

For reasons intrinsic or extrinsic, the learner accepts the challenge of finding out.

III Gathering Resources and Information

The learner marshals what he or she already knows which may be relevant to the problem, and then may ask questions of books and people, observe potentially profitable activities and processes, and seek instruction.

IV *Formulating an Hypothesis or a Plan*

By trying ideas out in the imagination, through talking and writing, by modelling, etc., the learner eventually approaches 'closure' on a certain plan of action. This is not always a logical and sequential formulation. It may arise through a kind of intuitive leap or 'gestalt'.

V *Applying the Hypothesis*

The learner tests the plan or hypothesis in action and evaluates its success by seeing if the problem is solved, by seeking the evaluation of a respected 'judge', or by comparison with the efforts of others.

VI *Reflection on Consequences*

The learner may further modify the hypothesis, or make minor adjustments according to consequences. By reflection on the learning experience, the learner may also come to articulate more clearly the principles underlying the operation.

These six phases do not account for the wealth of incidental or accidental learning which occurs inside and outside schools. Such learning becomes part of those latent resources which often 'come to the surface' when a problem is confronted.

The crucial difference between the 'reinforcement' theory and the 'hypothesis' theory is that the latter sees the learner as an active 'scientist', making and testing hypotheses, while the former sees learners as dependent on teachers who undertake to modify existing behaviour.

Good teachers operating according to the 'hypothesis' theory might be judged according to the following criteria:

- introduces new material so that it becomes problematic to the children
- helps the children to define broad goals
- assists children to marshal their own resources and to share their present understandings
- encourages children to ask questions
- directs children, where necessary, to potentially profitable sources of information, demonstration and instruction

- thinks aloud, demonstrates, answers and teaches when this is requested, explicitly or implicitly, by the learners
- values error-making as an important aspect of hypothesising
- encourages children to use a variety of learning media in the process of understanding new information
- allows a wide variety of products which demonstrate understanding
- arranges for shared reflection on and analysis of the learning experience and the products.

With such a teacher, the child might develop the following attitudes towards self and towards learning:

- I already know a good deal which may be relevant
- others, including teacher, have knowledge which I can share
- it is important to ask questions, to observe, and to entertain 'guesses'
- talking, writing, drawing, modelling, imagining, filming, enacting, etc. help me to sort out my ideas
- error-making is a part of learning
- teacher will help me if he/she can
- thinking about the experience afterwards helps to make the product better next time
- learning involves tenacity
- I have my own learning style
- teacher cannot learn for me.

On Language

Children learn language by using it to make sense and by having access to help when they can't make sense. In other words, children learn to talk by listening to the language around them and eventually trying out their own hypothesis about how to say it. This version is not at first the full adult version but some kind of contraction. 'Want milk' will over time, through continual access to the full version, gradually be modified to become 'May I have a glass of milk please, mummy?' If the relationship between children and those in power, older siblings, parents, teachers, is such that the children are suppressed, contained and treated as language-deficient underlings, it is likely that they will stop talking and thereby cut themselves off from their chief means of thinking and learning (talk as an hypothesis in action) and their chief means of learning language (which is learnt in use).

Children talk best and most when they have something to say to someone who genuinely signals interest and caring. Children talk least when they are made not to like themselves or to feel inferior. Adults are the same. To give an insight into the kinds of abilities I would look for in a good language teacher, I include ten questions that I would ask in evaluating teachers of my children:

- Does the teacher care about and for children?
- Does the teacher value production of meaningful language as the key to language learning and literacy?
- Does the teacher deliberately challenge children to work out 'what it means'?
- Is the teacher continually showing children how she/he does it (thinking aloud in front of the children)?
- Do the children know why they are doing what they are doing?
- Does the teacher have a 'tracking' rather than a 'motivating' approach to language development?
- Does the teacher get children 'intending' rather than 'motivating' them?
- Are there obligatory periods of reflection where teacher and children talk about 'how good it was' and 'how it works'?
- Are there many 'voices' in the classroom (literature, drama, visitors, radio, T.V., etc.)?
- Is the classroom like a workshop where children are busy crafting language, using language and making sense (where teacher is the senior *craftsperson*)?

We learn language by using language for a *purpose*: to make sense. We make, or *craft*, meaning and it helps if there's a 'master' craftsperson to consult when we are in trouble. Practising bits and pieces of language, filling in blank spaces, unjumbling jumbled words, doing exercises from 'word power', etc., are largely illusory language learning experiences. Let's give up substitutes, then, and do 'the real thing'. Provided this happens, we can – all of us – be confident that we are providing the best conditions for truly powerful, 'hyperactive' learning.

10

THE CURRICULUM AS NARRATIVE

Originally a Working Party Report written with assistance from Barry Dwyer, Denise Hallion, Bernard Newsome, Barry Carozzi and other working party members from a national conference on Developing Communicative Competence. It was jointly convened in 1979, by the University of New England and the Armidale CAE.

There is a pithy statement which goes something like this:

'Everything that is loved grows.'

If we apply this statement to language we soon learn the difference between allowing children's language to develop like a brightly coloured mosaic encompassing many diverse skills as opposed to the more tightly structured but almost sterile skills-based programmes, many of which are still found within our schools today.[1]

The Group Process

After hearing a wide range of papers on aspects of oral communication[2], a group of teachers met to make connections between theory and the questions which teachers must answer. Without cynicism we seriously asked, 'So what?'

Two people decided to seek out a class somewhere in Armidale in order to test Andrew Wilkinson's principle that the situation calls forth the language[3]. Armed with video cameras, they went out to the frontiers and returned later with convincing and lively documentation of children vigorously using a wide range of language functions within a 'space exploration' scenario. Their film proved to be an excellent way of reminding us all of the amazing capacity and resources of children when they are engaged in something they really want to do.

While the two forward scouts worked in real classrooms, the rest of us tenaciously reflected on our own teaching in order to clarify problems and then to seek some possible answers.

We decided to proceed in the following way:

- Clarify our broad principles of learning and, specifically, our principles of language learning.
- Develop a model or framework of curriculum composing consistent with these principles.
- Generate some possible units of work within the framework and, at the same time, establish criteria by which these units might be evaluated.
- Reflect upon the value of the group process and product.

Issues

The conference papers soon revealed a fundamental tension between what might be termed a 'communications' curriculum model based on sequenced instruction for communication competence and a 'language-development' model based on the creation of conditions for the progressive realisation of 'meaning potential'. Michael Halliday[4] had suggested strongly that one cannot directly teach a communication skill without trivialising it to the level of Dale Carnegie-type tricks, sometimes called 'good manners'. He also warned against hasty translation of new taxonomies and theories of communication into curriculum schema. 'Project English' and its fate in the USA might warn us how unprofitable this can be. Halliday is not suggesting the teachers simply love language and let it grow. It is the teacher's task to create conditions which will encourage 'meaning potential' to be realised and then to help the learners to 'de-automatise' the language by reflecting on how it works and the rules which govern it.

On the other hand, Barbara Leib-Brilhart spoke on the need for teachers to be well-armed with theory and structured curriculum at a time when the community is seeking more stringent accountability. By law, in America, schools are bound to develop 'oracy'. Teachers therefore need to have confidence in tackling the huge territory of 'oral communication'. To assist them, enlightened maps are being made, setting out appropriate sequences and pathways. It must be said that our Working Party feared that such guides for teachers could be harmful if they are not assimilated into a curriculum based on sound principles of language and learning.

Two related questions emerged for our Working Party:
- How does one learn the 'skills' of oral communication?

- What kind of curriculum will best promote abilities in oral communication?

A third question was left for another Working Party:

- What information and understandings do teachers need in order to teach oral communication?

Learning Principles and Principles of Language Learning

By a process of reflecting on our own learning and the observed learning of children when they are deliberately engaged in trying to understand or do something, we agreed that all intentional learning proceeds, not necessarily in a linear fashion, through the following phases and that each phase is accompanied by progressive evaluation by the learner:

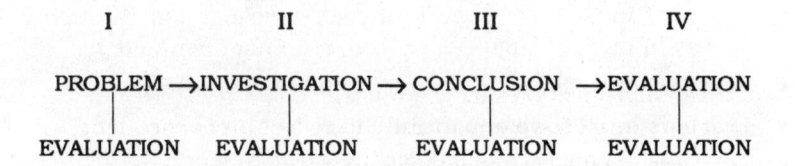

```
       I              II              III              IV

   PROBLEM  → INVESTIGATION →  CONCLUSION   → EVALUATION
      |             |              |               |
  EVALUATION   EVALUATION     EVALUATION      EVALUATION
```

Incidental learning, will, of course, be going on all the time.

Learning begins when the learner intends to take up an intrinsic or extrinsic challenge to solve a problem, whether this problem be of the kind 'Why is this so?' or 'How can I make that work for me?' In evaluating the problem, the learner will call on previous knowledge and attempt to identify the key questions and areas to be investigated. The evaluation will also include estimation of the possibility of success, an estimation that will be affected by the learner's past history as a learner. Should the estimation lead to a negative prognosis, the investigation is likely to be abandoned.

Entering into the investigation, the learner may ask questions, observe, explore, read, seek tuition, practise, make errors, reflect, plan, etc., evaluating all the time the degree to which the investigation is leading to a likely hypothesis or plan of action which will succeed.

The conclusion is some kind of test either through direct application or through a more academic process which satisfies the learner that something has been understood. Satisfaction might not be achieved until the solution has been evaluated in a variety of settings. Feedback from 'significant others' is likely to be a strong feature of the evaluation.

The learner will then evaluate the whole process and its conclusion in order to assess what is still to be learnt or modified and, possibly, in order to note false alleys and mazes which might be avoided next time. In reflecting on the process there will be a strong tendency to order and make sense of the 'story'.

Such learning only takes place if the learner has the confidence to struggle and persevere; has enough security and interim success; has access to potentially profitable areas of investigation; and has a strong tolerance of error.

To simplify, the following key principles or assumptions emerged:

- Learners must intend to learn and to find a solution (learning begins with a problematic).
- Learners must have opportunity for investigation through a variety of media (language, senses, art, enactment, etc.).
- Learners must have opportunity to test hypotheses.
- Learners must have opportunity to reflect on consequences.
- Learners need to be tenacious and, ultimately, secure.
- Question asking and error making are essential to learning.

Our principles of language learning are consistent with these general learning principles:

- We learn language by using it for a purpose and through having the opportunity to reflect on how it works.
- We learn language in social interaction where we have the opportunity to observe how it functions.
- We improve our competence in language by modifying our behaviour in the light of our evaluation of its effectiveness.
- Skills or abilities are learnt when the learner is attempting a whole task which requires those skills and abilities.

Towards a General Curriculum Model: A Guide for Teachers

The group now took up the challenge of transforming these learning principles into principles of curriculum design and development. To do this, we reflected upon our own curriculum composing processes, from the initial conception of an idea for a unit of work through to the enactment of the curriculum in the classroom. We found that two metaphors kept recurring as we attempted to clarify what happens. The curriculum planning and implementation seemed like an unfolding *narrative*, a kind of *fiction* which is eventually modified and realised in collaboration with our students. For the learners, the curriculum is a kind of *journey* through challenging new *territory*.

After teasing out what we saw as the key elements and stages in the evolution of the curriculum and then, as a test case, imagining a teacher who sets out to teach a six week unit on 'messages', we constructed the following guide to curriculum development for the classroom teacher, generalisable to the teaching of any subject at any level. Although the guide is written as a recipe, it does not claim to be *The Way*.

A Suggested Sequence for Curriculum Planning for the Teacher

First Stage: Incubating

- Work within the framework of the generalised learning sequence and learning principles (as above).
- Whatever the starting problem (e.g. a desire to improve competence in message giving and taking), next pay attention to:
    (a) the nature of the class
    (b) the present concerns and activities in the classroom
    (c) the *content* or *situation* around which practice in the skill will be possible
    (d) the general *life* question(s) which will be addressed during the unit of work
    (e) the nature of the topic and the territory to be explored, including the opportunities and potential for exploration inherent in it
    (f) an analysis of the central speech function which will be practised (for teacher's clarification rather than as matter for direct teaching).
- Working on the principle that sub-skills should not be taught incrementally, but that children should attempt the global act in as authentic a setting as possible, begin to compose a 'fiction' or 'narrative' of what might happen, considering the sequence of (*problem > investigation > conclusion >evaluation*) in which sequence negotiation with the learners may occur at any point.

- Decide where the central focus of the unit will rest, keeping the mind on what children might be able to say and do as a result of the investigation.
- In making the fiction in your head (or on paper), reach fairly firm closure on the broad goals to be pursued (e.g. 'the children will be able to *say*, with more confidence and insight, when they are being unfairly manipulated in a speech act' or 'the children will have practised composing messages, transforming messages, delivering messages and receiving messages').
- This already requires that you begin to 'feel' or 'sense' the likely scenario and the broad plot of the curriculum unit.
- It also requires imaginative 'indwelling' in the minds of the children and the adoption of a 'pre-disciplinary' understanding of the 'world' to be explored (e.g. 'What is significant about messages from a child's point of view?')
- In beginning to 'tighten up' on the fiction, you might find it helpful to consider the following elements:
  (a) content
  (b) justification (including the underlying philosophical question which will lie beneath the exploration)
  (c) products (in terms of 'can do' and 'can say')
  (d) skills and media to be practised (in broad terms, not as minute objectives) in coming to be able to say and do
  (e) resources (beginning with the resources of teacher and children).
- The 'fiction' writing about the process should be sufficiently general and tentatively held so that you do not invest it with too much certainty before consulting the class.
- In considering the process, ask the following questions:
  (a) How might the 'territory' be presented to invite exploration and to present challenges?
  (b) How will I ensure that children have the opportunity to use a variety of media if necessary (e.g. talk, writing, film/TV, music, enactment, etc.) to build up understandings?
  (c) What are my constraints? (including the children's present abilities, time, the classroom context, etc.).

(d) In what medium or media will the children present their conclusions?

Second Stage: Clarifying and Negotiating

At this stage the proposition is taken to the class and, according to your intention, negotiation can take place. Children's modifications and contributions can be considered and, where possible, accommodated (e.g. resource ideas, process ideas, conclusion ideas, evaluation ideas). This activity will involve marshalling what is presently known and clarifying the 'problematic'.

Third Stage: Programming

At this point you may, for official purposes, or for clarifying of the 'plot', then take away the children's information and prepare a structured programme with fairly firm sequencing and timing.

Fourth Stage: Enacting

The unit now begins to unfold, with you and children evaluating and re-shaping where necessary.

Fifth Stage: Evaluating

You and the class may reflect upon the unit. You may now add retrospective information to the initial programme.

A Unit of Work in Oral Communication with Criteria for Evaluation

At this point our working party divided into three groups, one to prepare a detailed programme on 'messages' for 12 year olds, one to develop a unit appropriate for seven year olds, and one to generate a set of criteria for evaluation based on our articulated principles (see Appendix).

Sadly, we did not record our discussions, transcripts of which would have been striking documentation of the complexity of the curriculum composing process. Such documentation is needed as a reminder to those who may stand outside schools and classrooms attempting to measure and prescribe. What follows is obviously only a shadow of all that really happened...

In dealing with the curriculum for seven year olds, the group began by focussing on one particular child in a school at which one of the group members was a teacher. This child seemed unable to communicate and to be unable to understand simple instructions.

The group began to reflect on the possible reasons for this by asking questions of the teacher. It was established that the school was in a so-called 'disadvantaged' industrial area and that many of the children shared this girl's sense of personal inadequacy. Teachers at this school saw many children as deficient in their abilities to communicate with confidence and clarity.

As the discussion went deeper, and as we came to 'indwell' with more empathy, our focus changed from considering ways of giving these children some skills to reflecting upon the possible deep-seated causes of the present behaviour.

Eventually, we began to feel that fearfulness might be behind the children's lack of confidence, allied with the view that they have nothing personal to offer. And so, starting with what was seen to be a fundamental cause, rather than with a notion of some 'surface' communication skills to be taught, we set about devising a unit of work around the theme of 'Monsters', where the major content would be a story read to the class together with the subsequent anecdotes which the children might offer.

Once this had been decided, we followed the suggested sequence of our guide for curriculum planning in building up the 'fiction' of what might happen. We felt that in coming to terms with their own fantasies about monsters, the children might also be coming to terms with fears closer to home, gaining confidence and releasing 'meaning potential' in the process.

We envisaged a sequence beginning with the reading of *Where the Wild Things Are*, through various explorations of 'my awfullest monster', to a class celebration where a class-constructed monster might be burned. The lasting product was to be a class book containing pictures of monsters made by individuals.

Conclusions

We reflected with some satisfaction that our own Working Party 'curriculum' had been consistent with our principles. We had proceeded from the problematic towards some tangible products through a process of investigation and testing out. We did enough to convince us that, whether or not teachers take up the details of our guides, the process through which we went has value in itself for those who wish to arm themselves with a coherent theory and a sound structure in the face of depredations from employers, academics, the community and sceptical colleagues.

In retrospect, we feel that we have developed a framework in which communication skills are seen in the proper perspective of the larger communication acts which they serve and in which oral communication itself is seen in the context of the wider curriculum. A teacher might, using our framework, take such taxonomies as provided by Dr Leib-Brilhart and her colleagues and incorporate appropriate aspects of skill development into the larger 'narrative' of a curriculum unit.

Our model enables us to take account of John Skull's description of the complexity of the speech act, to apply in context some of the maps of language as described by Bill Crocker, and to manipulate curriculum scenarios in order to make increased demands on language, as Astrid Wooton advocates. It protects us from the trivialising of oral communication teaching into a Professor Higgins-type approach where students might merely practice 'how to win friends and influence people'.

I'd temporarily wind up ACER projects, CDC projects, and the system's curriculum-development teams and spend all the money saved on a nationwide advertising campaign. I don't want much to be in life if people can't talk about it with me. What does it profit a person if s/he escapes lung cancer or heart disease but is left with withered utterance? Talk, be in it. Quite seriously, ignorance, persisting mythologies and ingrained fears about talk are our greatest enemy.

NOTES

1. Sr. Denise Hallion (Working Party member).

2. See W.J. Crocker, 'Developing Communicative Competence: Papers from Invitation Conference held to discuss the teaching of oral communication skills to children', The University of New England, Armidale, N.S.W., 1980. The papers referred to here are included in this collection, with the exception of the Halliday reference (see Note 4).

3. Andrew Wilkinson, *The Foundations of Language*, Oxford University Press, London, 1971.

4. Michael Halliday, 'How Children Learn Language', in K.D. Watson and R.D. Eagleson (eds), *English in Secondary Schools: Today and Tomorrow*, E.T.A. (N.S.W.), 1977.

APPENDIX: SOME CRITERIA FOR EVALUATING A CURRICULUM UNIT

In drawing up criteria for evaluating a unit, we considered not only the initial planning by the teacher but also the continuing interaction between teacher and students. The principle that learners must intend to take up the challenge led us to place great emphasis on the teacher's obligation not only to explain in detail the 'journey' to be taken but also, wherever possible, to allow the learners to help plan aspects of the itinerary. The degree to which a teacher might enter into such collaboration and negotiation would obviously depend on the age level, the previous experience of the class, and the constraints operating within the school and its community.

The following thirty questions proved to be a rigorous and illuminating challenge to those who had planned units of work:

- Does it allow teachers and children to value worthwhile aspects of the human condition? (Does it raise 'important' or significant general questions?)
- Does it allow children to be informed of what teacher intends and of the rationale for the work?
- Does it allow for children to be clear about the broad goals and purposes?
- Does it provide challenge and does it allow children to define the problematic?
- Does it allow for negotiation (or explanation of non-negotiation) about content, processes, products, resources and evaluation within the constraints (school, context, teacher, children, external requirements)?
- Does it allow for the class, groups and individuals to investigate the territory through the use of a variety of media in exploratory ways?
- Does it allow for children early in the 'narrative' to marshal and share what they already know and can do? (Especially through anecdote.)

- Does it allow children access to potentially profitable experiences (Such as observation visits, 'spectator' activities, etc.)?
- Does it allow children to practise the use of skills and media with respect to a task which has a clearly understood purpose?
- Does it allow, indeed ensure, error-making, risk-taking, and guessing within a supportive context?
- Does it allow for children to make tentative formulations?
- Does it allow for children to present, perform or show their knowledge or products to audiences which will provide feedback?
- Does it allow opportunities for reflection? (On consequences, on interim formulations, on possible alternative ways of construing, etc.)
- Does it allow for possible celebration? (Of a child's work, of another's work, of a group's work, of aspects of human endeavour, etc.)
- Does it allow for, and expect, unforeseen outcomes in terms of class, group or individual learning and doing?
- Does it allow for teacher demonstration, explanation, thinking aloud when this is needed? (For class, group or individuals.)
- Does it ensure that children have access to additional information from a variety of sources?
- Are the children invited to value their own and others' work?
- Does it assume a teacher who is a trusted adult, co-learner and senior curriculum planner (with respect to children)?
- Is it based on the moral stance that power should be shared wherever possible?
- Does it allow peer-to-peer teaching, and collaboration and support?
- Does it allow for children to share the criteria by which the process and the outcomes are to be evaluated?
- Does it allow for teacher to participate in and perform some of the tasks set for children?
- Is the 'scenario' rich in possibility and clearly related to the world outside school?

10 The Curriculum as Narrative

- Are there possibilities for products and outcomes to be used or incorporated in further learning?
- Does it allow for consideration of subject-specific language, meta-language and theories about 'how it works' or 'why it is so'? (Understanding the medium *after* or *while* it is used?)
- Does it allow for teacher to act as 'umpire', final arbiter and classroom manager (in terms of organising time, resource, structures)?
- Is it based on an understanding of the importance of prediction and anticipation on the part of the learner?
- Does it serve to enrich the deepen the relationships within the classroom?

11

NEGOTIATING THE CURRICULUM

This is an article originally published, in 1978, in English in Australia. It owes much to the work of a National Working Party on the Role of Language and Learning in Education, convened by the Curriculum Development Centre, the members of which included Jon Cook, John Annells and Richard Campbell. This chapter should be read in conjunction with chapters 12 and 13, to trace the development in Garth's thinking on this issue.

Introduction

It is becoming fashionable for schools in Australia to produce language policies *across the curriculum*. Because I am now convinced that such policies will be ineffectual unless they are accompanied by changes to the school's administrative structure, its curriculum and its educational philosophy, I want to explore an issue that goes behind language to the eternal triangle of education: the *teacher*, the *child* and the *curriculum*.

This exploration owes a considerable debt to Professor James Britton, who offered valuable encouragement and advice in the early years of the work of the various 'language and learning' teams in Australia. Britton supported our growing belief that the more profitable question to put to whole school staffs is not 'How can we develop the child's language?' but '*How do children (and* for that matter, *we) learn?*'

The first question quite often threatens those teachers who consider themselves unqualified to teach language, and it can also lead to petty bickering about the perennial bogey surface-features of spelling, punctuation and 'proper' presentation. If language across the curriculum is associated with the English faculty, Sampson's 'Every teacher is a teacher of English' becomes a misleading focus.[1]

But put the second question, and all teachers, lecturers and directors-general are, or should be, equal. This is a question to which we all should have personal, articulate and perpetually speculative responses.

Allied to the question of 'How do children learn?' are further teasers, such as *'Under which conditions do children learn most effectively?'*, *'What is learning?'* and *'Do we all learn in the same way?'*

On Learning Theory

Since 1975 the Language Across the Curriculum project team in South Australia, and more recently the Curriculum and Learning Unit that grew out of it, have been asking teachers questions like this, as well as looking into official, departmental curriculum statements to see if any of these address themselves directly to what may loosely be called learning theory. Few departmental statements address learning theory. Certainly *teaching* theory abounds, either implicitly or explicitly, and it may be argued that, however tenuously, teaching theory must be based on some notion of how people learn. However, our team in South Australia concluded, on the basis of widespread inquiry, that few teachers can articulate what they assume about learning.

By having a learning theory I do not mean being able to précis Piaget, Skinner and Bruner. I mean being able to state one's own best-educated understanding as to how people come to internalise new information or to perform new operations. It can be argued that we come into the world *theorising*. Certainly Year 1 children can be easily be encouraged to talk about how they learnt to talk. Teachers likewise can examine the learning theory implicit in their classroom practice.

So I come closer to the topic of negotiating the curriculum through classroom practice. Imagine education-department curriculum guides, with no explicit learning theory, being taken by teachers with no explicit learning theory and turned into lessons for children who are not told the learning theory. Some of the best of these children then graduate to become teachers. And so on. Isn't it about time that we all tried to articulate what is surely there behind every curriculum unit, every assignment, every examination?

If we can tell ourselves our present theory, we can also tell it to our students in terms that they can understand, so that they can try it out to see if it works in helping them to learn. From our joint evaluation we can then modify the theory, and try again. So, collaboratively, teachers and students may build learning theories, if by 'theory' we mean a kind of working hypothesis.

But learning theory cannot be disconnected from the criteria used to select what is to be learnt and when (i.e. our theory about the *curriculum content*: the subject offerings and the subject sequencing). These, in turn, are framed by a theory about society and culture.

Professor Basil Bernstein talked about the framing and sequencing of curriculum[2]. He spoke of the way in which we often attribute divine universality to what may be simply culture-specific subject offerings and lock-step teaching sequences. When I look back on many years of work in schools, I think that education is an almost self-perpetuating chain of subjections. The education system is subject to the ingrained educational myths of society (deified into theories in the universities); and the children are subject to teachers who choreograph all the myths in subjects, each educational genre with its own ritual, language, sequences and decor, and each with its own value (e.g. classical physics is worth more than popular art, which is worth more than punk-rock, or sex education).

The aim of this essay is to suggest tentatively how this chain may be broken by articulating the mythologies or theories at all levels and then taking a constructively irreverent stance towards them. I have already suggested that teachers and children may collaboratively build learning theories. I now extend this to include curriculum theories and theories about society – and I mean this quite seriously *from Year 1 to Year 12*.

Summarising, I have so far questioned language as a way in to whole-school teacher development, and I have suggested learning as a more profitable topic. Learning is, or should be, inseparable from curriculum theory, but curriculum theory is shaped by the mythologies of a specific culture and based on *teaching*, handing down and initiating children into valued ways of looking at the world. Teachers who become their own learning theorists also need to become their own curriculum theorists.

Experiments by the Curriculum and Learning Unit in South Australia have shown interesting consequences when teachers, each having reflected on something recently learnt, together build up a learning theory, after which they are asked a simple question: *'How would you then fare as a learner in your own class?'* They are generally forced to conclude that schools are institutions of teaching, not of learning.

On Power

Before focusing specifically on the curriculum, it is necessary to reflect a little on power. It was not the brief of the Language Across the Curriculum project to inquire into the politics of education, but the project officers now believe that no discussion of language and learning can afford to ignore the structure of systems and schools.

We sat for hours reflecting upon teachers' problems, our own problems and data gathered in classrooms. Inevitably, we kept returning to the question of power relationships: inside the classroom, within schools, within the system and in society itself. Perhaps initially we were inclined too hastily to apportion blame to teachers; we would now want to question the very bases of our society.

With our interest in learning, we set out to gain insights into how teachers perceived knowledge and how they think wisdom is achieved. With exceptions, of course, we found that a kind of pharmaceutical metaphor is widely applicable. Teachers define the knowledge to be dealt with, prepare the medication, and dispense the knowledge according to the prescribed dosage.

Knowledge is perceived as transmittable, and the learner's mind as a passive receptacle. The assumption is that teachers *have* the knowledge and that children *have not*, the 'have nots' being dependent on the 'haves'.

Now, even when teachers profess humanism, democracy, respect for the learner and horror at the mere thought of manipulative behaviour, we have come to have doubts – not about the teachers' sincerity, but about their ability to perceive the power vested in them, simply because they are *adults* and control the dispensation of knowledge.

Indeed, we are beginning to wonder whether the outright autocrat is not less dangerous than some self-deluding humanists. At least the former may make the rules of the power game explicit. We looked closely at so-called 'child-centred' progressive teaching techniques, where teachers purport to take a largely 'facilitative' role. Here, teachers who still retain the significant, ultimate powers often pretend to divest themselves of power by giving limited decision-making opportunities to the children. For example, children may be free to choose one of several options without having the option to reject the options.

Moreover, many attractive learning packages in schools demand little creative, individual, teacher and learner contributions.

A crucial question arises: 'Are schools dedicated to the child's power to learn, and ultimately to learn independently of instruction and guidance?' I am sure that administrators and teachers throughout Australia would answer with an unequivocal 'yes'. Why is it, then, that we find dependent learning rather than inquiry and experiment? Why is it that we find so few questions from children? Why is it that *fact* is so often revered above *principle*? What is the reality?

On Constraints

The teachers with whom we have worked in South Australia have impressed us greatly with their concern to help children to learn and with their self-critical approach to the craft of teaching. Many devote themselves to education with awesome energy, but we are left with the feeling that, in isolation, these teachers have little power to affect the many feudal structures long embedded in both schools and the system. Sadly, we have talked to a good many teachers who are frustrated and often plagued with guilt because they are falling short of their ideals, when the real cause often lies not in themselves but in a subtle combination of various manifestations of external control. These may include a fragmented timetable, disguised streaming of children and teachers, external examinations, large classes or a limited choice of commercially-produced resources, all with an implicit, behaviourist learning theory. The more we have speculated about the nature of schools, the more we have come to believe that a massive deep-seated inertia, not of the school's wishing, persists – despite cosmetic changes from closed to open space, from 40 minute lessons to hour modules, from English to general studies. It is devilishly difficult to effect change, yet we feel that radical structural changes are needed to produce a school context in which language can flow powerfully between teachers and students in the pursuit of action knowledge.

For example, where individual teachers wish to change the emphasis from teacher as Examiner to teacher as Collaborative Evaluator with the students, they act in a broad context quite inimical to their intentions: students socialised for years into seeing the teacher as Judge, a school system geared to external reward for effort, and a society based on competition. Depending on their own personal charisma, teachers may begin to succeed in winning the confidence of some students, who may then feel aggravated by their other teachers; but the more usual result is that such teachers are devalued as soft or even slightly crazy. It is therefore very difficult for teachers to share their power with students, because society and schools are not based on such philosophy.

It is my belief that there are *some existing strategies that can be improved*. For instance, our reflections on power have led us to question our South Australian's strategy of working with *individual* teachers in the hope that good things will ripple out. There may be some rippling, but the steady hands of custom and ritual soon calm the waters.

To summarise again, I accept that there is an inevitable inequality between teacher and child and that teachers have wide powers. In turn, I see individual teachers as relatively powerless themselves within the governing frames of society and the education system, so they are often reduced to the status of intermediaries, translating society's values and initiating children into these values. Where administrators of the system, with respect to teachers, or teachers, with respect to children, purport to hand over powers, I believe that the harmful effects of their power may be increased, because the subjects of this power are likely to be more *mystified* about the actual sources of control.

On Demystification

Now, our specific concern in the South Australian team is to promote more open communication, more talk to exchange and seek information, and more questioning to relieve mystification. This follows from one of our basic assumptions: that learning is vitally connected with the language resources that can be brought to serve it.

A more equitable distribution of power (or at least a more healthy exercise of power), which we know can be used either benevolently to let in or maliciously to exclude, will not come while those *in* power monopolise the talking space (i.e. the language), thereby keeping other people in relative ignorance.

So, what should be done? I believe that there are three important areas of action:

- Strategies should be applied at *all levels* of the system and society. That is, politicians, parents, administrators, teachers and children all need to be brought into *discussions about how we learn*, if we are to raise the quality of thinking and learning in schools and society.

- There will always be inequalities of power both in schools and in society, and the harmful effects of power will be offset only *if those in power make quite explicit* the values, assumptions and criteria on which they base their actions. In this way others will have a better chance to defend themselves, more opportunity to question and more chance of negotiation, at least where the power figure is not totally despotic.
- Significant changes will come only *through collaboration at all levels.* Individual action is usually contained and rendered ineffectual when it begins to threaten the established order.

This does not mean that individual teachers should delay action until they can find support from their colleagues. At least, teachers can talk to their students openly about why they do what they do, about how they think people learn, and about the societal consequences of various behaviours.

I have found perhaps the most exciting and challenging strategy offered in the book *Language, Truth and Politics* by Trevor Pateman[3]. Pateman says that we should ourselves be able to do, and then in turn to be able to teach children how to do, the following:

- question an unreasonable assertion
- say that we don't understand if we don't understand
- pause to think
- say that we don't know if we don't know.

This should be accompanied by a good deal of thinking aloud in front of students, so that they can have open access to the teacher's thinking powers.

On Motivation versus Negotiation

Motivated Learning

Now, Model A represents the traditional curriculum model in which, after reflecting on past experience and the content to be taught, teacher A, within the practical constraints of school and society, intends to teach a certain programme..

Before teaching can proceed, the students must be motivated in some way. If the topic is 'Weather and Climate', this may be achieved by a trip to the local weather station, or by a lesson in which the coolers are turned off to draw attentions to the topic in hand. The powerful motivator thus *by indirections finds direction out,* and the

MODEL A: MOTIVATION

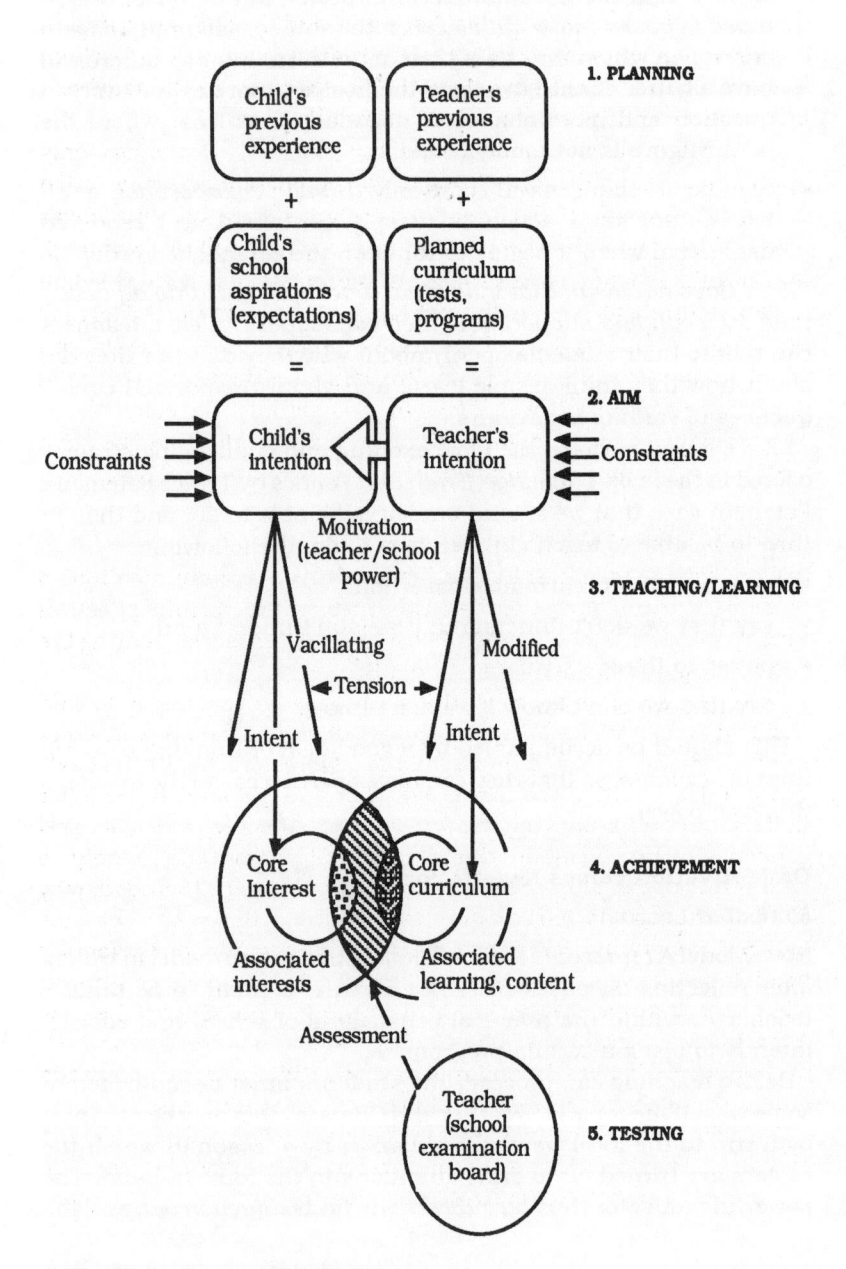

1. PLANNING

Child's previous experience + Teacher's previous experience
+
Child's school aspirations (expectations) + Planned curriculum (tests, programs)
=

2. AIM

Constraints → Child's intention ⇐ Teacher's intention ← Constraints

Motivation (teacher/school power)

3. TEACHING/LEARNING

Vacillating ↔ Tension ↔ Modified

Intent → Intent

4. ACHIEVEMENT

Core Interest — Core curriculum

Associated interests — Associated learning, content

Assessment

5. TESTING

Teacher (school examination board)

children, to varying degrees, come to intend roughly in the same direction as the teacher. Throughout the planned curriculum unit there is tension between the teacher's goal and the children's intent, but most students eventually receive marks or grades for written work, which tell them how close they have come to the teacher's intention. Sometimes the mark is externally decided.

As Model A shows, even at best the children's learnings only approximate to the teacher's goals, so the curriculum may touch only a little of each child's key and associated interests. This leaves a good deal of what has been learnt unexamined and undervalued, because the teacher, or external examiner, tests only what is set on the curriculum. Of course, the overlapping shown in the model may not occur at all, and the child is failed or subjected to remediation, which requires more intense motivation. In either case the child appears to have learnt much less than is actually the case.

Irrespective of the teaching style of the teacher, there will be great wastage if this model is applied.

Negotiated Learning

Armed with a Pateman-like outlook on open communication, a personal learning theory and an awareness of the harmful effects of inexplicit power, a teacher may develop strategies for negotiating the curriculum as represented in Model B.

Here, teacher B reflects in the same way as teacher A to find worthwhile curriculum content and strategies based on past experience, coming to fairly non-negotiable conclusions about the basic content of the unit. If the unit is 'Weather and Climate', the teacher finds some core input that should illustrate the key *principles* and *concepts* to be learnt. At this stage the teacher talks openly to children about the topic to be covered, why it is to be included, why it is important and what constraints prevail (e.g. it may be a set topic in H.S.C. geography; it may have been made obligatory by the faculty head; it may have to be finished in three weeks). The talk centres on what the children already know, how the teacher thinks the new information may be learnt, how the necessary tasks are to be shared, and what constraints the children have (e.g. 'We've got an enormous amount of reading in English this week').

The next step is for teacher and children to plan the unit, the activities, the goals, the assignments and the negotiable options. (Compare this with Model A, where this programming takes place

MODEL B: NEGOTIATION

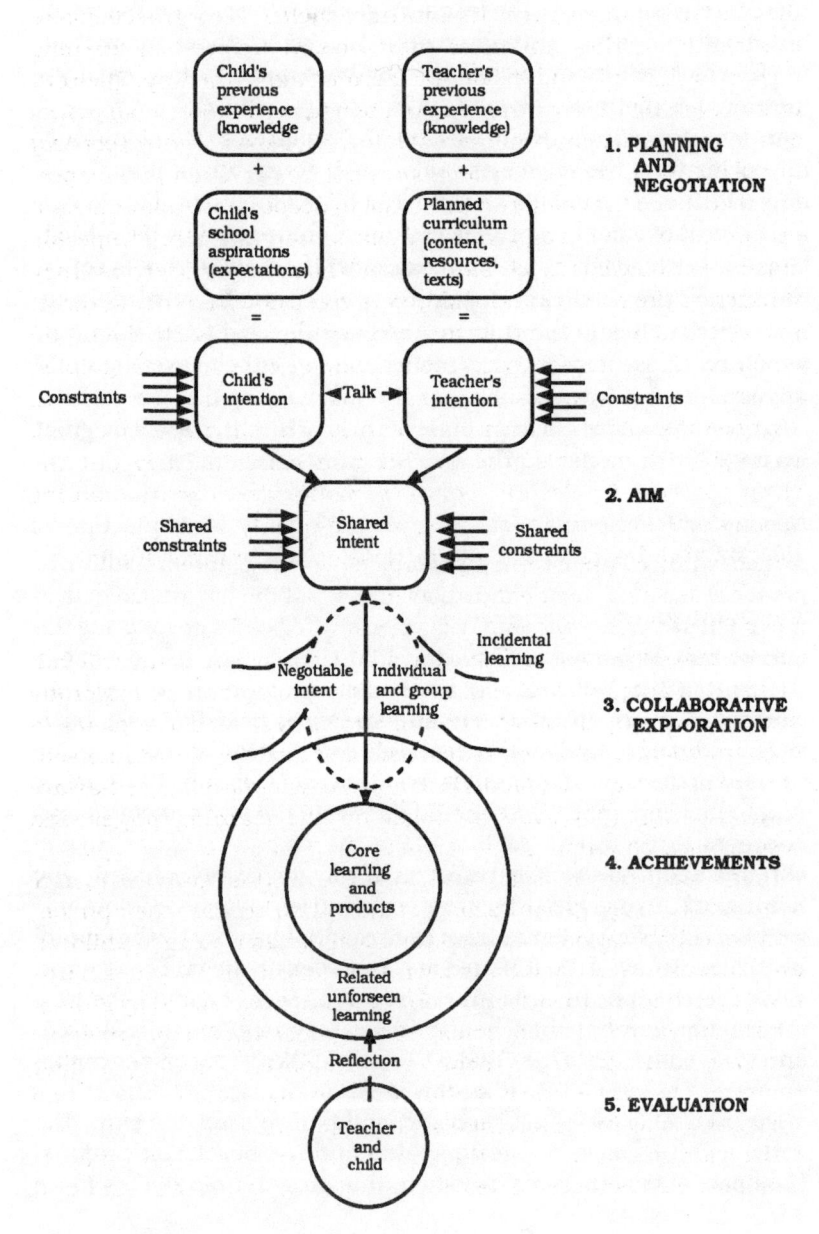

- Child's previous experience (knowledge)
- Teacher's previous experience (knowledge)

+

- Child's school aspirations (expectations)
- Planned curriculum (content, resources, texts)

=

Constraints → Child's intention ←Talk→ Teacher's intention ← Constraints

1. PLANNING AND NEGOTIATION

Shared constraints → Shared intent ← Shared constraints

2. AIM

Negotiable intent — Individual and group learning — Incidental learning

3. COLLABORATIVE EXPLORATION

Core learning and products

Related unforseen learning

4. ACHIEVEMENTS

Reflection

Teacher and child

5. EVALUATION

148 *Metaphors and Meanings*

without children present, before the sequence begins.) Collaboratively, a fairly tightly structured unit of work is prepared, in which the class, the groups, each child and the teacher all contract to make contributions. The unit takes into account unforeseen learning related to the topic and incidental learning along the way. The unit is, however, tightly constrained but open to negotiation at all points either by the teacher or children. *While the topic and central content are prescribed, specific outcomes cannot be set down in advance.* The broad aim that children will come to deeper understandings of certain key principles and concepts *can* be set down. Indeed, specific objectives would effectively sterilise such an approach, because they would lead the teacher and children to creep down a narrow, direct path, guide book in hand, rather than to explore boldly the broad territory of the topic. The teacher's main role in a negotiated curriculum is to give information and teach only when it is needed.

When the products of learning have been written, made, modelled, painted or dramatised, the teacher and children carry out the crucial process of reflection. This is when the class shares its valuing when there is comparison, respect for quality and rejection of inferior work by those who did it (class, group or individual).

On Quality

I think that Model A is a recipe for 'standards' where many will fail; Model B, if adopted, will lead to dynamic exploration and rigorous pursuit of quality by all who contract to be in it. Model A relates to both traditional, whole-class teachers and modern, individualised-transmission teachers; Model B relates to clear-thinking, self-aware teachers willing to make a wager on the learning power and resources of children.

These teachers do exist, and they do not just survive in our schools. They even generate more of their kind, because their philosophy of collaboration is applied to colleagues as well as to children and because what they do is seen to be effective. They are hardheaded, articulate theorisers about practice, not plagued by guilt at what they cannot do, nor defenceless against attackers, armed as they are with both their theory and the obvious quality of their practice. They have learnt the futility of trying to stand alone, and they know how to compromise without capitulating.

They are not prey to educational fads (e.g. the latest spate of language exercise texts). Their greatest allies are their students, and the parents of their students who are brought into the collaboration. They even get excellent examination results.

Conclusion

If teachers set out to teach according to a planned curriculum, without first engaging the interest of the students, the quality of learning will suffer. Student interest involves student investment and personal commitment.

Negotiating the curriculum means deliberately planning to invite students to contribute to, and to modify, the educational programme, so that they will have a real investment both in the learning journey and in the outcomes. Negotiation also means making explicit, and then confronting, the constraints of the learning context and the non-negotiable requirements that apply.

Once teachers act upon the belief that students should share with them a commitment to the curriculum, negotiation will follow naturally, whether the set curriculum is traditional or progressive, and whether the classroom is architecturally open or closed.

NOTES

1. See George Sampson, *English for the English*, London, Cambridge University Press, 1921.

2. At the National Language Development conference in Canberra, January 1978; see J. Maling-Keepes and B.D. Keepes (eds.), *Language in Education: the L.D.P. Phase 1*, CDC, Canberra, 1979.

3. Trevor Pateman, *Language, Truth and Politics*, Nottingham, Stroud and Pateman, 1975.

12
READING THE WHOLE CURRICULUM

A version of this paper was originally presented as a Keynote Address at the Australian Reading Association Conference, Darwin, in 1981. Originally, Michael Marland was to give the Address. However, he was unable to attend and Garth was called in at the last moment.

Introduction

As a precursor to this address, I invite you to reflect upon my title and make predictions about where we will be going together. This is my way of giving substance to the important pedagogical principle that an essential first step in learning is to activate what is already known and to arouse the learner's intention. In this instance, the task may be made difficult because my title is rather cryptic, but once you have begun to predict and anticipate I am confident that I will be talking to some thinking heads that are already starting to defend themselves against me. One of the things that I wish always to do as a teacher and as a conference speaker is gently to alienate my 'audience'. I want to do this so that people realise that what is happening is a *performance*. I could be charming and disarming, and set you at ease, but it is more important for you to be a little tense, geared up for dialogue and constructive contradiction.

My broad concern is with what is called 'language across the curriculum'. In 1972 I worked in London, partly on my own postgraduate research and partly as a consultant, with people like Nancy Martin, Harold Rosen and James Britton. I came back to Australia really fired up to try and make some of the new ideas work in Australia and in South Australia in particular. Since then, however, and over time, I have come to realise that the strategies that were being used, while they seemed fine, were easily marginalised, and hence I have sought to be more and more rigorous in my thinking about what needs to be done in order to secure these ideas and proposals. Even then, 'language across the curriculum' had been misinterpreted by many people in England, as happened in Australia, and now I no longer want to use the phrase because of its connotations and effects.

As I see it, that misinterpretation was basically like this: Let's have a policy for all faculties to make sure they correct fullstops, that they mark out spelling errors, that they look to neatness and tidiness and presentation of student writing, that they make sure they teach the vocabulary of the subject before they actually get into a text, and so on. Clearly such a view is naive and inadequate. All the same there is considerable pressure here in Australia, as elsewhere, particularly with the 'back to basics' and literacy scare, to get that kind of 'language across the curriculum' going in schools. The drive is to tighten up the game, as an instrument of further control. The changes essentially are cosmetic. Basically the school is still driven by the same values, the same relationships, and so the curriculum won't change at all, in any real way.

The language and learning movement, as I prefer to call it, was however trying to get across policies of a different and arguably far more fundamental kind. The focus was not: Let's improve literacy and language performance. It was: Let's improve learning by looking at how language affects and shapes learning. This involves school and faculty policies focussed on matters of thinking and meaning and learning.

In my own case I've moved in my work in South Australia from a project identified as 'language across the curriculum' to a Language and Learning Unit, and finally to a Curriculum and Learning Unit. That movement must be seen in strategic and possibly in symptomatic terms. We came to see that working at the language end was getting us into trouble. With regard to that last name change, the same ideas and values were driving us as before, but now we were more sensitive to the fact that if the structures and relationships in schools aren't changed, you can't get into changing the kinds of language usage and you can't get into improving the quality of learning. So the policies that the Curriculum and Learning Unit was promoting focussed on the need for all faculties to expose their criteria to students, for teachers and students collaboratively to set goals, for negotiation, and for changes to the content and methods of assessment so that what is valued is congruent with what is espoused. For instance, if you say you value group work and student investigation, you had better start setting assessments and assignments on the basis of those values because, until you do, as is the evaluation so is the curriculum.

Such a change in perspective involves increasing the range of learning media which we get students using to power into, and through, new territories. As it is, schools are very much language-bound institutions; but here it is a case of using any medium to learn with, not just language. It involves an action research emphasis in terms of which faculties undertake small scale inquiries, as do students, into matters of concern to them. Related to this is a focus on teachers learning, teachers as researchers and deliberate learners, teachers theorising and researching their own practices. It involves arguments and debates in and across faculties about such things as the difference between understanding and recitation. Increasingly it has been a matter of improving school and classroom relationships and structures as an absolute essential before getting into these other concerns, as the necessary basis for moving in these directions. Involving people in new modes of relationship inevitably forces them into new modes of language usage and new kinds of interchange with others (notably, teachers with students), leading in turn to qualitatively different forms of language learning; in the end, it also improves full stops and commas and spelling. Hence the book *Negotiating the Curriculum*, where teachers from all over Australia (in particular, the southern states) experimented with changing relationships with students and the way they treated the curriculum. As different options in terms of relationship were opened up, so too the language use was opened up and widened, the learning improved and the learners empowered. All this has led me to a clearer understanding of why the 'language across the curriculum' movement failed.

Terrorism

So much for the introduction. I want to present two quotations now, taken from the Preface to Roland Barthes' *S/Z: an essay*. I've amended them slightly:

> Only when we know – and it is a knowledge gained by taking pains, by renouncing what Freud calls instinctual gratification – what we are doing when we [are learning or being taught], are we free to enjoy what we [learn or are being taught]. As long as our enjoyment is – or is said to be – instinctive it is not enjoyment, it is terrorism.

In questioning the superficiality of much work in language reform, then, I'm going to be addressing matters of terrorism – *educational terrorism*.

The second quotation is as follows:

> We require an education in [curriculum] as in sentiments in order to discover that what we assumed – with the complicity of our teachers – was nature was in fact culture, that what was given was no more than a way of taking.

Curriculum is never 'natural', or inevitable. That is an important point as I see it. Many students don't question the curriculum; it is simply there to be taken, they *receive* it, and they never question that it is made by someone. That may be the case with many teachers too.

Virtuous Circles

So with these two quotations in mind, I set about revisiting Michael Marland's book *Language Across the Curriculum*. I was mindful that this was much closer to the Bullock Report, being published in 1977, and that it related principally to a British educational climate which may bear little resemblance to Australia in the blustery conditions of 1981.

Language Across the Curriculum was written specifically to aid schools in their quest to take up the Bullock committee's Recommendation 139 which is as follows:

> To bring this understanding [of linguistic processes in learning and of the demands of specific subjects] every secondary school should develop a policy for language across the curriculum. The responsibility for this policy should be embodied in the organisational structure of the school.

Marland very nicely puts the rationale for 'language across the curriculum':

> The aim of a 'language across the curriculum' policy is simply...to create a *'virtuous circle'*: if a school devotes thought and time to assisting language development, learning in all areas will be helped; if attention is given to language in the content and skill subjects, language development will be assisted powerfully by the context and purposes of those subjects.

At the risk of appearing presumptuous I want to argue that the Bullock Committee, with fine intentions, got it wrong, or at least recommended the wrong way of tackling the problem. Indeed, I believe that Bullock got the problem itself wrong, stating it at too superficial a level while looking through the wrong lens – the 'language lens, rather than the 'learning' lens.

In order to create a little more tension here at the outset, I want to suggest that Marland (circa 1977) was running around in a much too limited virtuous circle. I am presuming in the light of his chosen title 'Reading, Learning and the Whole Curriculum' that in 1981 he may have been about to widen and deepen the 'language across the curriculum' question. It was in trying to create my own version of the 'virtuous circle' that I decided to, in the same action, collapse, conflate and distort his title: hence, *Reading the Whole Curriculum*.

I want to address some deep-seated problems of educational terrorism and educational primitiveness. This means taking liberties with the word 'reading' so that it encompasses the 'reading' of culture itself, only part of which is the world of books. And I am about to enter into vicious school circles by looking through the *learning* lens, not primarily through the language lens as Bullock (1975) and Marland (1977) did.

What does it profit a school to tamper with the surface words of lessons and occasional texts when the curriculum itself remains a closed book? What is the sense in unpacking the meaning of 'photosynthesis' if the school itself is meaningless?

First, let me compose my virtuous circle:

> If a school devotes thought and time to assisting the students' development in reading its culture and curriculum, then the school itself, in order to do this, will have to be more sensitive in its reading of each child's culture and intentions; if the school is sensitive to each child's culture and intentions, then learning and thinking in each subject area will be enhanced and language will grow to match new thinking and new learning.

That is, language development in school depends on the student's ability to 'read' the school culture. When I am in a culture I cannot 'read', I tend to be silent. I cannot 'read' well from a culture which shields its work and does not hand up its calculations and processing along with the finished products. Such a culture will terrorise me, until I can unlock its secrets.

The Reading Process and the Curriculum as 'Text'

To unlock its secrets, I must use my brain. I have thought deeply about the reading process (as represented by Clay, Smith, Goodman and all that happy psycholinguistic crowd) and also about the composing process (as represented by Graves, Britton, Moffett and so on). I extract from both processes a common theory of learning which I find congruent with the work of Dewey, Vygotsky and Bruner. I think a great deal about brains and, in my basic commonsensical way, I disturb and excite myself by the thought that, of course, human brains being the same biological instrument will all go about processing the world in the same way if they have not been damaged – a salutary antidote to the 'we are all different' school. I am not wanting to get into the argument about learning styles – but I do want to say that I think that across cultures we might be surprised to find that human brains operate in much the same way.

Aha! So human beings will learn to read the world as they learn to read books. The discovery is illuminating and liberating when I shine it on the problems of the student 'reader' in the embrace of the school's curriculum, with teachers as crucial go-betweens.

What happens then if we take what we now know about how children come to be good readers and, seeing what strategies they use, translate these into reading the curriculum? Let me pursue some isomorphic operations in this regard.

I have taken four questions that Marie Clay asks about reading, with reference to beginning readers. These are questions young readers are encouraged to ask, particularly when they are in trouble. First, a semantic cue: *Does it make sense?* We talk about children 'barking' at texts where they actually read (aloud) the words but make no sense of them, nor of the text. So, how many students in our schools are just barking at the curriculum? The next question involves a syntactic cue-ing. *Can you say that?* Or is it bad manners? Have I just said something, or done something, that is against the rules? Am I allowed to say or do that in this school, or is it considered bad manners, a school sin or taboo? In other words, do I know the sanctions and rules and particular syntactical operations of this school? The next one is: *Does it look right?* This involves a kind of visual cue-system. In curriculum terms, is this the sort of product that gets rewards in this school? Have I now produced something that looks right and is appropriate? The final question, a prediction cue, is: *What comes next?* Or rather: What do I expect to come next? Is this a curriculum story which I am comprehending? Is it like a novel where I can see the way it is unfolding and have a notion of what comes next? Am I able to prepare myself for the next encounter in some way that will be *useful*?

When you start to ask such questions of the school's curriculum,

DIAGRAM 1: TERRORISM OR LIBERATION?

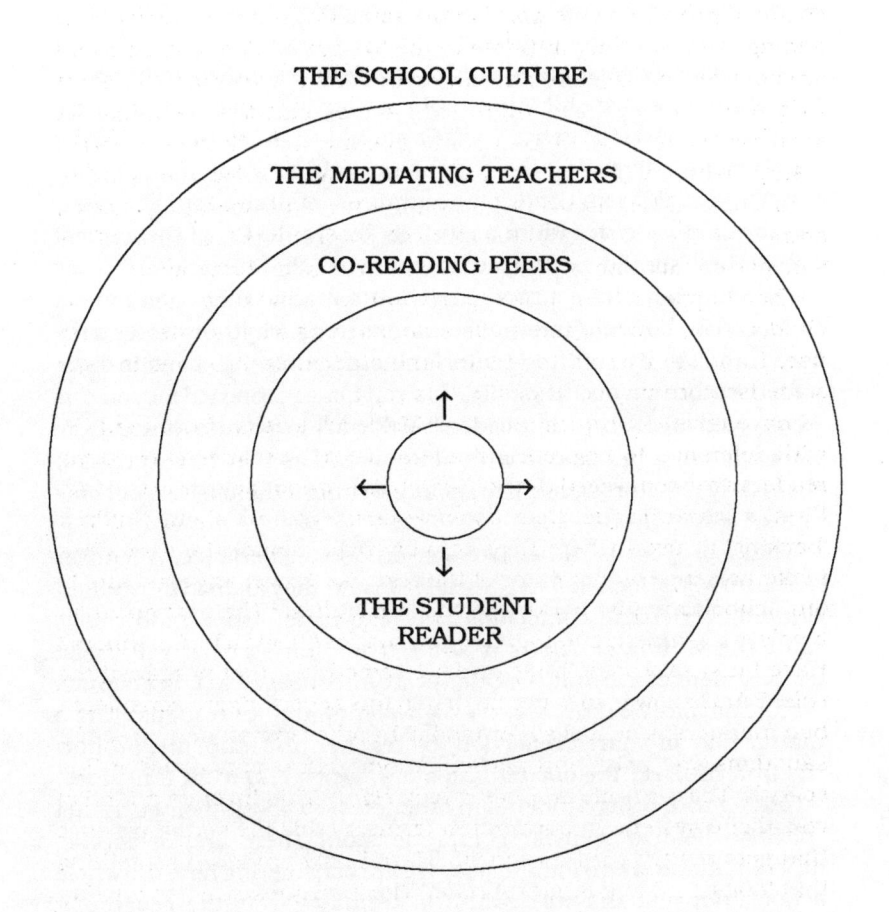

THE SCHOOL CULTURE

THE MEDIATING TEACHERS

CO-READING PEERS

THE STUDENT READER

it is no longer possible to believe that it is 'natural'. You have to become, like the audience at a Brechtian play, a healthily alienated inquirer who knows that the curriculum is a performance generated within the school's culture, a demonstration with palpable designs on you. It is no longer a *given*; it is a way of *taking*, now that you have learnt to act on it.

Some further isomorphisms.

Beginning 'composition' should accompany beginning 'reading'. In the same sense that children should be starting to write at the same time as they start to read, so they should begin to write with the curriculum, composing the curriculum, at the same time as they learn to read it. From Grade One onwards, children should be starting to compose curriculum as well as receive it. From the earliest times they should be helped to compose the curriculum. They should therefore have a good curriculum read to them every week, so that they begin to internalise the patterns, rhythms and structures of the 'story'. In Grade One, for instance, the teacher sits down with the students and says, 'This is what I have proposed for you this week', and talks about it. Students will start to get into the act from the early times of this curriculum event and as they have it read to them they will start wanting to get into writing it themselves, or some of it at least.

What I propose is rather like shared book experience. A teacher holds up a Big Book in front of students and they all read it together. Shared curriculum composing and reading is also a 'good thing'. After the writing or telling of the curriculum story, it will assist development of learning if students are encouraged to talk about its strengths and weaknesses, its high points and its troughs. It is a matter here of shared reflection, by teacher *and* students, on how the unit of work, the curriculum story, went, and what it means.

Talking with other students in other classes about their curricula will also help to increase comprehension. There are, of course, different kinds of curriculum text. We are considering here the whole school, not just the curriculum in terms of, say, the geography course for the year. For instance, the school assembly is a text that has to be read – you have to know what the school assembly is, what the rules are in school assemblies, how to predict school assemblies, and how school assemblies make sense or otherwise. Similarly with the geography lesson, the art excursion to the gallery, the sports period, the school choir, the lunchtime ritual – all school texts which students have to learn to read.

Each text requires special reading strategies. Reading is not something you get once and for all. For each sub-culture there are new strategies. You only learn them by trying new keys, until you achieve, in Jerome Bruner's terms, 'the unlocking of capacities by techniques that come from exposure to the specialised environment of culture'. What we must do for students is unlock their capacity to read a culture by techniques that come from immersion in and exposure to the 'specialised environment' of the culture. So, if you want them to learn the genre of the geography lesson, they have first to be exposed to it and then allowed to talk about it, to see how it works so that they can unlock and control it. You could be exposed to it forever and still not be able to really read it, unless someone gets alongside you and explains it to you, and helps to answer your questions about what is going on. In other words, we should always get students 'casing' new texts and new ideas when we introduce them – they have to have the opportunity to case the joint. As each new sub-culture is unlocked, so the students' intellectual potency is increased, as they unlock more and more of the texts in store. Donald Graves has said: 'Student adventurousness and creativity is directly proportional to teacher predictability'. This could be said, I think, for schooling generally. The more predictable the school, the more intellectually adventurous the students will be.

By this argument it is the responsibility of each teacher to teach students how to read the special sub-cultures through which and in which they teach. So it is the science faculty's responsibility to teach the sub-culture of science – what science textbooks are like, what happens in science, how to behave scientifically, and why this is the case. This presupposes that they can and will also teach the general culture of the school. If an opportunity comes up in a science lesson to teach something about the school as well as about science, then the teacher does it – as would, of course, teachers generally, regardless of subject area or level. That is what my particular lens tells me. It is more than a fancy way of re-stating the truisms of the reading-in-the-content-area fraternity and the Bullock Committee. It raises the aspirations and the challenge quite a few notches, transcending linguistic chauvinism.

The Complicity of Tact

The model in Diagram 2 will help me explain what I have termed, perhaps over-dramatically, the kind of educational terrorism and

DIAGRAM 2: THE COMPLICITY OF TACT

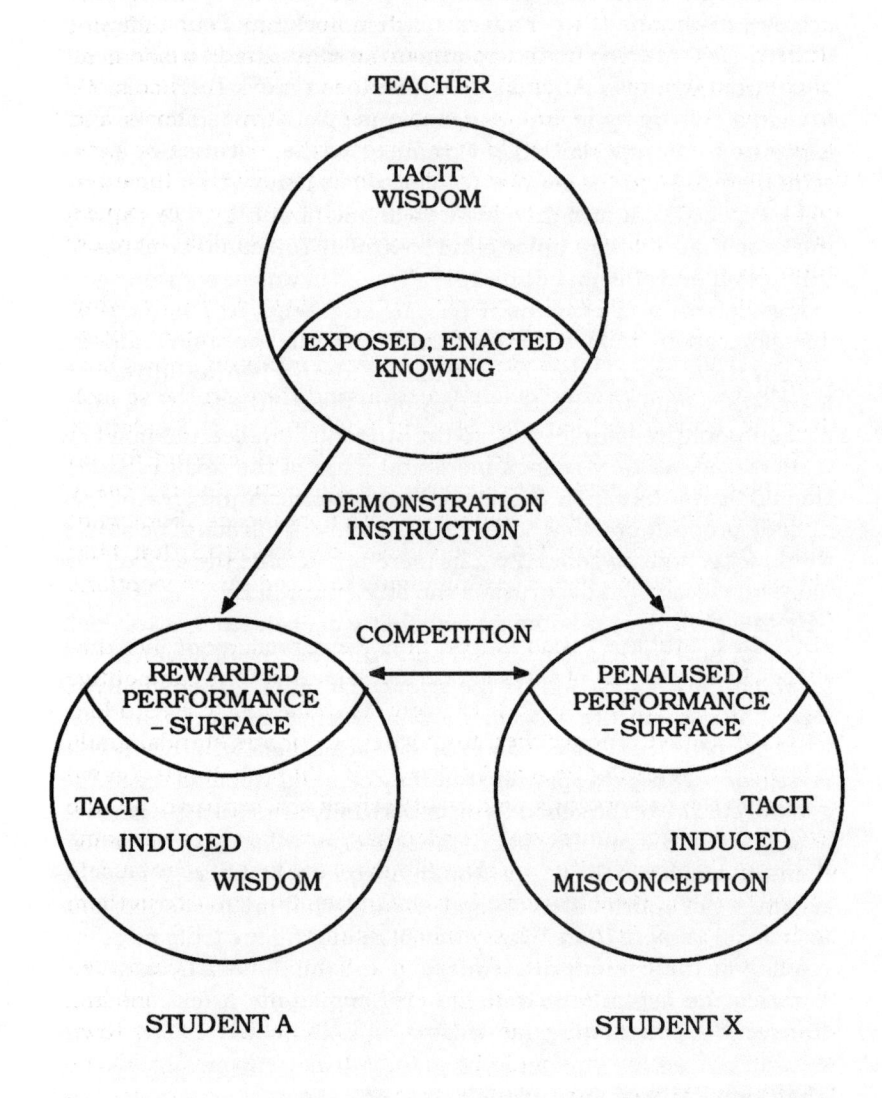

TEACHER

TACIT WISDOM

EXPOSED, ENACTED KNOWING

DEMONSTRATION
INSTRUCTION

COMPETITION

REWARDED PERFORMANCE – SURFACE

TACIT INDUCED WISDOM

PENALISED PERFORMANCE – SURFACE

TACIT INDUCED MISCONCEPTION

STUDENT A

STUDENT X

primitiveness that occurs when teachers do not accept the obligation of taking students behind the scenes of their teaching set. In what I call the complicity of tact, which I see as one of the vicious circles in schooling, we have a teacher and two very different students. The teacher has an enormous amount of tacit wisdom, as teachers do generally. After all, we have all been through schools. We are 'experts', the most knowledgeable people about schools and school cultures that you could ever come across, because we have been through twelve years of schooling, through tertiary education, and now we are back in schools as teachers. Indeed, we only expose or enact, or actually demonstrate, a very small part of what we really know about schools.

Student A is the one who succeeds. He or she has 'know-how', what I call tacit induced wisdom because it is wisdom that has never been made explicit and yet it *works*, the student in question knows how to please the teacher and gets rewards in and through the school. Over here in competition with Student A is Student X. Student X keeps coming across comments like this: 'I was looking for an integrated history essay; please write an integrated history essay next time.' He or she keeps coming up with hypotheses about what might get rewards, but isn't even close to relating to that tacit wisdom, and indeed keeps getting tacitly induced *misconceptions* about schooling.

Somehow Student A has tapped into the complicity of tact that makes for and is part of school success. Because of the competitive framework in which they work, Student A is not going to let Student X into the secret. The teacher, from where he or she stands, tends to let neither one into the secret. It is almost as if schooling is a game of finding the password, a politics of secrecy and surprise. So, the teacher doesn't or can't reveal the necessary secrets, or reveals some of them only by way of the surprise tactics of testing; Student A gets access to them, somehow or other, and doesn't or can't pass them on to Student X. Hence, the complicity of tact.

If we won't take students, all students, behind our teaching set, then they are being terrorised, however benign our intentions are. Consider the curriculum as a kind of Hollywood western town teaching set. What we should be doing, I believe, is saying, 'Come behind here and I'll show you how it works'. By that I mean, letting students into one's seemingly magic curriculum tricks, or, to put it another way, leaving uncovered the footprints so often carefully dusted over. The God in the machine is really only an experienced mortal and it would be a relief to so many tribal sinners to know it. So many vain sacrifices and fruitless rain dances would thus be rendered unnecessary.

Part of the seeming magic of the teacher comes from a lifetime of immersion in the culture of schools so that countless little short-cuts and nuances have become transparent components of the taken-for-granted, lost, as it were, and therefore very inaccessible to an outside reader. We as teachers are so immersed in schools and schooling that we take it for granted. We take for granted the very culture in which we work and live. We breeze through it so immaculately that we can't understand, or perhaps don't understand as much as we might like, how difficult it is for students. And yet it is those short-cuts and nuances which allow the teacher to operate so confidently and smoothly, to breeze so immaculately through the culture of the school and the more rarefied sub-culture of the specific curriculum area. We breeze through the school, but how much *more* immaculate are we in our specialist area, our own particular territory?

Now Student A, the one who succeeds, the high flyer, often the teacher's privileged friend, nuts out a working theory of how to do it in order to please. The tacit wisdom (and it is tacit because the underpinnings are so rarely talked about) may not contain the same tricks as the teacher's, but it serves as reliable scaffolding. It *works.* One may speculate on how this wisdom was induced, and where it came from. Was it from talking to peers, or from privileged private conversation with the teacher, or from parents in the know? Whatever the source of wisdom, Student A contrasts sharply with Student X, who fails. Betrayed by a head full of induced misconceptions, Student X is tenaciously all the time looking for clues, for analogies, for explanatory stories, and somehow misses the boat or catches the wrong train of thought.

What is more, there is a vicious circle in operation which will keep this student terrorised. Because of the competition and knowledge capitalism of the classroom, Student A is not likely to let on. 'I'm all right, Jack. Go crack the code yourself.' The teacher, for different reasons – which bear thinking about – blocks, or does not see, the need to provide access to his or her wisdom. Perhaps he or she is not even aware of what wisdom is needed because it is, or seems, so simple. Thus, Student X is a remedial curriculum reader, a cultural retard, and part of a complicity of tact. For Student X is also silent about the muddle and chaos beneath the surface of incompetence.

Behind the Scenes

What are some of the features of the unilluminated underground of schools? Let me use two illustrations.

A maths teacher whom we taped, as part of the language across the curriculum project in the mid-seventies in South Australia, spend half an hour in monologue/demonstration teaching equations, solving for x, the unknown (e.g. $2x + 4 = 10$). He pursued, at some length, the analogy that it was like unwrapping a Christmas parcel, layer by layer, until you came to the unknown present and recognised its value. This seemed to be a generous attempt to offer the students some cognitive footholds. At the end of the demonstration, we took one student who said he could do it and put him with another who could not do it. We asked the competent student to re-teach the lesson; it took less than two minutes. The conversation went something like this:

Student M: Do you understand what to do?

Student N: No, Haven't got a clue.

Student M: Well, You see this problem $(2x + 3 = 4)$?

Student N: Yeah.

Student M: Well, you see, where it says plus, you take it over the other side and say minus. And when it's times on this side you take it over the other side and divide.

Student N: Oh. Is that all? Now I understand.

We know, of course, that Student N didn't understand in the way the idealistic teacher might have wished, but all the same Student M knows, at a ruthlessly honest level, that mathematics at secondary level is largely a matter of twigging the formula. So Student M dispensed with the embroidery and gave access to a simple piece of know-how. The teacher possibly did it this way as a student, but may have forgotten, or have learnt to see it as impure!

Diagram 3 shoes a mathematical puzzle which was put to a group of fourteen year olds. A painter is asked to paint an area around a circular window. The space is bounded by tangents on either side of the window extending to the top and bottom of the window and

DIAGRAM 3: USING INTUITION

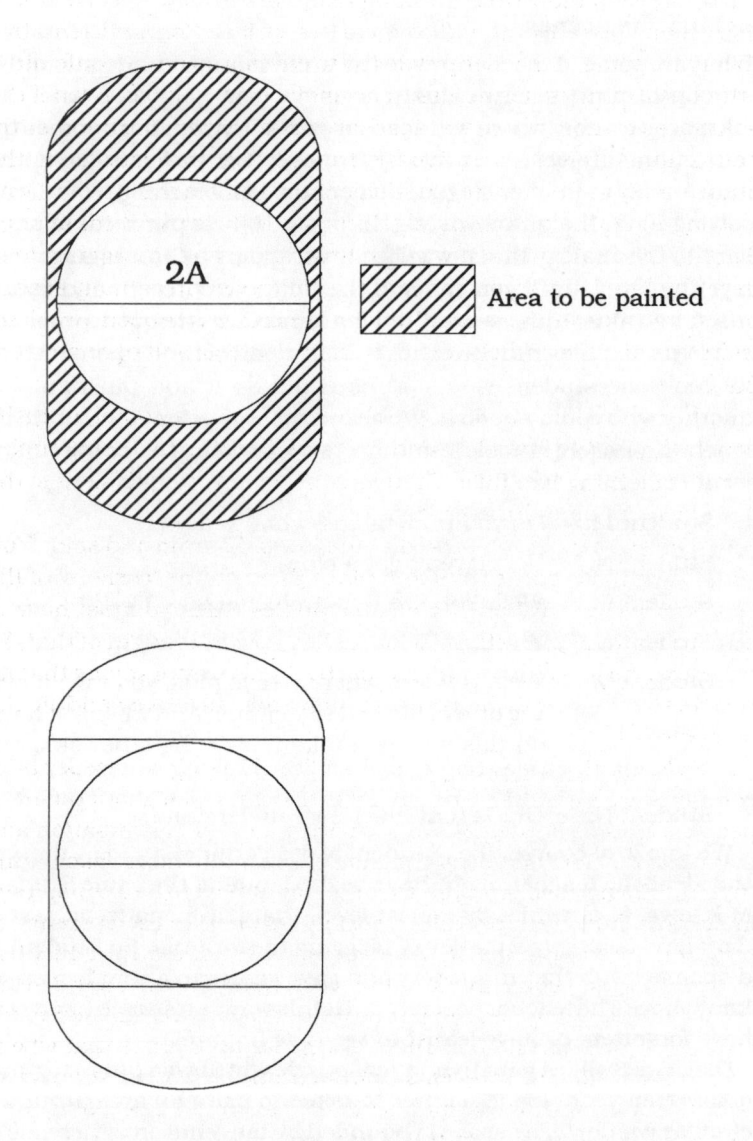

2A

////// Area to be painted

WHAT EXACTLY IS THE AREA TO BE PAINTED?

closed by two semi-circles as shown. The diameter of the window is 2a. What exactly is the area to be painted?

To hear each individual thinking aloud about how to solve it is a marvellous lesson in the idiosyncrasies of intuition and tentative theory building. A teacher privileged to eavesdrop on the unfolding, faltering strategies has access to normally tacit wisdom. Even if the solution was not found, the teacher has many and various entry points for authentic and productive teaching dialogue with the students. How much more illuminating for all if the teacher, too, was a vulnerable thinker from scratch, in a collaborative think-along? Each individual student's wisdom is increased by the aggregate of new thinking by all those involved. The more we can actually expose students to various people thinking around a common problem, therefore, the more likely it is that their thinking will become more subtle.

The neat solution to the problem comes from completing the square around the window and realising that the two semi-circles equal the area of the circle. Therefore the square is equivalent to the area to be painted. Answer: $4a^2$.

My twelve year old son looked at the lower diagram and said: 'You could take those corner bits and place them on the 'corners' of the semi-circles so that they became rectangles. Then you just have to add the rectangles together.' When asked how he thought of that, he said: 'Oh, it's just a matter of perspective' – his way of saying that he couldn't prove it, but he could *see* how the corners would fit the semi-circles...

The moral of this example is that the thinking antecedents of solutions are exceedingly rich in folk wisdom, clues about different people's reading strategies, and opportunities for conversation and comparison. How one does the magic is usually more fascinating then the magic itself. And yet, there seems almost to be a conspiracy in schools, and even in western society, to devalue the currency of intuition by concealing it. As expressed by a maths educator: 'Although most people think inductively, nevertheless after discovering some fact they tend to shroud it in the language of deductive thought' (Plumpton, 1973). The message for teachers is that whenever presenting new problems and territories, they must strive to become naive and pre-formal again. 'What would I be doing, and feeling, if I was coming to this fresh again?' That is, re-create, as much as possible, what it was like for them themselves, in engaging with new knowledge of this kind. Strangely inefficient as it may seem, this pre-disciplinary frame of mind will allow students also to be inductive and will offer many points of collaboration between teacher, as reborn student, and learner.

Helping Too Little, and Helping Too Much

I close with two more points – one about the asceticism of schools, and the other about indulgence. The ghastly taboo of cheating seems to have so warped many teachers' minds that they withhold many of their well-oiled 'cheating' devices. Teachers know brilliantly, thoroughly, fiendishly the wiles of the reading hunter. They know how to regress to pick up important clues, they know how to gut, how to skim, how to use sign-posts, how to read cover blurbs, how to sample, and how to give the appearance of knowing – the art of judicious blustering. All these are very useful coping and struggling strategies which any experienced student needs in the armoury. Such is the hypocrisy or miserliness of schooling, however, that these strategies are rarely openly and generously offered to students. Are we ashamed then of our own subterfuges?

On the other hand, there is the over-indulgence of those who find it hard to withhold clues or assistance. We teachers seem to have a very low threshold of patience in front of a cogitating, pained mind. We jump in with a clue and unwittingly administer a mind-opiate which, if habituated, will enslave the student to authority and governing imaginations.

The independent, powerful reader can struggle through the boundaries of new cultures largely unaided. 'The vividness of "aha" is inversely proportional to the number of clues provided' (Deans, 1973). It seems to me, therefore, much more powerful for learners to come to 'aha' without too many clues.

Summary

In summary, I have argued that the language across the curriculum movement has been trivialised and contained because it looked at *language problems* in schools rather than at *learning problems*. I have drawn an analogy between the characteristics of a powerful, independent reader and a student who has learnt to read the culture of the school, submitting that most learning acts in school will have a low voltage unless they are carried out with an understanding of how the school works. Therefore, in the interests of powerful learning, teachers are obliged to teach students how to read the culture of the school, the subject and specific texts. In order to do this, teachers have to make explicit to themselves what they may have so long taken for granted about schools, their own subject and their own learning strategies. It is argued that the more information and understanding students have about these 'secrets', the more adventurous and powerful will be their learning.

And so, teachers looking through the culture and learning lens will, in every teaching act, be contributing to students' ability to read *the whole curriculum*. They will know the place of their words, their sentences, their paragraphs and their chapters in the massive novel of school life.

Reading the whole curriculum is a matter of becoming self-conscious, healthily alienated explorers of the text of school which must be seen not as 'given' or 'natural' but as *constructed*. It is a matter of learning how to take from it, to build, and then to act to control and transform one's own life. In this context, learning word-attack skills on photosynthesis may be significant. Without such a perspective, however, reading is likely to be very much an act of terrorism.

REFERENCES

Chapman, L.R. (ed.), *The Process of Learning Mathematics*, Pergamon Press, 1973.

Deans, J.F. 'A Note on Discovery', in Chapman (ed.), *op. cit.*

Howard, Richard, 'Preface' to Roland Barthes, *S/Z/: an essay*, Hill and Wang, 1974.

Marland, Michael, *Language Across the Curriculum*, Heinemann, 1977.

Plumpton, C. 'Generalization and Structure', in Chapman (ed.), *op. cit.*

13

NEGOTIATION REVISITED

In 1982, a special edition of Interpretations, the Journal of the English Teachers Association of Western Australia, was devoted to issues in curriculum negotiation. Garth used the opportunity to reflect on his original formulation of 'negotiating the curriculum' in 1978.

In 1978, I wrote the paper 'Negotiating the Curriculum' – now included in the book *Negotiating the Curriculum*[1] – as a base paper of historical interest.

In 1978, this paper represented my position after five years of experimentation in South Australian schools on matters related to the slogans 'language across the curriculum' and 'language and learning'. Having worked with Nancy Martin in 1972/73 as a consultant to the Schools Council Writing project which was following through on the London Institute of Education research of the late sixties, I came back to Australia in 1973 determined to continue experimenting with ways of helping teachers to develop their own theories-in-practice and their capacities to engage with the theories of others. I was not convinced that the model being used in the United Kingdom would effectively take root and grow in schools because it seemed to underestimate the power of institutions to stultify and contain, and because it represented a view of the world which was decidedly subversive to the point of being explosive (in terms of its advocacy of changed student/teacher relationships in which students might be more empowered and less acted upon). It was, therefore, likely to be rejected by most parents, most teachers and most administrators because it promised to weaken control and lead to a dilution of institutionally approved courses and curricula. Furthermore, it was likely to be rejected initially by most students because it required them to think and act and because it broke the established rules of what teachers and students usually do.

In working on the Language Across the Curriculum Project in South Australia (1975-76) (an attempt to intensify and strengthen the United Kingdom model by working in depth in four schools), I became increasingly aware of two major problems:

- Without changes to the structure of the system and the schools, individual change in schools is unlikely to spread far beyond the individual classroom and indeed is likely to be contained or curtailed by the application of sanctions within the institution.
- To work with receptive individuals on problems associated with *language* in education is insufficient if it does not lead to fundamental examination of *learning, knowledge* and the *curriculum*.

The ideas implicit in 'Negotiating the Curriculum' developed logically, in retrospect, out of attempts to address the second problem. Some attempt is also made within the present work on negotiation to take account of the first problem, but it is more on the nature of self-defence strategies for negotiating teachers than on developing ways of effecting structural change in schools and systems. The extend to which education in negotiation is education for disillusionment is, therefore, an abiding concern.

It is appropriate and salutary for me, then, a decade after my consciousness-raising period in the United Kingdom, to consider some vexed questions and difficulties which continue to flourish in the territory of negotiation.

Negotiation as 'Conning'

A major tenet behind 'negotiation' is that those in power should be as explicit as possible about the designs they have on students. It is contended that where power figures withhold information and intentions, the relatively powerless are likely to be worked over without the chance of defending themselves. The phrase 'coming clean' is common in the rhetoric of negotiators.

But at what point does one say, 'Enough'? Teaching could become one massive confessional, plumbing the depths of teachers' and students' psyches if one were to take 'coming clean' to its limits.

Each teacher will have personal and pragmatic reasons for establishing thresholds of explicitness beyond which a kind of trust or unspoken understanding will have to operate. Each student, too, will have 'boundaries of tact'. Indeed, the student's most powerful method of defence is tacit resistance, if not internal rebellion.

Now it is a common ploy of some unscrupulous manipulators to give a convincing portrayal of 'coming clean' themselves in order to lull the manipulated into divulging information. Pseudo explicitness, or calculated explicitness, is in this way used to render the relatively powerless even more powerless because they have innocently offered up their major weapon, information about themselves (a modern equivalent of giving the witchdoctors one's name).

In a mediated exchange which I had with Dorothy Heathcote, some time ago, I questioned her failure to be explicit, particularly pointing to her ploy of divesting herself of the role of teacher and then taking up a role-play power position within the children's drama. My view is that, by seemingly divesting herself of teacher power, she has in fact increased it by playing crypto-teacher within the fiction. She can therefore control at a more covert level. Heathcote in answering this criticism replied that she had no need to negotiate explicitly because the children *trusted* her implicitly and because her deepest intentions were to *empower* and *liberate* them. It was a kind of 'ends-to-justify-means' argument. My response was to claim that, no matter how loving and noble one is, trust needs continually to be negotiated and affirmed. As an Australian citizen under a regime which will always claim to have honourable intentions towards me, I will continually strive to have these intentions, at the deepest level, made explicit.

Nevertheless one cannot legislate for honesty in education or society. And for that matter most people will admit to a relatively slender knowledge of themselves. If we daily 'con' and 'delude' ourselves, we will inevitably 'con' and 'delude' others. This kind of reasoning has led some of my colleagues to eschew the whole idea of negotiation as a game which is inevitably illusory. They contend that one should simply, in a no-nonsense way, get on with the teaching without the convolutions of meta-education and justifying commentary.

You will in the end teach what you are. Negotiation will only dress up what you believe about life, society and learning. If your basic urge is to control, you will use negotiation to control. If your basic urge is to empower you will tend to empower[2]. I agree with this conclusion. But I strongly believe that *negotiation strategies will amplify the power of a teacher to achieve his or her basic urges*. In the case of the controller, the techniques outlined in *Negotiating The Curriculum* will be press-ganged into the service of control by means of limited pseudo-negotiation. In the case of the liberator, the techniques will be taken up more authentically, in the spirit which I support, in the service of teaching children how to amplify their own power.

There is an enormous amount of work to be done in revealing how authorities and power-mongers appropriate to contain. The history of the women's movement and the responses of cunning men are illuminating in this regard.

I suspect that a major flaw in the present 'negotiation movement' in education is that we have started by trying to raise the consciousness (indirectly the power) of the relatively more *powerful*, the teachers, where the more radical drive would be to raise the consciousness of the relatively *powerless*, the students, by teaching them the secrets of questioning, bargaining, calling bluffs, citing evidence and banding together. That is, of course, what teachers, the relatively powerless, need to learn in negotiating with administrators and politicians, the relatively powerful.

My defence against those who inevitably point to the abuses and misappropriation of 'negotiation' is that we had to start somewhere. It is also to point in reply to the many effective and powerful teachers who are constructively and deliberately negotiating, acting and resisting in classrooms across Australia.

Changing Profiles of Power

I would now like to write a book on *Negotiating The Hidden Curriculum* in which I would complicate the quite simplistic monodimensional view of power projected in *Negotiating The Curriculum*. In global socio-political terms, teachers are more powerful than students, boys more powerful than girls, Anglo-Australians than Aborigines, the employers than the employed. But a micro-analysis of the moment-to-moment dance between, say, teacher and student will show fascinating fluctuations in the balance of power, a shifting drama of point and counterpoint, changing patterns of initiation and response. If ethnographers could develop a kind of x-ray lens to probe the psyche, I am sure they would uncover quite amazing flows and ebbs of affect and primal resistance in teachers and taught from moment to moment. Behind the facade of overt action and response, beneath what I have called elsewhere 'the complicity of tact'[5], deepseated emotions and stereotypical and idiosyncratic aspects of the individual's socialisation will be operating to change and reverse the profiles of power and control.

We all know the phenomenon of the child who is able brilliantly to tug at the heartstrings of a parent who has shown him or herself to be vulnerable to certain overtures. We all know how the 'bad vibes' accompanying a certain name can carry-over and be applied to any innocent wearer of that label. We all know the personal panic and disintegration of control which can occur when, despite ourselves, we let someone else 'get to us'.

Thus while we may reasonably predict that teachers will, by and large, appropriate the conch shell in schools, there will be strong pockets of individual or group terrorisation, subjugation, manipulation and charming of teachers.

There will therefore be, in both the *affective* and *cognitive* tensions in the classroom, fluctuations in the permissioning and commissioning sanctions. Covertly and overtly teachers will signal differentially, according to context of situation and the participants in the unfolding drama, what is *permitted* as well as what is *required*. There are times when you may laugh and times when you may disagree. Likewise, students will differentially give permission and issue commissions to the teacher. So one child will commission attention and another permit the teacher to come close.

Furthermore, it is now clear that boys and girls are differentially permitted and commissioned in classrooms[4].

Negotiating The Curriculum oversimplifies the question of power and largely ignores the negotiation of affection. It puts forward strategies for engaging minds without a deep exploration of how 'hearts' are engaged or how heart and mind interpenetrate. We now need some detailed interactional analysis of changing profiles of power in classrooms, where some attempt is made to uncover the deep motives of both teacher and student. A picture would emerge, I believe, showing students far more actively and aggressively manipulating and resisting than is implied in *Negotiating The Curriculum*[5].

Besides recognising the changing profiles of power, there is also a need to analyse and define power with greater subtlety. The term is used rather loosely in *Negotiating The Curriculum*. We need to get a better purchase on the various categories or genres of power. There is legal power, experiential or informational power, charismatic power, physical power, public power, private power, deliberate power, accidental power, personal power and group power. With a clearer map of power, we could analyse the classroom dance with more precision.

In this article and in *Negotiating the Curriculum*, I generally refer to power as the capacity to construe, resist, control and act upon one's existential world, but this does get mixed up with notions of conferred power, and social and legal status.

The Tyranny of Tact

While there are problems for teachers in 'coming clean', there are far more profound problems when teachers remain silent about themselves and the curriculum.

It is interesting to note that the 'direct instruction' lobby in education is highly critical of most teachers for withholding information and instruction and forcing children indirectly to find out how to do things. The 'direct instructors' advocate explicit and systematic instruction of that which is to be learnt. Learning, they say, only happens when there is teaching.

Now *Negotiating The Curriculum* similarly contends that to withhold information is to jeopardise learning. It, too, advocates the deliberate demonstration and explication of that which the teacher wishes to be learnt. But unlike the 'direct instruction' school, it sees the initial *intention* of the learner to learn as an absolutely necessary condition of teaching and the consciousness of the problematic as a precursor to instruction. When intention is aroused, and the problematic recognised, instruction and demonstration are potent. These two fundamentally opposed camps share, for different reasons, a critique of teacher indirection.

The more I examine present teaching in Australia, the more depressed I become about what almost seems a teacher conspiracy not to *tell*. It is, of course, not a conspiracy. Most teachers are unaware of the elaborate rituals which have been developed in education to make knowledge and technique mystical. The major strategy, perpetrated under the banner of rigour, is to make passing a privatised game of finding the password. The prizes go to those who by private enterprise (with no officially defined cheating or *sharing*) find out the teachers' secrets. The best students will find secret entrances to the teacher's very self, learning how to predict moods, how to read quirks and nuances, how to win affection. Those who fail will be relatively illiterate 'readers' of their teacher, continually tricked, tripped and thwarted, their at first frantic guesses gradually retreating into withdrawal or becoming transformed into rebellion against a seemingly unjust or unfathomable deity.

Donald Graves, in an address I heard in Chicago in April 1982, asserted that there is, according to his observation, a clear link between teacher predictability and student adventurousness. The easier it is to 'read' a teacher, the more likely it is that students will back their own judgement and plug into their own power.

Negotiating The Curriculum advocates explicit, unprincipled, and therefore consistent, teacher behaviour which strives to make the educational programme principled and predictable for students who have been involved in its construction. It does not, however, go far enough in its rationale for negotiation. Clearly while teaching, say, Science, negotiating teachers are also teaching negotiation, but, by the tenets expressed above, learning how to negotiate will be impeded if teachers fail to make explicit and to teach students *deliberately* how they negotiate.

If teachers negotiate and yet remain silent about the skills and strategies of negotiation, they are withholding the keys to the desired kingdom. Some students will work it out for themselves but many others may remain 'magicked' by the process.

In this way 'negotiating the curriculum' can become yet another conservative instrument keeping the student dependent.

The radical negotiator must willinging and wittingly supply the very weapons which could lead to mutiny – explicit demonstration of the tricks. However, the radical negotiator fights *with* the children and so it is not likely to be a gift to the enemy but rather a strengthening of our team.

Teachers who cannot and do not negotiate effectively within their own school will not be able to teach negotiation.

The Alienation Effect

I have continuing uncertainties about questions of comradeship and charisma. At present, I feel that it is necessary for teachers to foster a Brechtian-type alienation effect in the theatre of education.

This involves showing children that the curriculum is not natural but constructed and in many ways arbitrary. It also means teachers showing that they themselves are fallible, vulnerable and not to be fully believed (in the sense that there is no ultimate truth, or that truth is always relative).

If children are bound to teachers by charm, unquestioning love or various other ties ranging from respect to awe, they are likely to be subjugated through the act of belonging. The children in belonging to the teacher make the teacher responsible for them and thereby are less responsible for themselves.

If we are to teach children to be subtly alienated from us, I suppose that we must be subtly alienated from ourselves, forever catching ourselves out in acts of self-delusion or faulty theories. We must be continually going beyond ourselves, attempting to become gently estranged from our present convictions.

Yet we must do this with affection for ourselves, avoiding schizophrenia and disintegration. I think.

Empowering Teachers

Bill Green in an unpublished paper on theory/practice relations6 raises some very healthy doubts about the early days of 'negotiating the curriculum':

> A researcher proposes and outlines a strategy, and a teacher, perhaps attracted more by the rhetoric at the early stages, attempts to apply it directly, more as a 'formula' than as an invitation for focussed theorisation, or re-theorisation, of the basic proposal; an invitation, that is, to 'ownership'. It is more than likely, in any case, for anyone, and perhaps even despite some initial engagement with the idea, that it won't work straight off, which more often than not discourages the teacher who subsequently abandons it or else dismisses it as 'good in theory'. The end result is both researcher and teacher are frustrated in their mutual attempt to enhance learning by what is essentially a communicative failure; moreover, the distance between them widens, as does the antagonism and conflict. (p. 25)

This raises the very question which faces all educators. How can teachers teach so that children learn? How can teacher educator/ researchers like me effect teacher development in the field of negotiation?

Green's analysis is, I believe, a caricature of what can happen to teachers who take up explicit or implicit invitations to try aspects of negotiation. My own studies of how people come to take up new ideas, and eventually to make these their own, suggests that the evolution from information or idea to understanding can occur in an infinity of patterns. The ignition stage is particularly various across teachers I have observed. A common characteristic, however, is that each teacher had had some degree of anxiety about his or her present teaching. Whether they are attracted by the rhetoric, or convinced by the logic, or in need of salvation, or suddenly made bold to do what they have always felt, or moved by the possibility of recognition by the administration, potential negotiators are operating out of some form of professional anxiety ('anxiety' in the sense of disequilibrium). New ideas are never taken up mindlessly. Teachers are, like all humans, possessed of intelligence. The focus, as Green suggests, may not be on 're-theorising practice' but it will be on *something*, and in this regard the new idea will always be tried as a working hypothesis with respect to some aspect of the area of anxiety. It may be tried in the hope that it will solve discipline problems. It may be tried in the hope that it will cure jaundice about teaching. It may be seen as a new technique to extend the repertoire.

Disillusionment and antagonism are not the only outcomes of initial failure. I have known some teachers who have re-formulated the problem, consulted 'the makers' and tried again. I have known others who have put it aside and come back to it later. Indeed, I have known few who have written off the idea or those who suggested it. It is more likely for them to write off themselves, or the school, or the present point in history. Even if they reject it they do not, I suggest, reject the imagination which led them to consider it possible. That possibility remains, maybe a little like a burr beneath the skin of a rhinoceros, to cause nagging discomfort and dissatisfaction with what is.

Green suggests that when something is taken up as a formula, a likely story of failure has begun. I used to think so, too. But so many teachers I have worked with have grown and been empowered from 'negotiating' beginnings which have been self-consciously formularistic that I need to wonder. Wondering leads me back to Vygotsky[7] and his writings about scientific and spontaneous concepts. Teachers have the job, according to Vygotsky, of introducing pre-formed 'scientific' concepts and challenging the learners to leap up from their platform of spontaneous, everyday concepts to make connections. He presents the picture of learners at first using the scientific concepts awkwardly and relatively empty of meaning. Gradually, through multiple applications and encounters in different contexts, the scientific concepts become invested with personal meaning until they are used spontaneously.

The intention of the learner to make sense, to switch to Polanyi's image[8], unlocks tacit powers which allow the learner to move to a higher level of consciousness and ability to act.

Crucial to the encounter between teacher and learners is, I believe, the *relationship* which exists while the learner is moving from formula to formulation. The teacher must indwell in the problems of the learner and be able to recreate in his or her mind the thoughts and feelings of one who is coming to this territory for the first time. The teacher (or the 'researcher') will ideally 'stay in there' to support, to encourage reflection, to explain interim failure, and to help the learner perceive any positive effects which are emerging.

The picture Green paints is likely to occur if the learner is not supported in this way.

If I had time and space, I could continue to complicate the story of how new ideas from research or elsewhere eventually come to be taken up.

I believed that I am involved in a continual struggle to *disconfirm* my present hard-won formulae which in more generous moments I call theories. I self-consciously struggle, as I am struggling now, to re-formulate. It is this view of the world and myself that I bring to my teaching. I recognise what ideas and formulae have done for me, at the same time fearing that a fixed formula will do for me.

In a long-term relationship with those whom I profess to teach, I will teach the need for alternating *tight* and *loose* construing of the world, a continual, empowering breaking free after closure. As a hit-and-run purveyor of new rhetoric and slogans, I am a menace.

What Next?

Theories of negotiation must grow within theories of society. Negotiation with children must be accompanied by negotiation with parents, administrators and politicians. Teachers must come to feel the power of documentation and production after reflection. Children must be 'taught' to negotiate.

NOTES

1. Ashton-Scholastic, 1982.
2. It should be noted that there is a great difference between those who wish to empower children to join their side and those who wish to empower children to work out what side, if any, they wish to fight on.
3. 'Reading the Whole Curriculum', this volume.

4. Dale Spender et al., *Learning to Lose*, Pergamon Press, London, 1981.

5. Henry Giroux has written compellingly on such issues in a fairly recent article: 'Hegemony, Resistance and the Paradox of Educational Reform', *Interchange*, Vol. 12, No. 2-3, 1981.

6. Bill Green, 'Theory and Practice: Introducing the Kewdale Project', April, 1982. (Unpublished ms.)

7. L.S. Vygotsky, *Thought and Language*, M.I.T. Press, 1962.

8. Michael Polanyi, *Personal Knowledge: Towards a Post-Critical Philosophy*, Routledge and Kegan Paul, 1958.

14

TEACHING AGAINST THE GRAIN

An address to the annual conference of the South Pacific Association for Teacher Education, in Canberra, 1984.

Only dead fish swim with the stream[1].

We are subjected to the production of truth through power and we cannot exercise power except through the production of truth.[2]

We are concerned, rather, with the insurrection of knowledges that are opposed primarily not to contents, methods or concepts of a science, but to the effects of the centralising powers which are linked to the institution and functioning of an organised scientific discourse within a society such as ours.[3]

...there is something else to which we are witness, and which we might describe as an *insurrection of subjugated knowledges.*[4]

Besides teaching, the only profession which has not codified its practices, in the sense of establishing commonly accepted principles and procedures, is prostitution. 'And a good thing, it is,' you might argue. 'Teaching is an art which defies codification. Serendipity, panache, style, idiosyncrasy, artistry and ingenuity are what teaching thrives on.' You may see teaching as a variegated impressionistic art form.

You may accordingly see codification of education as a lethal form of hardening of the categories; an attempt to establish the clinic in the classroom; a manifestation of 1984. As benevolent anarchists you may give three cheers for the chaos that gives you room to move.

Let me try to disturb such thinking a little. Do you think you could recognise a teaching act if you saw one? Could you identify a piece of work done by a student in school, as opposed to other kinds of work? If you could eavesdrop on language at work, without the benefit of visuals, could you identify school talk amongst other kinds of talk? I think, with confidence, that in most cases I could. So much for eccentricity and flair. You see, I have a *theory.*

The Teaching Habit

Codified it may not be, but teaching is probably the most massively habituated of all professions and the tertiary sector probably demonstrates this most dramatically. Most citizens in this country, for example, could give a convincing account of *how schools are*, and *what teachers do*. The teaching/learning game may not be written down but it is deeply inscribed in our minds and hearts. We *know* it, from the inside. And, I suggest, people have known it quintessentially ever since there were schools. It is so taken-for-granted that the few cosmetic changes we have tried over the years take on a falsely exaggerated aura of the spectacular in contrast with the ongoing frenzied ceremonial drumming of the school humdrum. We tend to be so intrigued by the superficial change that we do not see that it is the old habit with a new image. By and large, what were the individualised cartoon-embroidered worksheets of the open-space era but the former textbooks dismembered and re-deployed? Behaviourist psychology informed the textbooks and it simply powered on uninterrupted through the cards. That same behaviourism based on animal training permeates much of the 'new' computer software overlaid with complementary metaphors of seek-and-destroy, win-and-lose. Learning is an aggressive competition business.

The deep-seated habits of schooling have remained deep-seated because they work. They allow schools to do their job of socialising the citizenry into acceptable modes of behaviour and relating with values appropriate to the western capitalist 'way of life'. They allow schools to sort, 'level' and allocate. There is a common code and, indeed, a common curriculum at the deep level. Teaching as a genre has a recognisable grammar and distinct conventions.

Public Lies

A fascinating aspect of education, however, is that we do not acknowledge publicly what we do. We pretend, to each other, and to the community, to do something else. The rhetoric of systems bears little relationship to what happens. In Australia the rhetoric, which adds up to a public discourse, is established in curriculum guidelines, discussion papers, policy statements and various manifestos endorsed by Directors-General and Ministers of Education. It purports that schools are institutions of learning; places that foster personal development, independence, rationality, democracy and co-operation.

In the public mediated spiel of our profession, we elevate dreams to the level of intentions and facts and thereby commit our teachers to collusion in hypocrisy, condemning them to varying degrees of guilt, shame or cynicism.

Meanwhile, at the local level parents, who know what stakes their children are running for, tend to talk with teachers about what really happens, and what really matters; about discipline, homework, marks and job aspirations.

In South Australia, if teachers concertedly practised the injunctions of the policy document 'Our Schools and Their Purposes' we would have an educational revolution, just as we would, if the Schools Commission plans for Participation and Equity were effected in schools, or the Victorian Green papers. Interestingly such documents have very few 'teeth'. They are signposted wishes without the state machinery to enforce them. Thus schools are shaped by what society expects (as opposed to the Department's espousals); by what is ultimately valued and assessed; and by what teachers *can* do.

Indeed, the system has inbuilt 'teeth' which all but ensure the non-adoption of its own proposed innovations. Teachers are disciplined and 'normalised' in various ways. There are, for instance, subtle and not so subtle promotional and peer opinion penalties for risk-taking teachers who seek to increase student powers and rights. Furthermore, just as the working classes can be shown in various ways to collude in their own oppression, so students often tyrannise teachers back into modes of teaching which do not require them to exert mental labour and which keep them ignorant. The fragmentation of time into brief lessons bites into intentions to explore and speculate, reinforcing habits of dictation and recitation. Teachers on all sides are enticed to go with the grain.

Interrupting the Discourse

If you find the foregoing depiction of education to be a little sweeping, a little bleak, a distortion of what you think happens, remember that this is a paper about the importance of interruption; about reading our more precious fictions *against* the grain to expose absurdities, false constructions and incongruencies. My oppositional reading of teaching leads me to such provocations. It does not mean that I see no strategic gains in education; it is not to belittle dreaming; and it is certainly not to underestimate the many teachers who, while compelled to play various games to preserve their livelihood, still resist and subvert creatively in the privacy of their own classrooms. My counter reading does help me, however, to understand the courage and energy required by teachers to interrupt the many rituals which waft like musak through the halls of education.

Returning to my opening point, I want to argue that to assist teachers' liberation it would help if we began by codifying and explaining, if possible, what actually happens in the act of teaching. I have suggested that there is a clear code but that it remains unarticulated so that false representations made by systems and schools go relatively unchallenged. Because it is unarticulated, it is not easily accessible to critique, to deconstruction, to productive interruption, and therefore to systematic and deliberate improvement. Because we have not espoused the theory behind our present practice, we tend to remain spellbound by habit. And there is the strong possibility that, having developed the habit of not looking closely, we may be inclined ingenuously and unwittingly to tell lies about what we do.

There are various options for doing something constructive about this. One view of society and power relationships suggests that a ruling hegemony generated out of the economic interests of the wealthy class is imposed on the lower orders and determines local relationships. Therefore the attack must be directed at the wider political-economic structures. A counter view, argued by the late Michel Foucault, suggests that micro relationships built up at the local level are eventually organised into ensembles of power which take on the aura of what is right and true at a global level. These are held in place by an accepted high-status discourse, or orthodoxy. Should Foucault's analysis be accurate or even partly accurate, then in education we might well begin to unravel the given orthodoxy in *local contexts* if we find the established orthodoxy oppressive or toxic. The task in education is made more complex, I believe, because the official discourse of education, as purveyed by systems, is a front, behind which a 'crypto' discourse effectively rules (i.e. what everyone *knows* about education). The local irritant antilanguages of teachers, therefore, must be opposed to this crypto ruling discourse, not to the overt decoy discourse of the system. Indeed, in many cases, the words of the system can be appropriated by teachers to give strength to their opposition. Much of what the system says is already in opposition to what schools do and has a quite considerable subversive potential.

The Consequences of Opposition

In reading education against the grain, one could go in at any level to interrupt and expose complacencies which have been ingrained through habit. One could, for instance, disassemble the notion of class year-levels and reveal its pathologies. My recent research has required micro-analysis of one teacher and one class over an extended period. The teacher in question would be categorised, in comparison with most of her colleagues, as 'different' if not 'perverse'. For instance, she negotiates tasks with students, hands over planning responsibilities, employs group work, uses oral productions as alternative bases of assessment, and permits movement within established rules.

Within her school she is already teaching against the grain, but both she and I in watching replays of video-taped lessons can see many ways in which 'institutional contamination' is carried into the classroom. Alert as this teacher is, and articulate in her personal counter theories of education, she is likely from moment to moment to drop into modes of relating, controlling and shaping which belong to the set of educational constructs that she is trying to overthrow. This is not at all surprising, since her socialisation into education through school, tertiary institutions and now in school again, has been saturated with reinforcements of such constructs as 'teacher is the centre of attention', 'quiet work is good work', 'every error should be corrected', and so on.

Furthermore, the degree to which she actually and effectively opposes these constructs is the degree to which she is considered to be educationally 'ill' if not insane. She recounts, for instance, a time some years ago when, experimenting with group work which generated some noise, she became, unknown to her, the subject of concerned closet-talk between certain members of the school hierarchy because 'she was not coping'. She was innocently going about her work, quite excited by the achievements of her students as they struggled with her to meet the challenges of new structures and demands, while a rising tide of patronising sympathy grew amongst her colleagues. She had the educational equivalent of 'B.O.'. When through the frankness of a colleague this was revealed to her, she was appalled. For a time, she doubted her own educational sanity and reverted to normality. Thankfully, her admirable courage and rebelliousness reasserted itself, bolstered now with new wisdom about the institution of education.

Even when one has the will and courage to begin teaching against the grain, it is necessary to go further, to confront the problem of *students* who begin to read school against the grain. If the teacher succeeds in demonstrating to the class the benefits of a different classroom style, then it is likely that there will be insurrections of this new knowledge in the classes of other teachers. The students will begin to question and make demands. There are usually patent consequences for such impudence. In order to arm students to cope with the consequences of contradiction and complaint, the teacher must delicately teach the politics of tact without appearing disloyal to her colleagues. Students must be taught how to question 'with respect', to suggest without offence, and to endure, without losing sight of the ultimate goal, when they have no power to transform.

By way of illustration of deep-seated hypnotic features of schooling, I shall now briefly present and discuss some things which I have discovered by standing critically against the flow of the teaching tide.

Ticks, Praise and Good-Work Stamps

The innocent tick is not so innocent. In education it is as natural as the air we breathe, and yet, I suggest, its toxicity is high. What is its philosophy, its psychology and its politics? Philosophically, the tick reinforces the view that there is truth and that someone knows it; psychologically, it is directly related to Pavlov and his dogs; politically, it is an instrument of power, control and distribution of wealth (if we consider ticks to be promissory notes for Marks).

In all respects the tick is the teacher's seal of authority. The licence to tick is granted at the point of graduation. It is similar to the right to hear confession in that it confers on the teacher the divinity of judging good and bad and assessing penalty. Every tick implies a cross and every cross underlines painfully the absence of a tick. The tick therefore is an instrument destined to create anxiety. Always niggling at the edges of one's present satisfaction with the awarded tick is the contemplation of a future where it is withheld. As one nears the end of schooling, the poignancy of ticking on to Year 12 can see those crossed over into the workforce coping with a society where the ticking industry is very frugal indeed.

The tick is also the equivalent of a pedagogical grunt of pleasure. It is a very lazy form of instructional intercourse. In terms of meaning or capacity to assist the learner to transcend or go beyond, it is relatively impotent. Indeed, rather than providing new conceptions, it conserves and confirms the already achieved. There is an invitation in its very fibre for more of the same.

It is, of course, highly addictive for the recipient and often leads supplicants into various forms of prostitution, such as sticking together strips of other people's words.

Above all, it demands that the learner engage with, and focus on, authority. The teacher has paradigms, standards, models, algorithms and facts to which the novice must approximate. Knowledge exists outside the learner but can be found by following a trail of ticks, presuming one knows where the ticks are pointing.

A clear indication of the helplessness that attends rampant ticking is the student who hands up a test or an essay or an assignment with crossed fingers. He or she really *does not know* whether it is likely to be any good. Teacher, *deus ex machina*, will decide.

Ticking is a member of the wider family of Praise which includes good-work stamps, early minutes, glowing remarks in reports, and a considerable armoury of privileges most of which owe their inspiration to behaviourist psychology or religious adoration. Being adored is a very demanding and precarious business. Note also that 'Praise' comes from the Latin word for 'price' or 'prize'. There is a price to pay for prizes. 'Uneasy lies the head that wears the crown.'

When prizes are publicly distributed in classrooms, their worth is directly proportional to the number of people who do not get them. Prizes increase fear on the one hand and despair on the other.

Very young children, let us say in practising a somersault, do not require praise. They simply need *acknowledgement* that they have done a somersault. Over time, however, we socialise them into expecting more.

The question arises as to whether Praise can be used for peaceful and good purposes.

Perhaps the genuine expression of pleasure *in private* is acceptable and justifiable, and sufficient?

Asking Questions

Can you imagine a classroom where the teacher *never* asks questions or at least only asks questions where he or she really needs the information? After reading school questions against the grain, I am inclined to invite teachers to declare a moratorium on traditional questioning as an experiment for a few months. I believe that quite remarkable positive changes would occur in the dynamics of the classroom, that learning power would increase, and that teachers would begin to teach at quite different points in the programme.

Having observed classrooms over many years, I am struck by the power of questions to control, shape and direct. A very high proportion of questions in schools come from the teachers as opposed to the students, who tend to be left with the 'when-do-you-want-it-handed-in?' type of question. Of these teachers' questions, most are bogus questions if we define a question as a request for information or opinion where the asker does not have the information or seeks an opinion without knowing what it will be.

That is, the teachers ask questions to which they know the answers; for checking to see if they are being followed; to create productive tension ('you might be asked next'); to keep the class awake; and to move the exposition to its premeditated conclusions.

Thus, one can see questions being asked by the teacher *to further his or her experiment* which is usually 'how to get through the required work and achieve good results'.

Taking a distanced stance in classrooms, it can be seen that students are 'powered' at by barrages of questions which operate variously as electric fences, invitations to compete for prizes, prods, signposts and clues.

Where one finds a teacher who has made a study (personally or formally) of questioning, some improvement may found in that more *open* as opposed to *closed* questions are asked. Yet, a closer examination of the open question, the genuine invitation to speculation, shows that we are still witnessing a quite formidable power play. Speculation is invited on questions and territory *defined by the teacher*. The drift is still 'come with me' and 'attend to what I think is important'.

So, if there is unhealthiness in teacher questioning, how does one assess health?

My learning theory leads me to the fairly uncontroversial view that question-asking in areas of the problematic is essential to deliberate learning. A sign of health and deliberate learning in schools would then be classes where students ask questions about what they do not know and where teachers and others try to answer them.

A revolution will have occurred when teachers change the question-asking balance, *even* to a 50:50 sharing.

Programming

At music concerts we attend knowing what the programme will be in broad terms. When we arrive, we have access to a more detailed account of what we are about to receive. Restaurants specify an elective programme. Within limits we may influence our own eating programme. A programme is by definition a public written announcement of a sequence of events.

Schools are places of continual programming and sequencing. One of the most crucial times of the year is the establishing of the time-table and the allocating of classes. Another crucial time which pre-dates this is the time of decision-making about what subjects will be on the programme. In most cases, there have been prior choices about what kind of course will be offered within the subject field and quite often course outlines, written away from the school, are adopted.

Course offerings tend to be fairly stable and non-negotiable from year to year in the majority of cases. Curriculum review on a large scale is rare. Timetabling has traditionally been the province of one or two senior administrators. The timetable is often used as a means of explaining why certain teaching allocations have to be made. Apart from timetable tyranny, there is more or less negotiation with teachers depending on the school when it comes to allocation.

Eventually a teacher faces the task of programming within these broader programme frames. He or she, at worse, may be allocated a course written elsewhere, to teach to a class at a level not desired, at times which are not ideal, towards objectives or tests which are considered inappropriate. At best, he or she, through consultation, may have been allocated a desired course with a desired class with a fair degree of autonomy to devise content, processes and objectives.

Both these teachers, at worst and at best, however, have the task of programming details within their *assigned* challenge.

All this is by way of tracing where the eventual programme put before the clients, the students, comes from in order to assess how much they know about it and what power they have to influence it.

Good teachers and mere functionaries alike, it seems to me after many years of observation and talking with them, tend to programme *in private* in terms of the scope of the whole year and for the week-to-week schedules. Some of these teachers divulge some or part of what they have in mind. Many others, apart from giving some broad directions, tend to spring the programme on the clients, surprising them even from day to day.

As an extended experiment, I have asked hundreds of students in hundreds of classes at all levels to tell me what they are doing, why they are doing it, and what is coming next. With very few exceptions, I must conclude that compared with music goers or restaurant patrons students are in the dark about the programme. At its bleakest, schooling appears to be a process by which teachers who have had very little say in the school programme present programmes that children guess at. The best of these programmes are stimulating and presented by talented motivators, but there is usually an unspoken assumption that the programme as planned will be done. That is, with respect to programming the clients are more acted upon than acted.

Now if we want students deliberately to learn what we think is worthwhile, it seems only commonsense that they are more likely to do this if *they know* what we want and how we intend to teach them. If they share our designs, they can cooperate with us to bring them into being.

If they do not know our designs, then we are placed in a very dominant position of having secrets which we eke out piecemeal while our clients variously suppose, recline or decline.

As programmers, ins this sense, we are purveyors of rat psychology. We need to bring to this kind of regime a cunning of enticements, sanctions and probes. The intention is ours and the challenge is to woo the students to become participants in our privately composed fantasy.

Given the prevalence of this kind of regime, you can imagine what would happen if teachers started to programme against the grain. In my own recent research I have watched a class initially reject the implementation of a new programming practice. The teacher, imbued with a desire to empower students by explaining her intentions in great specificity and by inviting co-programming within clear boundaries, found that the students *did not listen* when she explained the programme. It seemed that, habituated to waiting to be told what to do, they put their minds into neutral while she gave a rationale for the work. I tested this by interviewing selected students after each lesson. Clearly they did not see co-programming as a legitimate school activity.

A lesser teacher would have abandoned the experiment but this teacher, recognising that she had to break through the habit barrier, persisted. Slowly the students' reading of the curriculum and their ownership of the planning improved. By the end of the year they will be quite proficient planners and programmers in their own right. They will know much more powerfully how to indwell in the minds of teachers and how to influence programmes in their own interests.

I hope by now that you have got my drift – or should I say, 'counter drift'. It had been my initial intention also to plough against the habits of correction, against the notion of successful learning experiences, against helping, against motivation, against the habits of homework and against the school surveillance industry. As it is, I shall leave you to imagine what I might have said.

By my own example, I should now urge you to read me against the grain if, by chance, I have begun to carry you along with my ardour. I should also read myself against the grain. Notice, for instance, my selective reading of the school, bolstered by seductively mixed metaphor, in order to paint the required picture of mindlessness in education. Had I decided instead to deliver a paper celebrating teacher struggle, I might just as easily have composed a moving account of the brilliance of 'poly-attentive' teachers able to make thousands of delicate decisions each day and superb in their capacity to understand the problems of their students.[5]

Then again I could even now write a piece debunking the exaggerated importance I have given to the tick. Surely most teachers use the tick in conjunction with a whole range of devices to help them cope with the problem of communicating efficiently to large numbers of students. How can it be so sinister, if the user does not have sinister intentions?

In reading myself against the grain, I would also need to expose the discourse, the version of the truth, which drives my thinking. I would need to place myself in the camp of anti-behaviourism, with an epistemology that sees knowledge as constructed by knowers, with a view of teachers as researchers and scientists, and with a somewhat romantic vision of a questioning, cooperating, interruptive society. My work is polemical, tendentious and palpably designed to unsettle.

With all these readings, counter-readings and meta-counter-readings, what have I said? Let me summarise.

Summary

Education is not codified. There are clearly established codes operating in education but they are not written down. This make it hard for us to examine their 'rightness'. In the absence of codification of what we do (if you like, in the absence of a science of teaching), we tell ourselves that we are practising the *art* of teaching.

'Are' respects each person's right to practise his or her own art. Criticism of method, style or content is, in this context, almost an obscenity. Certainly, one artist to another must be very tactful. Ironically, however, teaching under the umbrella of art is massively habituated and stereotypical. Take away the decorations, and teaching from decade to decade is largely reproduction.

If teaching were codified, there would be the possibility of deliberate experimentation in order to question the established codes and conventions. The science cannot be advanced because we cannot see the frontier.

As it is, the embedded codes carry us along largely unregarded while we compose personal and public discourses about what we think we do, or what we would like to think we do, or what we would like other people to think we do. These 'decoy' discourses create within the profession various distortions. If we begin to believe them, they will move us actually to see supportive evidence in our classrooms and to disregard unpalatable cues. If we don't believe them, we are forced to lead a double teaching life, tinged with varying degrees of frustration, guilt or shame. Furthermore, serious diversions of teacher energy are called upon by schools in order to sustain illusions. Many hours are spent in the writing of policies, manifestos, submissions and success stories. Committees, largely muffled by tact, skirt around specific instances of noxious teaching and deal with 'meta' issues.

In order to break these various complicities of tact and illusion, in order to liberate teachers from the tyranny of a decadent discourse, I advocate a revolution in explicitness and honesty which will require, initially, concerted perversity and courage. We need to call education at all levels *as it is*. We need to make opaque many of the presently transparent follies and absurdities that flow through our system. And perhaps the best technique for doing this is to begin swimming against the flow.

Of course, exposing the absurdity is not to exorcise it. Having taught against the grain, and having discovered the source of some oppression, pragmatics and survival may require us to return to the oppressive regime. But at least now, it will be a witting compromise containing a time bomb. The thought has been seeded and hence, as Michel Foucault says:

> Even before exhorting or merely sounding an alarm, thought, at the level of its existence, in its very dawning, is in itself an action – a perilous act.[6]

NOTE

1. Malcolm Muggeridge!
2. Michel Foucault, *Knowledge/Power*, The Harvester Press, Brighton, 1980 (p. 43).
3. *Ibid.* (p. 84)
4. *Ibid.* (p. 81)
5. See 'English Teaching: Art and Science', this volume.
6. Michel Foucault, from the preface, *Language, Counter Memory, Practice (selected essays and interviews by Michel Foucault)*, Cornell University Press, New York, 1977.

SECTION THREE
On Teacher Education

15

TEACHERS LEARNING

The text which follows can be seen as a synthesis of Garth's views both on teachers as learners and on language development. It was prepared as a contribution to a comprehensive book on language and education. For various reasons the book was not completed. Hence, this text is published here for the first time.

Specialists are becoming better at describing the ideal in the field of language and education, as they learn more about how language is learnt and how it changes with contexts and purposes. Official curriculum guides now state admirable goals and present a vision of children emerging from our classrooms as confident, literate, independent thinkers equipped with the ability to solve problems and make transformations using the media and methods of the various subject-disciplines. Even where the implications for language development are not already stated, the values expressed are in line with the insights of the linguistic revolution of the sixties and seventies which showed language learners to be very much inquirers and initiators in their own language development. Between the advocacy and the action, however, falls a curtain. It is a curtain of questions and doubts, a veil of 'Yes, buts':

- 'Yes, but how can you achieve intensive oral language use with a class of twenty-five?'
- 'Yes, but what if I'm the only teacher using these approaches?'
- 'Yes, but our school assessment scheme does not value these things.'
- 'Yes, but it is so different from the way I was taught and so I don't know where to begin.'
- 'Yes, but what does it mean in practice to set up situations which will make new language demands?'
- 'Yes, but I was not trained in linguistics and I don't know what to look for.'
- 'Yes, but schools value control and discipline and quiet and all this group work will lead to chaos.'

- 'Yes, but the parents want us to teach by the old methods.'
- 'Yes, but I haven't got time for exploration in and through language. I've got to get through the course.'
- 'Yes, but I'm not a creative and outgoing kind of person.'
- 'Yes, but I've also got to contend with a class of mixed abilities, different socio-economic backgrounds, different countries of origin and different aspirations.'

Etc.

Such responses are not to be seen as mere rationalisation of failure to act. They are, by and large, the realities of pragmatists who cannot indulge in unfettered imaginings of what might be. They underline the fact that teaching is a constrained and contested act.

The War With Contexts

Teachers are continually at war with *contexts*, trying to make them hospitable to their intentions. Classrooms without air-conditioning, inflexible timetables, resources representing a discredited view of language, school policies which value correctness over sense, societal pressures (to go back or go forward or go somewhere else), system's injunctions made flesh by inspectors and others, university entrance requirements (felt even in Year One), and the value systems of western society itself – all such micro and macro influences bear in upon the teacher and the class where the drama of the curriculum is enacted.

Eventually, no matter how brilliant and resourceful the teacher, the classroom action will always represent some kind of uneasy armistice between personal knowledge and intentions on the one hand and contextual and interpersonal demands on the other. Relationships between principal and staff, teacher and teacher, teacher and children, children and children, and teacher and parent, require each teacher to test potential acts carefully against the inevitable boundaries of tact, ethics, resources, rights and responsibilities.

This all amounts to the observation that understanding about language development is but one factor in shaping what teachers do. Many of our graduates from tertiary institutions are entering schools with a sound theoretical grasp of principles of language development but, without the ability to apply such principles in complex and variable contexts, theirs could be an education for disillusionment and eventual cynicism.

This paper speaks directly to teachers in training and those teachers in service who wish to transform 'Yes, but...' into 'Yes, and therefore...', with respect to new classroom practice consistent with what they now know about language development. After presenting features of the ideal classroom for language development and their implications for teacher knowledge and skills, five case studies of teachers learning will be presented and analysed in order to indicate ways in which teachers may progress from their present practices towards the ideal. From this analysis a set of guidelines for learning about language teaching will be constructed.

The ideal as presented here will, of course, change over time as we all learn more. Movement towards the ideal is only achieved through continuing transformations and testing in practice.

Developing as a Teacher

As language learners compose texts in oral and written language, constructing passages of meaning, so teachers learn progressively how to compose teaching acts which include the planning of units of work as well as their enactment with children. What teachers compose in their heads or on paper is eventually jointly negotiated and acted out with children. Just a language always operates in contexts which contain, shape and demand, so does teaching. Just as meaning in language is jointly constructed by participants in the exchange, so meaning in teaching is jointly constructed by teachers and children.

In teaching exchanges, the teacher tends to make the major initiations but there is ample research to show that students can and do dramatically affect what is taught and how it is taught. Curriculum construction may begin away from the students, but the moment the teacher enters the classroom, the intentions of the children are brought to bear on the teaching/learning act.

Just as in conversation one continually monitors the reception and interpretation of one's working, so in teaching the teacher 'reads' the unfolding curriculum in order to evaluate what is happening and to predict what might happen.

In the beginning, intending or novice teachers may operate somewhat like a beginning reader, going through some of the motions of the act but not necessarily comprehending a great deal. The first teaching acts of the novice may have some features of 'well-formed' teaching (such as: question asking, blackboard work and expectations of response), but may fail to engage the learners.

Much as young children have been shown to progress through a series of interim grammars, teachers may be seen to move through progressive stages of the 'grammar' of teaching, creating, over time, more and more subtly rule-governed curriculum sequences which have predictable shape and cohesiveness. Just as the young gradually learn how language varies with situation and purpose, developing communicative competence, so teachers learn how to vary their teaching with situation and purpose, thereby developing teaching competence.

What I am advocating is a *functional approach* to learning about language teaching where, from the earliest stages, intending or practising teachers work on the construction of *teaching sequences* in authentic *contexts* and *settings* for recognisable *purposes*. More and more subtle curriculum making is achieved through continuing *construction, reflection* on that construction, and consideration of the teaching of others in ever expanding new contexts.

Specifically in the field of language in education, teachers will bring to their curriculum construction what they presently understand about language, language learning, and language in use, as well as knowledge about their own capacities, human behaviour, schools, time management, resources, and so on.

The Ideal Classroom for Language Development

On the basis of what is now considerable research, it is possible to construct an image of the ideal classroom for language development. Such a classroom, when knowledge about language has been translated into appropriate methodology, would be, at least: active and interactive, collaborative, functional and purposive, exploratory, reflective, multi-modal, negotiated, contextually supportive, observed and tracked, experience-based, text-aware, conceptually demanding, unbounded and cumulative.

Each of these characteristics requires specific knowledge and skills in the area of general teaching and with respect to language in use. Each raises critical questions for teachers who aspire towards the ideal.

ACTIVE AND INTERACTIVE

Classroom Characteristics

The children use language actively in practical ways to produce effects and to get things done. In the process they interact with their teacher(s), fellow students, other classes and other adults as they construct meaning.

Knowledge and Skills

The teacher knows that language is learnt in interaction and must be actively manipulated by the learner. He/she knows how to allow for optimum activity and interaction without reaching disruptive levels of noise and movement.

Challenges

The conventions of traditional teaching require class teacher control of language interactions in classrooms. The norm is teacher 'out front' and children answering, in turn, according to teacher requirements. Silence is valued and bad reports often refer to 'talking in class'. In constructing new teaching sequences consistent with the need for action and interaction, the teacher has the challenge of convincing parents, other staff members and the children themselves that new classroom conventions are needed. The classroom has to be transformed into a new order which patently works to promote better language learning and learning through language. Such a classroom will have its own new distinctive rhythms and patterns of whole-class, small-group and one-to-one language exchanges.

COLLABORATIVE

Classroom Characteristics

Children work together in pairs, groups and as a class on projects to research, to make and to publish materials. They share and cooperatively evaluate each other's work. In working together and sharing, their language is extended and challenged as they negotiate, contradict and compromise.

Knowledge and Skills

The teacher knows that language is learnt more readily in a purposive community of language users, and that group problem-solving makes many demands on the resources of language. He/she knows how to organise different kinds of groups for different purposes, how to develop children's ability to work in groups, and how to manage time and resources needed by collaborating learners.

Challenges

The collaborative classroom contrasts with a privatised regime where sharing is often construed as 'cheating', where the injunction to 'get on with your work' is customary, and where the teacher is sole arbiter on the quality of individual assignments. The collaborative classroom requires considerable shifts in responsibility. The teacher throws more responsibility onto groups for their own discipline for the quality of their work. Specifically, children will need to be taught in detail how to work in groups for differing purposes and how to monitor their own group dynamics.

EXPERIENCED-BASED

Classroom Characteristics

Whenever children are engaged in new language learning, they activate what they already know and relate it to the new. Often, they experience at first hand that which they are to investigate. This may take the form of an excursion or, more vicariously, a film or an enactment.

Knowledge and Skills

Teachers are aware that children can only operate on what they know through experience. This requires developed skills in activating what children already know and can do in order to provide bridges into new territories. New experiences create the need for new thinking and new language.

Challenges

A good deal of wasteful teaching occurs where teachers do not rigorously check what the children already know before they begin a new unit. Learning power is much diminished when the teaching process does not allow learners to have their present related learnings acknowledged and legitimated as entry points to the new. Teachers operating on this understanding will clarify present learning bases *and* develop ways of extending these bases.

TEXT-AWARE

Classroom Characteristics

Children are encouraged to read and make texts (oral and written) and then, when appropriate, to talk about the characteristics and conventions of the text. Their main drive is always, however, to make sense of the text, to understand its meaning. Whenever new texts are introduced, children are helped to approach them deliberately and systematically.

Knowledge and Skills

The teacher knows that children before age five already have a language to comment on language, and that they have also acquired a good deal of knowledge about language. It is his/her task as a teacher to extend and formalise this. This requires the teacher to be capable of close commentary on text and to teach children how to recognise and use features of text.

Challenges

Just as teachers call upon students to be deliberately and critically conscious of the text of the curriculum (through negotiation), they will in a 'text-aware' classroom spend considerable time in 'casing' new kinds of oral and written texts which are brought into the classroom. Much as the naturalist will deliberately and systematically wish to 'place' new species, so the student needs to get a purchase on the special features of, say, a science textbook, as opposed to a novel or an advertisement or a joke.

Thus the classroom will from time to time resemble a laboratory where new specimen texts are examined or old texts re-visited to reveal new insights.

FUNCTIONAL AND PURPOSIVE

Classroom Characteristics

Children read, write, speak and listen for purposes which they understand and intend to accomplish. The functions and purposes will reflect language functions and purposes outside classrooms, and will be continually extended as the children' language resources are developed.

Knowledge and Skills

The teacher knows about the functions of language and has a sound grasp of the linguistic demands inherent in different functions and purposes. This enables him/her to arrange contexts and situations which demand that language functions in certain ways to serve certain purposes. The teacher is able to modify language challenges to suit the differing capacities of individual students.

Challenges

This classroom contrasts with the 'deferred gratification' model where children habitually practise constituent parts of language texts so that eventually they will be able to put them together for real purposes. 'Deferred gratification' works on the principle that you may not understand why you are doing these exercises but one day it will all make sense. The functional classroom is based on the premise that language is best learnt in use for purposes where the *consequences* will be potent sources of information about how to do it better next time. The challenge is to enact classroom sequences where the consequences are not ticks and crosses or good work stamps but bona fide *responses* in terms of actions, or answers which take account of what the student *means*. A litmus test is to ask students what they are doing and why. If they respond in terms of 'this is what teacher has set today' rather than in terms of 'this is what I'm intending to do and this is how I'll know if it works', then it is likely that the classroom serves the functions, purposes and intentions of the teacher. If children are not to be more acted upon than acting, they need to be allowed opportunities to initiate and to affect the course of events.

EXPLORATORY

Classroom Characteristics

Children use reading, writing, speaking and listening to serve their thinking and formulating as they come to grips with new information, ideas and tasks. They are encouraged to make personal notes, to talk tentatively about emerging notions, and to seek out information which may extend their understanding.

Knowledge and Skills

The teacher appreciates the investigative function of language and knows that language and thinking are dynamically interdependent. Therefore he/she creates opportunity for exploratory language use and actively teaches children how to use language in the formulation of new ideas. He/she also knows that this kind of language should not be subjected to judgemental remarks with respect to its form.

Challenges

It is possible in many classrooms for children to gain rewards through recitation, through what Vygotsky has called 'empty verbalisation', where 'correct' formulae and formulations conceal conceptual bankruptcy. The exploratory classroom values *understanding*, what children *can say and do* as a result of their explorations, as they find themselves in similar but new contexts.

The challenge for the teacher is to construct a script in which the learners will be able to use their own familiar language to grasp the unfamiliar and to absorb it. This may require considerable shifts in the kinds of language 'allowed' in schools. Where dialect and the rich vernacular are outlawed, exploratory learning through language may also be outlawed.

A good test to ascertain the strength of an exploratory classroom is to take a count of the number of student-initiated questions being asked (as opposed to teacher-questioning).

REFLECTIVE

Classroom Characteristics

Children reflect upon and evaluate what they have learnt, how well language is working for them and how it works. They also reflect upon the different ways in which others use language, including reflections about different dialects and registers.

Knowledge and Skills

The teacher encourages learning about language through meta-linguistic commentary on language used or observed. This requires a working knowledge of linguistics, psycholinguistics and socio-linguistics so that the teacher can appropriately introduce concepts about language in use. Skill in shifting linguistic prejudices (e.g. with respect to dialectal difference) is required.

Challenges

If the overriding intention is to 'get through the course', the unfolding drama of the classroom will tend to be characterised by intensive presentations of *practice and production business* and *testing* where the test is a kind of coda signalling the end of a unit and heralding the beginning of the next. Depending on comments on the test and the process of 'going through the test' afterwards, there may be some opportunity for learners to reflect but it will be reflection in a regime where the 'pace is on'.

Where the teacher values joint reflection both during the process of learning new work and at the conclusion of a unit, there will be a different valuing of time in relation to content. The content may be covered more slowly to allow time for reflection and speculation, but theoretically there should be less need for later *revision* than necessary under the contrasting regime.

In constructing a 'reflective' programme, the teacher will need to develop a 'feel' for the appropriate patterns of planning, acting and reflecting from moment to moment and from day to day.

MULTI-MODAL

Classroom Characteristics

Children practise all four modes of reading, writing, speaking and listening and within this modes they experience a wide range of 'genres'. For example, they write notes, letters, stories, lists, reports, etc. and they read a wide range of texts. They also use a range of other communication media (enactment, film/video, dance, art, etc.).

Knowledge and Skills

The teacher knows that each of the four language modes interpenetrate and support each other, but also that each requires different capacities which need to be specifically developed. He/she also knows that new skills need to be developed with respect to each new kind of 'text' within each mode. Language potential is also stretched through transformations in and through other media. The teacher requires skills in programming for a range of social transactions covering the spectrum of modes and media.

Challenges

Classrooms and schools tend to be language-bound institutions. Traditionally, even within language itself they have tended to be institutions where, predominantly, teachers talk and children listen and read. Children are overwhelming assessed through the written mode.

Jerome Bruner has cogently argued that each time we apply a different medium (e.g. talk, drawing, enactment, model-making, diagramming, etc.) to an object or a body of knowledge, we intensify our knowledge and understanding of that which we are exploring.

The challenge to teachers, then, is to extend the opportunities of learners to apply a wide range of media (beyond language) in the exploration of the course content. Within language itself, a balanced use of reading, writing, speaking and listening is required. In particular, assessment through the oral mode in addition to writing needs to become part of the teaching repertoire.

NEGOTIATED

Classroom Characteristics

Children and teachers negotiate in two ways. What is meant needs continually to be negotiated. What is to be done and how it is to be done are also subject to negotiation to the point where children understand, accept and intend, and where teachers are aware of the constraints and aspirations of the children. At any time in the programme children and teacher can be seen in the process of re-negotiating and clarifying.

Knowledge and Skills

The teacher knows that there can be no direct transmission of his or her meanings to the learners, and that understanding must be built up collaboratively with them through a process of continuing checking and modification. The teacher also knows that if the children do not intend to learn or are unaware of what is expected of them, they will tend to be at odds with the teacher's intentions. Therefore he or she knows how to negotiate tasks and process to ensure maximum ownership. This requires the ability to teach students how to negotiate.

Challenges

A traditional and widely accepted model of programming involves the teacher or faculty planning a sequence of work which is then applied in the classroom. In this model, the learners *receive* what has been prepared, with little chance to affect the nature of the content, the processes, the pacing of the evolution.

A negotiated classroom will at least require the teacher to be quite explicit about plans at the beginning and then to seek continuing feedback from the learners as to its effectiveness during the process. A more advanced negotiator will develop methods of allowing the learners *to co-plan the curriculum* to the point where they are involved in helping to recommend and provide resources, in suggesting learning paths and even in the setting and assessing of assignments.

One test of the negotiated classroom is to observe it when the teacher is absent. If the learners continue purposefully with shared understanding of tasks and goals, the process is working.

CONTEXTUALLY SUPPORTIVE

Classroom Characteristics

Wherever possible, when children are learning to do things requiring new language they are immersed in a 'community' where that task is modelled, where examples are abundant, where use is intensive and where accompanying explorations are available. Contexts and settings are as authentic as possible.

Knowledge and Skills

The teacher knows that to practice skills clinically, away from context and purpose, is to jeopardise learning. He/she also knows that context is often rich in supporting clues *to assist in meaning making*. Access to example of others at work assists the apprentice learner. This requires a teacher who has skills in establishing a 'community' of workers in a setting which enriches and supports the tasks at hand. It also requires a teacher who can demonstrate and explain what is being done.

Challenges

Clearly, classrooms are institutionalised and specialised sites of learning but they can be transformed so that, in many ways, they simulate authentic out-of-school settings.

For instance, furniture can be arranged to support personal writing sessions, classroom decoration can reflect current tasks and topics, and excursions can help to widen the contexts of learning.

The less attenuated the teacher/learning interactions and exchanges, the more likely that learning will 'stick'. The challenge is to translate potent features of out-of-school contexts into the micro-society of the institution.

OBSERVED AND TRACKED

Classroom Characteristics

Children engage in one-to-one consultations with the teacher, discuss reading and writing, and share evaluations of their present progress. This helps to shape the directions and purposes of further classroom work.

Knowledge and Skills

The teacher knows that it is necessary to note and track the unfolding language and learning potential of the children. This requires skills in analysis of language in use, and pre-supposes that the teacher has a 'map' of language development which will guide him or her in encouraging the learner to attempt appropriate new tasks.

Challenges

The traditional classroom is documented before and after; before in a programme which records intentions and after in a 'marks book' where test results are entered with or without remarks.

In an observed and tracked classroom the challenge is to develop ways of recording and checking during the process of learning to enrich the data upon which further planning is based. In appraising work either in draft or in its finished form, the teacher will be looking to *diagnose the present learning strategies, cues and miscues being applied* as well as to assess *present performance*. (Folders of children's work, teacher journals, sample tapes of group work etc. may be part of the teacher's tracking and recording repertoire.)

CONCEPTUALLY DEMANDING

Classroom Characteristics

The children are continually being introduced to content, subject matter and tasks which require them to develop new concepts and to modify their existing constructs. There is a strong 'problem' oriented flavour to the classroom, requiring hypothesising and exploration.

Knowledge and Skills

The teacher knows that language development goes hand in hand with cognitive development. This then requires the teacher to select and introduce worthwhile and challenging content, potentially relatable, but sufficiently above the children's heads to require them to stretch their thinking and their language.

Challenges

Given the wide range of language performance and previous experiences, even in a selected or 'streamed' class, it is very difficult indeed to ensure that each child in the class is subject to conceptual demands.

A crucial part in the composition of any teaching sequence script is the selection of the content or territory to be explored and the texts which will be used to illuminate that content. Ideally there will be many possible entry points to the new territory and many possible challenges inherent in it, so that the students will be able to negotiate learning pathways and goals which will be stretching without being daunting.

UNBOUNDED

Classroom Characteristics

Children are using language and reflecting upon it in all areas of the curriculum, inside and outside the classroom. People from the community often visit the classroom and the class often goes out into the community. Children are not bound to speak in a certain way. Dialectal variations are permitted.

Knowledge and Skills

The teacher knows that the children will continue to learn language more powerfully in informal settings outside the school than within the school, but the school potential as a learning setting can be maximised by seeing all curriculum areas as contexts for learning language, learning through language and learning about language. The school can also be enriched by breaking down the boundaries and reducing the discontinuities between school and community. The teacher knows that ideally the classroom should be as linguistically various as the community.

Challenges

At the same time as selecting justifiable and challenging content, the teacher needs to imagine how the class can make connections and associations with aspects of other subjects, aspects of the community, and aspects of other cultures.

In constructing a programme, the teacher, in an unbounded classroom, will not be bound by the plan. The programme will always be open to reconstruction in the light of unfolding interests and opportunities.

CUMULATIVE

Classroom Characteristics

The classroom experiences and language activities seem to grow out of each other in a progression where earlier learnings are continually being recalled to service in new settings. Children get a sense of coherence rather than of the piecemeal aggregation of language skills.

Knowledge and Skills

The teacher knows that language resources are personal resources which grow organically in interaction with others. Language is not built through the addition of new 'blocks'. It is a growing reservoir. The teacher's task is to respect the integrity and coherence of each child's growing linguistic resource.

Challenges

The cumulative classroom will incorporate learning 'history' discussions, where teacher and students replay and revalue aspects of previous experience and learning as they relate to what is happening now.

Ideally, the teacher will have different linguistic expectations of each child in the class and will not be tyrannised by demands to bring each child up to a certain arbitrary standard by the end of the year.

The major challenge at the whole-class level is to plan the curriculum so that the new work grows logically and conceptually out of the preceding work and, at the individual level, to set new assignments which allow aspects of the preceding assignment to be incorporated.

Towards a Reflective Classroom

The section on the ideal classroom is by no means exhaustive, but it does indicate the scope of the transformations that teachers are being challenged to make in their teaching for language development.

While some teachers are managing these transformations with skill and excitement, others find themselves overwhelmed and paralysed by the enormity of the changes they face. Clearly, the way in for these teachers is not through the wholesale abandonment of their present regime but through smaller transformations where the experiments can be controlled.

This next section shows how some teachers, systematically but pragmatically, are taking up some of the challenges by adopting a *functional approach* to their own development.

SOME EXAMPLES OF TEACHERS LEARNING

Five brief case studies are considered. Key processes and principles in each study will be extracted and synthesised as a working guide to teachers wishing to design a learning programme using a functional approach. (N.B. These case studies are fictional constructions based on real examples.)

Case Study One

Twenty entrants to a college of advanced education undertake a B.Ed. course during which they will specialise in language in education. They intend to be primary teachers. The B.Ed. course is constructed upon a general principle that field work should precede or accompany instruction and academic input. All courses contain a large proportion of assessment by practicum, documentation of some practice, and investigation, with a theoretical explanation or interpretation. Although team teaching is not yet organisationally possible in the institution, lecturers in psychology, sociology, linguistics and 'the principles and practice of education' have collaborated in constructing the B.Ed. course section on language in education. Each course at each level is integrated with field-work activity and the student teachers know that they will be expected to bring data from their field-work into lectures, tutorials and seminars for theoretical consideration and analysis through the lenses of the specialist disciplines.

Before field-work (in the community and in schools) begins in year one, the students, regardless of specialisations, are obliged to take concurrently two compulsory ten week courses, one entitled 'Developing a Personal View of Learning' and the other entitled 'Basic Approaches to Field-Work'. The institution justifies this on the grounds that the two fundamental 'generators' in a teacher's continuing growth in the profession are: a personally owned and continually modified theory or view of learning, and a grasp of the principles and practice of enquiry into any aspect of teaching and learning. Throughout the teachers' career as formal students during preservice years and as learning teachers beyond, these basic tools will be continually called upon in the development of new hypotheses and plans directed towards solving the presently problematic.

The initial course on developing a personal view of learning is assessed by means of an assignment in which the student teacher outlines his or her own view of learning, optimum conditions for learning and principles underpinning learning *as experienced by the learner*, giving personal examples with an accompanying analysis of what happened. The assignment also requires the students to generate a list of criteria by which they will begin to evaluate the teachers of all courses at the institution, teachers observed during field-work, and themselves when they begin practice teaching. During the three years of the B.Ed. course they are required continually to modify and expand this initial assignment.

Their final assignment after three years will be to re-present their personal learning statement, indicating how and why it has been modified over three years.

And so, before they begin 'reading' teaching and learning interactions in society and schools and to focus on language in education,

they are required to reflect upon *themselves* as learners:
The process of the course is as follows:
- Each student writes in note form the evolution of a piece of deliberate learning which he or she remembers well. (The learning can be of an academic or a practical nature.)
- The lecturer requires students to share each other's accounts and to ask each other clarifying questions.
- Students then write out a full account of the learning, extracting from it a map of the progress of the learning with notes on conditions and personal feelings that applied at various stages.
- The lecturer then puts them all through a small programme of work requiring them to come to an understanding of some new content (e.g. the reading of an article on the concept of 'register' in linguistic theory). The lecturer attempts to model a teaching/learning sequence consistent with his or her own principles.
- All students then reflect upon themselves as learners during this process, relating the experiment to their first piece of writing and offering the lecturer a critique of the teaching they have just experienced. They make notes and modify their original statement as necessary.
- All students then experience being taught a new manual skill (e.g. an art lecturer is conscripted to instruct them in one aspect of the techniques of brush work). This lecturer also attempts to teach according to his or her own principles.
- As for the 'academic' learning, the students reflect upon themselves as learners and the teacher as teacher.
- Finally students prepare their assignment for assessment.
- The document becomes a vital point of reference whenever the psychology lecturer in particular, or other lecturers, introduce insights and data from research or commentaries on new theoretical 'schools' of learning. It also becomes a key point of reference in the evaluation of episodes in the students' practice teaching.

The existence of this course in the institution has caused considerable ferment and discussion amongst staff. Noticeable modifications of teaching behaviours seem to be related to the frequent critiques offered by student teachers.

The question may be asked: 'What is the connection between this piece of learning and teaching for language development?' It was contended early in this discussion that teaching for language development goes far beyond a knowledge of language and specific language teaching skills. In developing towards the ideal classroom for language development, teachers will need to learn to construct the best possible context for learning *anything*. This requires a set of learning and teaching principles which will generate an infinite pattern of surface teaching strategies and sequences. Without such principles, the teaching regime in language development may be internally inconsistent. For instance, at one moment the children may be asked to complete language exercises, filling in the blank spaces in incomplete sentences, and then this might be followed by a one-to-one conference on writing in the style of Donald Gaves. This in itself is not evidence that the teacher lacks a coherent set of learning principles, but it suggests that this teacher may be one who acquires new items in the teaching repertoire without examining the view of language implicit in the technique.

This particular case study indicates one way in which teachers can begin to articulate and modify a personal view of learning which will underline all their language teaching and act as a generating plant for all their curriculum construction work.

There is a view of human learning implicit in the features of the ideal classroom for language development. To take any one of these features and try to implant it or add it to an existing classroom will be to put it at risk, if that classroom is based on a contrary or inconsistent view of language and learning.

Reflections on Case Study One

Taking this case as a model in teacher education, one can identify various processes and principles at work. The learning process has the following stages:
- Establishing the known
- Clarifying the problematic
- Experiencing something new
- Reflecting on the experience
- Developing a model (or hypothesis)
- Testing and evaluating the model.

The goal is a written product which is then to be tested and modified over a three year period. Students are required to talk, write, read, and listen in a variety of contexts. They write notes for themselves. They collaboratively construct models. Through the lessons in new work, they experience, observe and reflect. They use this experience, their own understandings, and the understandings of their teachers and peers as resources.

In terms of the features of an ideal classroom already articulated, this teacher-education classroom is active and interactive (sharing with peers), collaborative (small group and whole class assignments), purposive (developing a personal reference document), multi-modal (though largely language-oriented), exploratory (coming to tentative views), reflective (experience followed by analysis), experience-based (working from what they know), conceptually demanding (one assumes), cumulative (since it will be re-visited over three years), and contextually supportive (everyone is in it).

Significantly, it exemplifies the belief that learning to construct and read teaching acts involves learning to read oneself and others as learners. All future teaching for language development will be inspired by, generated from, and embedded in an explicit or implicit view of how people learn.

This particular programme is obviously predicated on the assumption that teachers will be better for having an explicit and personally 'owned' view of learners and learning.

Case Study Two

In the same institution, ten student teachers opt to take a course called 'Language Development in Early Childhood'. The reading list for the course includes the names of M.A.K. Halliday, Courtney Cazden, Kornei Chukovsky, and Roger Brown. The avowed aims of the course are:

- to come to an understanding of some of the language learning strategies of children between 0 and 5;
- to begin to construct a picture of the stages and nature of linguistic growth during these years;
- to reflect upon the role of adults and others in this learning process.

The twenty week course is constructed so that a ten week fieldwork project initially runs concurrently with a lecture/tutorial system in which key readings in the 'literature' are introduced, discussed and related, where appropriate, to the data being gathered by student teachers. Each student is helped to gain access to a home in which there is a child between 0 and 5. Parental permission is obtained after clear negotiation and clarification about the aims and limits of the investigation.

One student, Beth, is able to carry out a study of Mary, a five-year-old who was born with a quite severe hearing defect, detected early and eventually partially reversed with a strong hearing aid and intense tuition at a special centre which combines lip-reading techniques with patient support as the child learns to approximate more closely to well-formed pronunciation.

Beth discovers during an interview with the parents that Mary is presently undergoing an exciting surge of language development which is more characteristic of their now older children when they were between eighteen months and twenty-four months.

Mary is read to every day and takes great delight in music and singing, even though her own vocal reproductions are, in tone and pitch, difficult to reconcile with the original. Fortunately, the mother has kept a close record of 'mile posts' in Mary's development and gives Beth access to these. A feature of Mary's present language surge is the emergence *at five* of extended pre-sleep monologues in which she mixes talk with a range of incantations.

In consultation with her tutor, Beth is encouraged to gain parental consent to record some of these pre-sleep monologues, to transcribe them and then to analyse them *with the help of the parents*.

The parents agree, sharing Beth's curiosity as to the content and nature of the monologues, and so a tape recorder is arranged, Watergate-style, behind the bed-head.

In order to transcribe the tapes, Beth often has to resort to the mother or father for interpretations, and then, in the analysis, the work becomes necessarily collaborative with the parents who are needed to relate strips of unfolding text to previous incidents in Mary's life, to daily happenings, and so on.

Transcripts contain a fascinating mixture of direct reference to events, language 'exercise' work, creative compositions and reproduction of and variations upon songs, as well as re-told stories and jokes.

In lectures, Beth begins to make strong connections with the findings and insights of Kornei Chukovsky, and in tutorial work she is directed towards Ruth Weir's study, *Language in the Crib*, in which Weir analyses the pre-sleep monologues of one of her own children (at a much earlier age). Having completed her assignment, Beth needs no convincing that language development requires the child to create and generate new meanings. It cannot be explained by imitation theories. Beth now reads other case studies, such as Halliday's description of Nigel's linguistic development, with a strong sense of identification and curiosity as a fellow researcher.

Reflections on Case Study Two

Beth's learning path is as follows:
- Becoming curious (beginning to wonder)
- Establishing a goal (with the tutor)
- Collecting data
- Analysing and illuminating the data (by reading other commentators)
- Drawing conclusions (in an assignment).

While there are extrinsic pressures and requirements in the course, Beth's intrinsic interest takes hold and the study becomes strongly *intentional*.

With the help of the tutor, she increases, through exploration, her own reservoir of understanding of language development so that she can make pertinent connections with the work of theorists and researchers who might otherwise have been impermeable or irrelevant.

Her work is very much bound up with the analysis of texts which she collects (the learning sequence is *text-aware* and *reflective*). She works closely with her tutor and Mary's parents (*collaborative*). There is a strong field-work component (*experience-based*) and the emerging meanings have to be continuously checked out and verified (*negotiated*) The further Beth goes in her exploration, the more *unbounded* her sources.

The tutor works on the principle that theoretical input and information about language is best introduced after or concurrent with appropriate student field-work.

In Case Study One, intending teachers were developing a view of learning. Here Beth is developing, though personal observation and reflection, a view of language learning. She is developing concepts and views which will allow her to engage with other commentators and theorists on language learning. At the same time she is developing skills in observing, tracking, recording and diagnosing which will enhance her capacities as a teacher. Through her own investigations of Mary's language growth, she will have a rationale for the exploratory, reflected, collaborative and functional aspects of her classroom. She will also have an orientation of *text awareness*.

Case Study Three

John, a third year student teacher with an interest in drama as a way of promoting language development in the primary school, is allocated to a fairly conservative school in a working class area for a six week block of teaching. This will be followed by a special ten week elective on 'Drama and Language Development'. As preparation for the elective, John has undertaken to try some drama with the Year Five class (nine-year-olds) to which he has been allocated for observation and practice. The teacher to whom he is apprenticed is happy to let John try some drama but is privately sceptical, knowing the problems of discipline and control which beginning teachers usually encounter.

In previous years John has been part of an extra-curricula 'learning through doing' drama group at his college. This group has specialised in improvisations, some of which are shaped and eventually performed publicly. He is convinced that the linguistic processes and interactions which accompany the journey from idea to improvisation to public performance would oblige young people to expand their linguistic resources. He is confident that he has the knowledge and skills necessary to guide children through this kind of work.

After a week of observation to familiarise himself with the class, John is given a one hour slot in the programme for three days running in order to try his first experiment in drama.

Inspired by Dorothy Heathcote's accounts of her work with working class children, he begins by telling them the beginning of a story of his own creation about pirates who find themselves shipwrecked on the proverbial coral island. He then asks them to volunteer to become specific characters. At this point, the activities room where this is taking place becomes more than mildly chaotic, as embryonic villains dangle from imaginary ropes swinging imaginary swords, tumbling wrestlers fight to the death, and some of the more timid scuffle off into the corners to observe the slaughter. John, confident to this point, suddenly realises that he has no skills in restoring order and is somewhat abashed when their usual teacher has to step in, cuff a few ears, re-establish the power structure and call the whole thing off.

In discussion after school, the class teacher and John talk about the incident. It becomes clear that this class has not had this kind of work since Year Two, and that they are always inclined to take a yard if offered an inch. The class teacher believes that John should begin conservatively with some whole-class reading of a scripted play, whereas John, like the young driver who has had an accident, thinks he should get back in and try again as soon as possible. He asks if there is any other teacher at the school who could help him, but finds that improvised drama is not a priority at this school. The principal suggests that John might like to contact the drama consultant based at a nearby teachers' centre.

John takes up this suggestion. The drama consultant encourages him to persevere, speaks with him about various successful programmes he knows, and offers him a copy of a new state curriculum guide for drama containing a section on 'ways in for beginning teachers'. The consultant arranges for John to visit an outstanding secondary teacher in a working class area where drama is successfully established. This teacher has played a key role in the writing of the system's drama guide.

The experienced teacher allows John to watch a beginning sequence with a reputedly 'tough' class. He notices that there is a tightly established routine – shoes off, sit in a circle, speak one at a time, clear indication of time limits, and so on. He also notices that the teacher begins with anecdotes from the children's experience and gradually negotiates a topic which the class is prepared to develop.

It seems to be particularly important that there is a purpose, a culmination point for all this. The finished product, some weeks hence, is to be performed before some classes from a local primary school. Jobs and responsibilities are allocated, goals established, and *then* the various groups break to begin improvisations. There is a sense of purpose, order and excitement in the room. There is still horseplay but the tension of the task seems to bring people back to business quickly.

When the secondary teacher hears that John belongs to a drama group at his college, she suggests he arrange a demonstration for the Year Five class. 'After all,' she says, 'how can these children be expected to discuss and improvise, if they are not shown what is expected and involved? It's also very important for them to know where they are going and where it might end.' The next week John persuades three of his friends to show the Year Fives the stages of a small improvisation from first discussion through to performance. He explains to them that they will need to watch closely because he intends them to have a go later. The children watch with surprising engagement, eavesdropping on the contradicting and compromising, the planning and trying, the shaping and polishing which occurs. Afterwards, they ask questions and indicate that they would like to try something.

The one hour slots are revised. John makes the rules very explicit, and the class decides to aim for a performance to the parents at the school open night in four week's time. They decide to explore the theme of 'Brothers and Sisters' which, unknown to them, happens to relate very closely to the official Social Studies programme.

It is not all smooth sailing but the process works well enough for a creditable performance to be held. More than the usual number of parents attend the open night, the children are pleased with themselves and John, exhausted, has some data to contribute to 'Drama and Language Development'.

Reflections on Case Study Three
John's learning evolves as follows:
- Intending and facing the problematic ('How do I teach them improvisation?)
- Formulating a plan
- Trial and error
- Reflection on 'error'
- Seeking further information, advice and observation
- Formulating a new plan
- Putting it to the test
- Evaluating the teaching

It is interesting to see how a contextually unsupportive situation is retrieved through the tenacity of the learner in seeking outside supports in the form of the drama consultant and the secondary teacher.

John's initial plans do not succeed because he has no pertinent experience to help him imagine where they will go wrong. It is significant that the opportunity to watch an experienced teacher at work, *once he knew his problem*, is a turning point in his learning. He can now construe a different programme which he can *imagine* working.

Wittingly or unwittingly, he employs this same principle of *demonstration* in his own teaching of the Year Fives.

His learning has been *exploratory*, strongly *purposive*, *reflective*, *multi-modal* (he acts, watches, improvises, talks), *collaborative* (supported by outsiders), and decidedly *experience-based*.

John had a good grasp of the role of drama in language development but he had not sufficiently *indwelt* in the problems of the learners. He was also somewhat naive about the intentions of ten year-olds. Because improvisation was not problematic to him, he had not imagined it being problematic to students. His eventual recognition of his own lack of empathy with children's view of the world helps him to compose a successful learning experience.

Here is an example of the war with contexts referred to earlier. John is very confident in his belief that improvised drama has much to offer in terms of promoting language development in the classroom. He has knowledge and skills in this area and is more than capable of teaching others how to do it, *if* those others will cooperate. He is capable of articulating the language theory which justifies the place of drama in the curriculum. What he lacks is a developed understanding of how to establish organisational and management structures, and how to mobilise the students' intentions and purposes.

So often new approaches to language teaching do not *take* in the classroom because the present school and classroom structures, and the present habits of teaching, are antipathetic to the new approaches. John wishes to set up an active/interactive regime in a traditional classroom. He also wishes to allow the incorporation and use of children's ideas, where this has not been the custom.

Like many teachers who try something new, he is first subject to the tyranny of the students who have not been taught to cope with the new regime. He has also to come to terms with the crisis of nerve which occurs when our present teaching skills are not sufficient to the new demands.

John's tenacity is fueled by his belief in the methods and process of drama. His solutions are found in developing a tighter regime of teaching and explaining the new requirements. The principles he eventually follows in introducing a *new form of teaching* are analogous to the principles which he follows in introducing a *new form of language* (improvised drama).

Case Study Four

Terry, a Year Nine science teacher, is dissatisfied with the performance of his class and feels that there is a good deal of recitation as opposed to understanding in the tests he applies each month. It happens, at this time, that an Innovations Project team is working in the school to investigate what it calls 'language across the curriculum'. One of the Project team members approaches him to see whether he is interested in conducting an enquiry into any aspects of language and learning which he considers to be a problem. He is about to say that he thinks language is the province of the English teacher, when he recalls a niggling feeling that the language of the current textbook may be one of the reasons for his class's poor performance in science. The text is particularly 'dense'.

The Project teacher seems eager to hear about this and together they examine the text in question. In discussion, it emerges that the next unit of work will deal with the chapter on *Light and Energy*. While the Project leader, Ruth, does not believe greatly in reading difficulty measures (because 'readability' seems to vary with intention and prior knowledge of context), she applies a simple measure devised by Fry to find that the chapter on *Light and Energy* would probably challenge most sixteen year-olds.

At this point Ruth injects into the conversation some of the notions of L.S. Vygotsky, who recognised that schools often produce 'empty verbalisation', responses from students where the words are 'correct' but clearly not understood. Teachers have the job, according to Vygotsky, of introducing pre-formed scientific concepts and challenging learners to leap up from their platform of spontaneous, everyday concepts to make connections. Ruth suggests that the present science text is asking the learners to leap too far, and that it may be necessary to provide a bridge by re-writing the text in language closer to the experience of the learners.

Terry is not keen to attempt this himself, but brightens at the suggestion that some of last year's students, now in Year Ten, might be given a project to re-write *Light and Energy* for the specific audience of this year's class.

An experiment has begun and Terry, being a scientist, is anxious to 'control the variables'. He decides to record certain pre-experiment data, the readability of the science text, and the previous average scores of each student on his teacher tests. He also collects some random samples of some previous answers. Before the experiment begins, he prepares a test on *Light and Energy* based on what he would have administered if he had taught as usual from the text. He has colleagues verify that it is of comparable difficulty with previous tests.

A group of three accomplished Year Ten students accept the re-writing assignment with interest, having been briefed on the reasons for the experiment. The re-written chapter, including new diagrams and illustrations, is typed and duplicated for the Year Nine class which is unaware of the source of the new text. On the Fry test, it emerges as having a 'reading age' of thirteen (theoretically 'spot on'). The teacher then teaches in the normal way from the new text and eventually sets his pre-prepared test.

Results show in all but two cases an improved grade of at least one grade on an A to E scale. In some instances there are quite dramatic improvements. Random samples of answers compared with earlier answers suggest that students are indeed writing with more understanding.

Ruth interviews several of the students after the new experiment. Most think that the teacher has written the new text. With one exception they judge it to be better than the formal text, more understandable, clearer and better organised.

Terry and Ruth collaborate to write up the experiment which eventually appears as an outcome of the Project available to teachers across the state. The booklet closely analyses the kinds of linguistic transformations carried out by the student writers. It is possible to learn from what they did.

Reflections on Case Study Four

Terry learns through:
- Negotiation and clarification of a problem
- Composing a plan for investigation
- Collecting 'base data'

- Applying the new approach
- Testing the outcomes of the new approach
- Reflecting on the new data and documenting the experiment.

It seems fair to conclude that Terry would never have entered upon this experiment without the gentle intervention of the Project officer who helps him imagine an experiment that may be *useful to him*. He enters into the project because it promises to throw light on a niggling problem.

It should also be noted that, apart from the initial 'seeding', the experiment is totally under the control of Terry. How much time and energy to invest, over and above his normal teaching load, is his own decision.

Ruth takes up some of the considerable burden of documentation in order to make Terry's work more widely accessible as a contribution to current wisdom about teaching.

This case study illustrates the principles of the learner owning the learning.

In terms of learning process, this is a case of *collaboration* (with the Project officer, the Year Tens and the class itself), *exploration, reflection, contextual support* (the back-up work of the Project officer), *observing and tracking* (interviewing the students), and *consciously examining and analysing text*. The task is delicately *negotiated.*

Whereas Beth, in case study two, adopts an investigative role *in preparation* for future teaching, Terry takes on action-research on the job with respect to a problematic aspect of language and learning.

With reference to the ideal classroom, he is experimenting with aspects of the *experience base* and *conceptual demands*. How can the language of instruction be brought into a more dynamic engagement with the present language and experience of students?

It is interesting to note that this learning experiment did not arise from the injunctions or advocacies of new curriculum guides or theoretical texts. The language knowledge of the outsider was fed into the problem in a *speculative manner* rather than as some kind of 'smart pill'!

The example is instructive in suggesting how curriculum advisers, consultants or key teachers may be of use to teachers, and how teachers might take up intentions to use experts and what they know.

Case Study Five

A national language curriculum development project is predicated on the belief that teachers should be involved in the development of national materials and that curriculum development must be accompanied by teacher development, that is, teacher learning.

One state negotiates to develop materials for teachers on writing development, using a network of thirty accomplished teachers to produce outcomes based on investigative work in their own classrooms.

After a year of preparation in which teachers undertake preliminary enquiries, the thirty teachers form six groups each focussing on a particular aspect of writing (Years 5 to 8) and each directed towards an outcome which could be taken up by other teachers to assist them in their professional development.

One group of three teachers based in the same primary school decides to explore in detail the notion of a 'community of writers', the idea that writing will develop best where children and teacher write together for many purposes, where writing is published, discussed, and re-drafted and where models of adult writers and adult writing are accessible.

The group knows that it has access to resource people who are part of the project team, to other groups in the project, to articles and books, to technical support (for sound taping, video taping and typing transcripts), and they know that there will be regular whole-project recall days when progress can be discussed. They know also, sometimes without delighted appreciation, that they are expected eventually to produce materials which will be useful for other teachers.

It is important to consider the value of the first preparatory year. As one teacher said:

> Because of my involvement in the project, I had to write, and it's a few years since I have done a significant amount of that! I have been encouraged to rediscover myself as a writer – warts and all.

The process of investigation and sharing had been illuminating:

> It came to me painfully... that a lot of us didn't really seem to know what we were about. People started to investigate themselves, what they believed... Talking to others I learned the names of things. I started to see what I was doing at a deeper level.

The first year had also been a time of coming to grips with the theories and thoughts of 'the heavies', as they were called:

> I went on humming and haaing and getting thoughts together. I had to think up a way of structuring my writing programme. I launched into reading... I got hold of a book by James Moffett and I spent about three nights reading that and that really affected the way I was thinking. Then in the holidays I met Don Graves... After all that I thought, 'Right I'll have to try something,' so I wrote about what I could do, the way I could organise the classroom, the questions about conferencing I wanted to ask.
>
> (Teacher, in Riordan, p. 2)

With this kind of experience behind them, the three teachers are prepared to construct something as close as possible to the ideal classroom for writing development. They let the children themselves into the experiment and co-opted them as community researchers, going out into their local community to interview adults in various occupations about how they use writing and what they thought about writing when they were at school.

The teachers and children invite locally prominent writers, novelists and poets, to come to the school and talk about how they compose. They have these occasions video-taped and these tapes later become a formal outcome for use by other teachers.

The children themselves are investigators into their own composing processes, gradually becoming more articulate about the significance of seeking interim opinions and publishing.

In all aspects of the life of the classroom, authentic opportunities to write are taken up and exploited.

At the end of the second year of the project, the teachers document what they have done and offer a similar *process* to other teachers rather than a polished *answer* to the problem of writing development. Reflecting on the life of the project, one teacher puts it this way:

> The project has provided me with a supportive framework within which I could carry out classroom research. My own small-scale inquiry and observation was legitimised, and as I became more serious and thorough in carrying it out, I began to see how what I was going might be useful to other teachers and how, in turn, their enquiries might complement things happening in my

classroom. Perhaps more important than the encouragement I was given to experiment, was the provision of 'someone to tell it to'. The project linked me to a group of people who wanted to share classroom experience. It was important to me to have other teachers to talk to about what I wanted to try out in the classroom, the difficulties I was facing, to help me to reflect on what went wrong when I failed, and sometimes, to bask with me in the pleasure of success.

(Teacher, in Riordan, p. 26)

Reflections on Case Study Five

The group project has the following stages:
- Preparation, sharing of information, explanation
- Negotiation of specific tasks and goals
- Experimenting with new classroom activities (trial-and-error)
- Documentation of what happened for other teachers.

The three teachers in this case study are less at risk than the science teacher, Terry, because they have a very *rich context of support* (the legitimation of a national project, access to a wide network of local resource people, opportunity to meet and share regularly with peers, and, of course, their own support).

The theme of *sharing practice* with fellow teachers strongly pervades the enquiry. These teachers, having begun to learn very tentatively, develop as confident, assertive enquirers able to *commission help* (either from people or books) when they need it.

Their experiment breaks down traditional boundaries between teachers and researchers, schools and community, learners and teachers. It is *multi-modal*. They write, film, read, enact, talk, listen, observe, transcribe and interview directly and indirectly through their children. They regularly *interact* with their peers in the project. They are *purposive* in aiming to produce material for themselves and others. Their learning over two years has been *cumulative*, one experiment leading into the next.

Their learning is an experiment in the construction of new teaching sequences, within the continuing *context* of their own classrooms.

In the same sense that they are tenaciously seeking to secure more subtle readings of their own teaching, this learning is highly *text-aware*.

THE PRINCIPLES OF LEARNING TO TEACH

Looking back over these five case studies, it emerges that the features of an ideal language learning classroom apply also to the ideal conditions for teachers learning about teaching, if the case studies selected are considered to be exemplary models.

It can also be seen that, while each case study illustrates a different *style* of learning, the *processes* by which these teachers learn are common. The classic scientific method can be identified in each case:

| Problem and Clarification of Problem | → | Seeking data Researching and Planning | → | Trial, Error, and Testing | → | Reflection on Consequences |

While in some cases the learners recursively return to an earlier stage before progressing again, there is a clear progression from problem to reflection as represented above.

In examining the conditions under which the learning takes place, the following features can be identified:

- *Purpose* and the *intention to learn* keep the learners tenaciously 'on task'.
- *Outside supports* assist the tenacity of the learner.
- There is access to input, information, advice and *demonstration at the point of need*.
- In each case, *reflection* is strengthened through *written documentation* by the learners.
- In each case the enquiries are grounded in *practice in authentic settings*.
- In each case, learners seek to develop *finer explanations or theories about what happens*.
- *Hypothesising and predicting* are necessary in each case.
- In each case, the learner, appropriately supported and advised, *controls the learning* and takes responsibility for *using the learning*.
- Within the long-term enquiry, there are many opportunities for *incidental learning* and development of new skills.

- Learners in each case gain in power, through their own enquiries, to read and understand work by specialists in language and learning.

A Set of Guidelines for Learning Teachers in the Field of Language Development

This account has sought to show how some teachers are successfully building paths towards the ideal in language development.

In contrast with these deliberately experimenting teachers are many who remain trapped by a 'Yes, but...' frame of mind, who hear the rhetoric and advocacy and tend to believe it but are unable to construe practical paths towards the promised land.

It has been contended here that a functional approach to teacher education *grounded in practice* is necessary to break the reproductive cycle whereby today's teachers, with cosmetic changes, emulate their forebears and perpetuate outmoded views of language and learning.

The following set of criteria may be of use to student teachers or teachers who are designing learning projects for themselves and wish to adopt a functional approach.

Some Criteria for a Learning Project

- Have I been able to state clearly the problem which I face and the outcomes I hope to achieve?
- Have I clarified and consolidated what I already know about this area of my work, and can I state this as a set of operational principles or a rationale?
- Have I identified a person or persons who can support me in this work, who will respect my experience, values and attitudes and yet will offer constructive criticism?
- Have I identified the constraints acting upon me – political, social, structural, economic, time, etc – and have I considered how to handle them?
- Have I set out my plans in terms of how I intend to act and reflect on action?
- Have I identified sources of 'expertise' in terms of people, texts, sites of demonstration?

- Have I secured the support of authority figures who might otherwise block or divert my attentions?
- Have I negotiated clear contracts with all parties concerned – with respect to commitment, ownership of data, confidentiality, contribution? With children; parents; colleagues, administrators, supporters?
- Have I considered ways in which I might make available to others what I find?
- Have I anticipated ways in which I need to protect myself?
- Have I fully explained to the students what I intend, what part I wish them to play, and how it may benefit them?
- Do I have the required resources (people, money, books, equipment)?
- Will my proposed project allow points of conflict/tension/interest to surface and be considered?
- Can I imagine myself managing this work, given my present workload?
- Is my project going to be interesting?

Theory, Practice and Language Development

There is a pervasive myth about teachers being practitioners who are not interested in theory. I have shown here how at least some teachers value their own theory-in-practice. I suggest strongly that teachers in coming to terms with new approaches to language in education need to re-value theory, not as something 'out there' which experts have, but as their own present understanding of why they do what thy do.

In a recent report of his research into children's strategies when undertaking cloze tests on reading, Dr Brian Cambourne commented on 'fragment grabbing' behaviours in which many children arrived at a 'correct' conclusion on the basis of the fragment of language around the gap, and not on the basis of their construing of the *whole text* as it was unfolding. There is an analogous tendency amongst teachers who are not reading well the unfolding *text in context* of their own teaching. Such teachers often seek expedient, pragmatic solutions which seem to fit the moment, perhaps unaware of the inconsistencies and incoherences which would be apparent to one who viewed the behaviour as part of a wider text.

Inservice and preservice courses which purvey bits of teaching practice as good ideas or 'things to try', and which justify themselves on the basis of an avowed teacher demand for practical things ('We're not interested in theory'), tend to perpetuate fragment-grabbing behaviour and to impede the teachers' development as powerful planners and 'readers'. The approaches adopted by the teachers described here empower them to read their own teaching with more subtlety and to construct new potential programmes for investigative application in their classrooms.

The learning projects described in the five case studies depict teachers developing practical judgement which requires far more than the technical application of new knowledge about language and new skills. It requires that discernment which comes only from a complex apprehension of all the elements operating at the site of the action.

It is the teacher in context who must reconcile *what might be* (the ideal classroom) with what *is*; who must decide what is fitting.

Conclusion

This necessarily compacted account of teachers learning to become better teachers for language development contains some significant challenges. It has been suggested that the identifiable features of the ideal language classroom will also be identifiable features of the ideal 'teachers learning' project. The principles of language learning, it has been contended, are analogous to the principles of learning to teach.

If this isomorphism is accepted, there are clear implications for pre-service education, for in-service education and for curriculum projects in the field of language development, and elsewhere for that matter.

For instance, pre-service courses would not set out to teach the 'grammar' of the ideal classroom; to describe what is deemed to be 'correct' and to justify it in terms of 'the experts'. They would instead require students to investigate pertinent aspects of their own language learning and the language learning of children; to articulate what they already know; to recognise the problematic; to seek new information; and to conduct experiments to test developing hypotheses.

The institution's task by this analysis would be to direct and shape the investigative processes, to organise for collaboration, and to give access to information, research and critical evaluation *as it is commissioned*. There would be a consistent drive towards practice and reflection on practice in the quest for personal principles. Presentation of insights by specialists would tend to occur *after* exploration, at the point of need. Teaching, like language itself, would be treated as a continually developing resource.

Pre-service and in-service courses and curriculum projects would strive to illuminate, through inquiry, *learning to teach, learning through teaching and learning, about teaching*.

REFERENCES

Brown, Roger (1958) *Words and Things*, Glencoe, Ill: Free Press

Cazden, Courtney (1972) *Child Language and Education*, Holt, Rinehart and Winston.

Chukovsky, Kornei (1968) *From Two to Five*, Berkley, University of California Press.

Halliday, M.A.K. (1972) *Explorations in the Functions of Language*, London, Edward Arnold.

Riordan, Lorraine (1982) *Unpublished Evaluation of the Language Development Project in South Australia*.

Vygotsky, L.S. (1965) *Thought and Language*, Cambridge, Mass., M.I.T.

Weir, Ruth H. (1962) *Language in the Crib*, The Hague: Mouton & Co.

ATWOOD LIBRARY / BEAVER COLLEGE
PE1065 .B6 1988   MAIN
Boomer, Garth/Metaphors and meanings : e

3 3295 00085 7059